THE CARE AND FEEDING
OF YOUNG LADIES

THE CARE AND FEEDING
OF YOUNG LADIES

John Taylor

ILLUSTRATED BY DON ROBERTS

M. & J. HOBBS
in association with
MICHAEL JOSEPH

First published in Great Britain by M. & J. Hobbs,
25 Bridge Street, Walton-on-Thames,
in association with Michael Joseph Ltd
52 Bedford Square, London, W.C.1
1975

© 1975 by John Taylor

ISBN 0 7181 1268 7

Printed in Great Britain by
Northumberland Press Limited, Gateshead
and bound by Redwood Burn Limited,
Trowbridge and Esher

This book is dedicated to

Adele, Adrienne, Aileen, Alexandra, Alison, Amanda, Amy, Angela, Anita, Ann, Anna, Annabel, Anne, Audrey

Barbara, Beatrice, Berenice, Beatrice, Beryl, Beth, Betty, Beverley, Blanche, Bridget, Brigid

Candy, Carole, Caroline, Catherine, Cecilia, Charlotte, Charmian, Cherie, Cherry, Christine, Chrystal, Clara, Constance, Cynthia

Daphne, Deborah, Deidre, Denise, Diana, Diane, Dinah, Dora, Doreen, Dorothea, Dorothy, Dot, Drusilla

Edith, Edna, Eileen, Elaine, Elana, Eleanor, Elizabeth, Ellen, Elsie, Emma, Ernestine, Esme, Esther, Eva, Eveline

Faith, Fanny, Felicity, Fiona, Flora, Florence, Frances, Freda

Gabrielle, Gail, Gale, Georgina, Genevieve, Genevive, Geraldine, Germaine, Gertrude, Gloria, Grace, Greta

Hanna, Heather, Helen, Helena, Henriette, Hester, Hilary, Hilda, Holly

Ida, Inez, Inga, Ingrid, Iola, Irena, Irene, Isobel

Jacqueline, Jane, Janet, Jean, Jennifer, Jessica, Jill, Joan, Joanna, Joanne, Jocelyn, Josephine, Joyce, Judy, Julie, June

Katherine, Kathleen

Laura, Leona, Leonora, Lesley, Lillian, Linda, Liz, Lois, Lorna, Louise, Lucy, Lydia

Madeline, Maggie, Maggy, Marcia, Margaret, Marie, Marilyn, Marion, Marjorie, Mary, Maureen, Melissa, Millicent, Miriam, Miranda, Moira, Molly, Muriel, Myrna

Nadia, Nancy, Naomi, Nina, Nora, Norma

Olive, Olivia, Ophelia

Pamela, Patricia, Paula, Pauline, Peggy, Penelope, Phillippa, Phoebe, Phyllis, Polly, Priscilla, Prudence

Queenie

Rachel, Rebecca, Rhoda, Roberta, Rosalie, Rosalind, Rosamond, Rose, Rosemary, Roxanne, Ruth

Sabine, Sabrina, Sally, Sandra, Sara, Sheila, Shirley, Sibyl, Sonia, Sophie, Stella, Stephanie, Susan, Susanne, Suzan, Suzannah, Sylvia

Tabitha, Tessa, Theodora, Theresa, Tilly

Una, Unity

Valerie, Vera, Victoria, Vida, Viola, Violet, Virginia, Vivienne

Wendy, Winifred

Xenia

Yolanda, Yvonne

Zena, Zoë

ORDER IS STRICTLY ALPHABETICAL AND IN NO WAY
DENOTES PREFERENCE

ACKNOWLEDGEMENTS

Many of the ideas contained herein have been developed and rewritten from pieces originally published in *Weekend, Punch, Penthouse, She,* the old *Men Only,* and other media. I am humbly grateful to the editors for their original subsidy, and hope they won't want their money back.

John Taylor, March 1975

CONTENTS

Women bring us solace: but if it wasn't for women we wouldn't need it.

Don Herold

YOUNG LADIES
AND THEIR ATTAINMENT

THE STORY OF MY LIFE—FROM THE FILM OF THE SAME NAME—
is a tragic succession of my getting into trouble with girls
and *vice versa*. Yet the teenage mating ritual which began
this sorry tale had a kind of hilarious protocol.

Thirteen was indeed unlucky for some. The day the world
caught fire was the second Saturday of my thirteenth year—
when the first flood of sexual realisation urged me to consider
girls as something other than just very poor football players.

Hindsight dignifies the moment as the arrival of puberty,
but at the time it started out as simply an aimless stroll with
my boyhood friend and confidant Frankie ('Soft') Row.
We had joined together for what was in pre-Television days
the inevitable pastime of 'going for a walk', when we encountered near the bottom of Streatham Common a pair of
young ladies of such innocent beauty that the sun came out.
In the pretty little silk dresses of the period, each armed with
that junior symbol of femininity—a Dorothy Bag—they trig-
gered off in us an instinct for the mating ritual which until
that moment had slumbered dormant. Frankie and I regarded one another wordlessly for a moment and automatically engaged upon Phase One of tyro courtship. It is known
as Following Them.

The protocol of the chase is ingrained in the male human
psyche as deeply and as naturally as a cat's urge to dig a
hole, and we fell into station at that steadily regulated
distance which indicates to the quarry that interest is alight
but which yet gives clear space to break off the engagement
should we shamefacedly encounter a splinter group of our
gang coming in the opposite direction.

Neckties hanging out like the tongues of randy Alsatians,
hands stuck self-consciously in trousers pockets, we sauntered
in casual convoy for some mile and a half across the Common,
through the Rookery and into Norwood Grove; skylarking
in our respective couples but keeping close enough formation
to allow our prey to look over their shoulders at every hundred yard check point and go off into gale force giggles.

Exhausted at last by our relentless pursuit the young
ladies finally posed themselves upon a wooden bench bearing

13

the possessive insignia of the Wandsworth Borough Council, and commenced to refresh themselves from a paper bag containing two ounces of Sharp's Kreemy Toffees.

Frankie and I meanwhile took up our positions on a metal railing at some fifteen yards distance from the seat and set the scene for Phase Two. This is known as chi-yiking.

It consists of climbing up, vaulting over, or balancing upon the top rail of the fence whilst establishing personal contact via a cheeky plea for a couple of pieces of the Kreemy Toffee. This last request being at last blushingly acceded to, informal introduction was thus effected and the ritual clicked into Phase Three or that facet of human courtship where it is necessary for the male animal to establish physical superiority.

This was accomplished very simply by Frankie making off with one of the Dorothy Bags, which had been laid neatly upon the edge of the borough council bench specifically for that purpose.

Now the courtship took on a more active turn, the owner of the bag scampering in simulated squealing fury from one male to the other as we casually tossed the bag back and forth between us. Only when she had sunk at last into despondent resignation, and begun to make a sulky way back to her companion, did I manifest an unspoken admiration by whacking her across the bottom with a rolled up copy of *The Wizard*.

Our cards now clearly on the table, Frankie and myself surrendered entirely to the arrival of puberty and proffered the suggestion that we should all four meet up next day and Go For A Walk. Having overcome the anxious disapproval of one of the young ladies (there is always one who hangs back a little) Frankie and I returned homewards with the first of Life's milestones in our pockets and the decision that that evening, in the secret of his garden shed, we should try our first cigarette.

In the leisured years of youth, we played us a waiting game. We let the old world take a couple of twirls and went for walks until habit became a trap and one day a man woke up married. The years between have shown how a Walk now goes only as far as the garage, and nothing but confusion embraces the once simple rituals of courtship. Too often, nowadays, what began in promise ends in frustration. No longer do the simple symbolisms, like asking a girl to go for a walk, establish that your intentions are far from honourable. For all its permissiveness—possibly *because* of its permissiveness—modern life promises too much and surrenders too little.

Indeed, in the pursuit of love, a deal of wasted time might be salvaged by applying to all young ladies those ready reference symbols with which hotels are categorised by the Automobile Association.

A One Star Young Lady, for example, would be the kind of young lady who not only has very little of what a man wants in a woman, but who clings to it grimly nevertheless. A Two Star Young Lady, on the other hand, would be the kind of girl who, having all necessary physical appurtenances but not necessarily having them arranged in aesthetic harmony, might be acceptable in either the privacy of your own flat or the privacy of hers, but whom the bubble reputation might prefer not to be seen escorting in any public place.

Three star would be better: This would mean a girl of clear physical and physiognomical attraction who, given only the barest amount of fuss, would regard a male/female relationship as at least a matter of give and take (or take and give, to get the variants in their normal sequence).

A four star young lady represents beauty, a figure of exquisite symmetry, a stunning sense of dress, a deep sense of male economy, a liking for your friends coupled with unswerving devotion to yourself, a hundred thousand quid in trust, a flat in Albany, a deeply lusty nature and a clean bill of health.

A five star young lady would be a young lady with four stars plus a preparedness to stand her own round of drinks.

Some of the other Guide Book abbreviations, indeed, might fit neatly into the scheme:

B and B—for Bed and Breakfast—at once has a pertinent ring. **c-d** for 'collection and delivery service' would mean she owns her own car. **G** for 'garage accommodation' facilitates the necessity for using your own car. **Ld** for 'last time dinner can be ordered' gives a rough idea of how late in the evening she might be contacted; and **np** for 'night porter' offers at once information on the embarrassment quotient involved in tipping the doorman to keep his blasted mouth shut.

We means 'weekends', of course, and **Not Pets** means that she does not pet.

Unlicen. stands for 'unlicentious'; **TV** for 'too virtuous'; and **Highly Recommended** simply means that she plays the field. **(T)**, for 'Temperance', is less than encouraging; and **Sc**, or 'service charge', would indicate a young lady who should be contacted only as a last resort.

My projected work *How to Acquire a Young Lady of Your Very Own*—to be published in seven volumes and Morocco leather—is a task of such dedicated research and prodigious investigation that I may never live to complete it.

However, when my time comes that is the way I want to go. In the meantime, some of the earlier chapters of the work may need to be completely rewritten in order to incorporate a report on a grisly development of recent years called 'Computer Dating'.

In all parts of the world organisations have emerged offering to find for their sad clientele a Mr. or Mrs. Right by the simple process of feeding data into the passionless maw of a computer, and standing by until the chuntering machine regurgitates the facts in the simplified form of a name and address.

Whether the system has as much dignity as a brisk Paul Jones or the more traditional process of standing on the corner watching all the girls go by, depends upon whether a girl's sensibilities are less bruised by a bleep than by a long low whistle.

But the major handicap, as I see it, is that a computer, for all its tidy logic, needs to be programmed. And the girl you are likely to get suggested to you is going to depend entirely on what kind of girl you suggest you want. And who knows what's good for him?

There may be a smattering of trick psychology questions among the programmed quiz, but how—in the choosing of a girl—can one ignore such essential qualifications as Vital

Statistics? And these, coupled with the trick questions aimed at bringing out into the open what a man is *really* after, is generally going to produce a desire for Sophia Loren every time.

Too, these computer investigations incorporate questions regarding the previous sex experiences of their subjects— and one cannot help but wonder how far the answers to such questions are to be trusted.

The Kinsey Report was regarded as highly suspicious in some quarters because it was considered that an aberrant quizzee might be too ashamed to reveal his bizarre preferences, or a frustrated wallflower might add imagined embellishment to a life of stark frustration.

The truth always lies slightly off centre; and once the interlocutor begins to make allowances for what he thinks might be the truth and what he thinks might be imagination, the process is no longer trustworthy.

It has always seemed pertinent to me that the only Poll which ever measured in advance exactly the result of a U.S. Presidential election was that of a flour mill in Missouri which offered retail sacks of flour bearing alternative pictures of either Tom Dewey or Harry Truman. Truman's majority was finally established exactly in the percentage of the buyers who chose Harry's picture in preference to Tom's. Here, you will see, there was no intrusion of high falutin' psychological questions; only the simple choice between one and another.

I mistrust Computer Choice, therefore, because I am convinced that deep down a man already knows perfectly well what he wants. Indeed the absurdity of the Research Men is best illustrated by the reasonably well known story of the multi-millionaire who instructed a research firm to find him the finest secretary in the world, no expense spared.

They launched a vast advertising campaign; applied medical, academic and professional examinations to several thousand applicants, hand-sifted through a short list of several hundred, and finally reduced the possibilities to three girls amongst whom prime suitability seemed to be divided equally.

Stumped, they decided upon a tie-breaker with the millionaire himself present, and submitted each of the girls in turn to a simple test. 'What is One and One?'

The first girl immediately answered, 'Two.'

The second girl considered for a moment and replied at last, 'Two.'

The third girl said, 'It could be two. It could be one point one. In figurative form it would be eleven. Or in fractional terms it could be One over One—which resolves itself into the entity ...'

The psychiatrists explained to the millionaire:

'You see—we have here entirely similar professional qualifications, but basic character dissimilarities which you must consider yourself in terms of the quality of personality and temperament which will best resolve your business requirements.

'The first girl answered at once, directly, and without qualification. She is forthright, determined, confident, unswayed by the possibility of half tone. But in consequence she is potentially rash, possibly arrogant, presumably not entirely responsible in your absence.

'The second girl revealed by her slight hesitation a readiness to consider possibilities beyond the immediate. She is more thoughtful, more inclined to weigh up a situation prior to taking action. But this very quality offers the shortcoming of not acting immediately in a crisis.

'The third girl explored potential to the ultimate—bespeaking a mind of such comprehensiveness as to ensure the most minute briefings in matters of business, but perhaps applying to matters of lesser concern more particular concentration than they may sometimes merit. You must make your decision in terms of how these varying qualities and characteristics are most likely to suit the girl's duties.'

The multi-millionaire said: 'I'll have the blonde with the big tits.'

Here, you will note, the prepossession with vital statistics was all—and it may be that I can be of small use to the young man seeking a young lady if all he is concerned with is quantity rather than quality.

Reducing the beautiful mechanical marvel which is young

womanhood to a simple set of three measurements has nothing to recommend it unless their juxtaposition and disposition
are in themselves aesthetically arranged.

Marking off a girl as 37 inches from nipple to nipple, 23
in the navel region and the promise of a kind of diabolo
balance at hipline, is as uninformative in its terms as knowing that her nails grow .01714 inches in 24 hours; she has
222 bones; there are 3 million cells in an area of her skin
the size of a postage stamp; she exercises 7,000,000 brain
cells daily however dumb a blonde she may be; her brain
weighs about $5\frac{1}{2}$ pounds; her heart $\frac{1}{2}$ a pound; her liver 3
pounds; and in 24 hours her heart beats 103,680 times. To
the student of serious research, these figures may have some
fascination—all useless information does—but what really
matters is how they stack up when placed in propinquity.

Here again, who can be sure what is attractive in the eye
of the beholder? What is Beauty?

After deep consideration, Keats came up with one answer:
'Beauty is Truth, Truth Beauty,' he said—which clearly
establishes that they are each other but offers small assistance
in making concrete decisions.

Ideals of beauty, indeed, vary with the whims of fashion—
and if this book is to have any life at all it must hesitate to
come down in terms of any specific era. When one considers
those Edwardian coloured photographic postcards with the
huge bottomed ladies depicted so bravely thereon, one must
wonder that in a single lifetime preferences can swing to
the Twiggy figures of the mid-nineteen sixties.

One needs to be no more than fifty years old to have witnessed wild prepossession with the Bust with its conical
dunce-cap shapes in the nineteen fifties, its flat suppression
in the nineteen twenties, and its mercurial jigglings in the
bra.-less nineteen seventies—and little older to have witnessed
lower concentrations via the Bustle of the eighteen nineties,
and the buttocks emphasis of the Hot Pants and tight jeans
era.

The Eton Crop didn't suggest that hair was especially
arousing—but the reason why women are still expected to
wear hats in church is because women in mediaeval times
were forced to cover their heads lest their crowning glory

egg into a frenzy of concupiscence the susceptible male kneeling in the next pew. It takes all sorts to make a history.

The Romans, for example, invented a kind of Three Point Plan which intractably outlined the physical necessities for attractiveness. Though today's aesthetics may coincide in many features, there are almost as many as are arguable.

The Romans required: 3 things RED: Lips; Cheeks; Nails. 3 things BLACK: Eyes; Eyebrows; Eyelashes. 3 things WIDE: Chest; Forehead; Space between Eyebrows. 3 things NARROW: Mouth; Waist; Ankles. 3 things THICK: Arms; Thighs; Calves. 3 things DELICATE: Fingers; Hair; Lips. 3 things LONG: Torso; Hair; Hands. 3 things SHORT: Teeth; Ears; Feet. 3 things SMALL: Nose; Head; Breasts.

Comprehensively considered there is not a great deal wrong with the listing possibly. But imagine in modern terms the acquisition of a young lady with Red Cheeks; Black Eyes; a Narrow Mouth; Thick Arms, Thighs and Calves; Delicate Lips; a long Torso; Short Teeth; and a Small Head and Small Breasts. Like this is not my bag, Man.

Better, therefore, that I should outline basic plans for the acquisition of young ladies identified by background and environment rather than by clear physical definition. For in each professional or social *genre* you may find wide enough physical declensions to please everybody.

It might be advisable, indeed, to base our discussion loosely on the following categories: SPORTSGIRL; HIPPY INTELLECTUAL; SECRETARY; FEMME FATALE; DEBUTANTE; and HOMELY or GIRL NEXT DOOR (see *Consumers' Guide* page 263.

How to acquire a Sportsgirl
First requirement is a Butch haircut. Eschew after-shave and its effeminate connotations. Smear yourself from head to foot with Sloan's Liniment, and search the sporting records for a vaguely familiar name who has excelled in an obscure sport like Pelota or Mud Wrestling. Claim him as yourself.

To avoid having to prove personal physical prowess, simulate a limp like Long John Silver's and hint darkly at records which would soon be shattered if you had but an inch of cartilage left in either leg. Butter her foolish belief that properly coached she might achieve five Olympic golds, and tell her ruefully that henceforth your own athletic life can be lived only through your Pat and Mike relationship.

The early stages of your courtship may be boring. You must time her over and over again as she clocks up twenty-two seconds for the eighty yards; you must nod wisely as she bangs every ball into the net, slices every drive straight into the club-house. You must limp along the side of the bath as she dog-paddles the width for a stunning ninety-two. But as her coach you have rigorous control upon her diet and her drinking—which ensures that no one else takes her to dinner, and she eats only what you are able to afford.

The gymnasiums are all closed on a Sunday night, of course, so rather than that she should break training it will be essential that she reports up to your place for a work-out. Wear your dressing gown with the wide sleeves and the apocryphal legend 'GOLDEN GLOVES, 1961' across the back— and circumspectly place the Gin bottle back in the sideboard. Remind her that alcohol is not to be indulged in during training; but stress the health and strength giving values of fruit juices and their vitamin derivatives.

This bottle of Grand Marnier, for example, is a concentrated Orange cordial manufactured by austere ascetics in France and absolutely crawling with Vitamin C. Get a couple of tumblerfuls of that down you, my dear, and then slip into your shorts and singlet.

Then give her a good rub down and show her those judo holds you were discussing this afternoon.

How to acquire a *Hippy Intellectual*
Wait for her at the British Museum Library, positioning yourself at the library steps with a tome heavy enough to render her partially insensible.

Let it slip from your nerveless fingers as she passes beneath. Forearmed as you are with your hip flask, you can be down the ladder and forcing Brandy between her teeth before the Librarian has got the waxed paper off his Aspirin. The combined effects of the blow and the alcohol will reduce her resistance and induce a rosy glow. She will be quite incapable of resisting your gallant demand that you see her safely home after the accident.

Introductions effected, it is now necessary to establish that you constitute enormous potential for intellectual improvement—for every Hippy wishes to proselytise. Your conversational ploys are as follows:

If she attempts to educate you in terms of Dada, reveal with a rueful smile that you are yourself an orphan. Should Brecht be mentioned, readily agree that it is indeed a braw, moonlecht necht—and suggest a nocturnal stroll. If Constable comes up in the conversation assert stoutly that your attentions are strictly honourable; and if she turns to Titian as a basis for communication, Bless her, simulate a fear she has caught cold from the treacherous night air, and suggest you wrap her up and take her home with you.

She is powerless to disagree because your four reactions have respectively (a) aroused her sympathy and her maternal instincts; (b) revealed your own romantic nature; (c) underlined your trustworthiness; and (d) shown your deep concern for her well-being. Furthermore, all have displayed an overwhelming cultural ignorance at once attractive to the do-gooder in every young lady.

How to acquire a Secretary

How to acquire a Secretary *for extra curricular activities,* that is.

A man's own secretary is almost inevitably in love with him in the first place. A woman's inferiority complex inevitably urges her to adore the man in command, and her perverse reaction to being ordered about by a male chauvinist pig forces her to rationalise his superiority.

Establishing attraction is therefore redundant. It is only necessary to break down the barrier of employer/employee relationship.

Glamour is your key to the situation. Change into your dinner jacket after asking her if she would be kind enough to work an hour late that evening. You have some figures you simply must take along to Lord Delpus at his dinner party tonight, and she is the only one who can help you.

That single assertion is almost enough to see her swoon dead away.

At about eight o'clock, assure her that everything is now under control, inform her that she is an absolute darling to come through in your hour of need, and suggest that as you have a good half hour to spare before you need report to Lord Delpus, you insist on buying her a drink before you put her on the bus to Tooting.

Emphasise the difference between your lives by taking her to somewhere she has read about in novelettes: the Savoy American Bar, The Post Office Tower, Annabel's. She will feel mousey and uncertain in her twin-set and sensible shoes against the splendour of your silk/mohair blend D.J. with the braided satin edges; but will be knocked out when you say, suddenly, 'Oh! Heavens! Lord Delpus is *such* a bore. I'll skip it—and let's you and I go on to Muriel's ...'

The inspired tattiness of the decor in Muriel's will make her feel like a queen at just the moment where the alcohol is beginning to give her confidence. Too, the mixture of drinking places will establish you as a democratic darling who is loved and accepted by one and all. Only the chi-yiking of other members when they see you in a D.J. may serve to tarnish the image. But take their chaff good humouredly (only registering names in memory for later retribution).

At dinner—which should be at an Italian or Spanish restaurant because any secretary has been to either country on a package deal and will expand more easily in a familiar atmosphere—your projection is Prince Charming. Use Number Three Smile (that sad, slightly cynical one which suggests a dark tragedy in your life) and let her catch you regarding her very seriously and attentively every now and then. Look away hurriedly once you've established that she's noticed. Do not even hold her hand before about 11.30— and then make it natural or accidental. Never at this stage follow up the eyes-meet situation with a brash grope.

Needless to say, a better effect will be created if you have always been a little gruff, a little more formal with her during office hours—with only those rare flashes of humour which show her what-might-have-been: a crazy, loving, easily-hurt guy whom Fate decided so cruelly to wound these many a long year past.

Let her drink anything. Do not so much as encourage her as suggest you are delighted to indulge the experiments of a lovely girl who has so sweetly escaped sophistication. You must evoke a situation where she is determined to get you. You must avoid a situation where she believes you are determined to get her.

If she asks for a Martini, be sure she gets one—a Martini *cocktail*, perhaps the most treacherous brew available. Unsure of herself, she may well ask for a Sherry—in which case order a Tio Pepe, the dryness of which will be quite foreign to her palate and will encourage her to switch.

Get her on the liqueurs if possible. They are (see elsewhere) the most insidious in that they taste nice and are therefore widely viewed as being non-alcoholic.

'I'll tell you what, Miss Fullbright—darling—have another piece of apple pie and a few glasses of Dutch custard over it. The Dutch always serve it in glasses, you know. They call it *advocaat*. Yes, isn't it a funny name. Just pour it on. Waiter—three more glasses of the *advocaat* please ...'

How to acquire a Homebody

I have tried a milk-round, which is possibly the simplest method of contacting housewives after their husbands have gone off to work. But the pay isn't much—and attempting to subsidise a couple of evenings a week at the *Terrazza* on the small change accumulated from overcharging on a pot of yoghurt is optimistic.

The door-to-door method, actually, is good for little more than getting across an urgent message. Dressed in my Young Encyclopaedia Salesman's Set I have rattled many a knocker with a copy of the A—BOA, hissed 'The China Garden at 8 o'clock', as she opened the door, and disappeared into the bushes as silently as I have appeared.

Timing is the essential attribute here. One day whilst I was concentrating on the garden path to establish a clear way of escape, I hissed the usual formula without waiting to see who was actually opening the door. I arrived at the China Garden to find the lady's husband waiting. A man

of aspiring academic ambitions, I managed to buy him off
with the A—BOA but the situation gave me quite a start;
and husbands are not generally in the mood to give you
much of a start.

Safer, perhaps, to concentrate on the pretty little home-
body who lives next door—a young lady whose most susceptible aspect must derive from her thirst for romance in terms
of the dramatic novelettes which are so often her only
companionship.

The adoption of a cloak and slouch hat as normal wear
is the main prop. and you must leave your house, secretly
but noisily enough for her to hear you, each night on the
stroke of Twelve. Do not return until the stroke of Four.
What you do out of the house during those hours is your
own problem; perhaps you could visit the wife of a night
worker, or sit up with a chic friend.

During the day push through her letterbox small boxes
addressed to yourself franked SMERSH, and leave curiously
worded messages for yourself at her phone number. Have
all your letters delivered to her by mistake as well. Mark
them TOP SECRET and when she knocks in neighbourly
fashion to pass them on, receive them inscrutably. Glance
quickly up and down the street behind her, say nothing,
and close the door without a word.

Next have a crate of Champagne delivered to your name
but at her address. Rest assured that she is by now so over-
whelmed with curiosity regarding your background that she
will be quite unable to resist the temptation of humping it
round personally.

On the morning planned for delivery, shave and dress with
special care. Wear the black Burton with the wide Prisoner
of Zenda lapels and the *I Zingari* necktie, but don't forget to
sew a Kilgour, French and Stanbury label inside your jacket.
Top it, perhaps, with either a Japanese Happi Coat or the
short silk dressing jacket with the tasselled sash and the arm-
insignia of a Ruritanian Admiral. Bunch your trusty Pyramid
hankie in your breast pocket to simulate the bulge of a
Biretta. Wait.

When she knocks, answer the door with a mask-like face,
but allow your cynical, handsome features to melt into a

charming smile as she stammers out her embarrassed explanation about how '... they've mixed up the addresses again ...' Suggest, gaily, that the least you can offer her by way of reward for her trouble, is just a glass or two of the Tattinger.

As she hesitates, glance over her shoulder vigilantly at something going on across the street, and taking her arm in a gentle but vice-like grip pull her firmly inside the front door along with the Champagne. Close the door, gumshoe over to the window, and peer very carefully through the side of the curtains.

Satisfied at last, turn to face her with a reassuring smile and lead her towards the champagne.

How to acquire a Femme Fatale
Here it is necessary to realise that nobody is impressed with what they have already. It is pointless, therefore, to attempt to flatter a femme fatale on the basis that you regard her as beautiful. Take it for granted, as she does, and emphasise continually the fact that you regard her as at least slightly stupid.

Ignore her obvious physical charms. But whenever she proffers an opinion or attempts to add to a conversation you are holding with a plainer girl, and to whom you are perversely giving all your attention, look faintly irritated at the interruption or turn away with a resolutely polite half-smile. Allow her to catch you winking at the plain girl.

Order the femme fatale a Pastis, a Pernod or a glass of sour Beaujolais. Make her stand drinking in crowded off-beat bars like the York Minster, where the crush is so intense as to prevent her lovely body from being appreciated, and where the obscure pronouncements of the indigenous intelligentsia will confuse her and develop her inferiority complex.

Her inferiority complex in terms of academic or cultural background is her weak spot, and should be attacked at every opportunity. Realising that her natural attributes are no result of her own achievement, she wishes basically to be loved for herself alone—so make it clear that you wouldn't touch her with a copy of Roget's *Thesaurus*.

This is the one girl to whom you can with impunity be outrageously churlish, if only because nobody has ever done it before, and never, *never*, make a pass at this one. Sulk a bit. Be moody. Simulate utter boredom. She will imagine she has done something to offend you and will try to make amends in the only way she knows how. Really sure of yourself when she tries to kiss you, you can even push her away a couple of times; though it is not advisable to overdo it.

How to acquire a Debutante

All daughters of important or successful men are in love with their fathers. So it is necessary for you to buck the old man's image without inducing resentment through shattering her illusions. Admire him in your conversations whilst emphasising slyly the generation gap. Wean her away from the social set with occasional and haphazard references to 'generations of in-breeding', 'chinless Charleys', and 'the drones'. Implant in her mind a fear of the genetic hazards of intermarriage between ancient noble families.

Take her to expensive places. She will have an idea that you can't afford it but will be impressed with the suggestion that money means nothing to you. It will put paid to the suspicion that you love her for her father alone. But whilst indulging her tastes stick resolutely to your own.

Alongside her Brandy Sour insist upon your pint of Best Bitter, a drink which at once suggests both virile plebeian practicality (Bitter) and qualitative selectivity (Best). Encourage her to acquire such tastes and 'Michael's introduced me to a different world ...'

Behind all the forceful independence, though, insert a streak of the helpless little boy. Always wear your tie knot slightly off centre and allow her to straighten it. Take advantage of the fact that a girl cannot indulge her maternal instincts in an admiration for a father figure. Comb your hair with careful untidiness and allow casual locks to fall constantly across your forehead. Brush it back impatiently throughout the evening and allow it to be shaken forward again every now and then. Later on, allow it to fall forward and leave it there. When she leans forward to brush it back into place you know you've got her.

*How to acquire a young lady when you are not on home
ground*

The short campaigns so far outlined have of course been
concentrated in terms of indigenous women. Yet, strangely,
the greatest necessity for female companionship is often felt
during periods of holiday or business trips away from a man's
home base.

For at the back of his mind, a man is always on the threshold of an adventure the moment he steps aboard a train,
a ship, or an aeroplane. Personally, I never leave home
without a burgeoning confidence that this time it will happen.
At the back of my mind is the incurable belief that tonight
I will enter the bar of the Wigan Hilton to find it empty
save for a stunning and busty brunette sighting me fond-eyed
along the barrel of her foot-long, jewelled, cigarette holder.

Our eyes will meet. My nonchalant nod, my casual invitation to join me for dinner, my sophisticated chatter, my
charming attentiveness; all will lead to that magical moment
when I wish her a quizzical good-night and she surreptitiously
slips into my hand the key to Room 504.

It has never happened, of course. But as the 11.16 for Hull
or some other exotic watering place diddley-dums its way
out of Kings Cross, hope springs eternal. I down my first
large Scotch in the Pullman, case the compartment for likely
offers, and console myself at their absence by stalwartly
assuring myself that Tonight is definitely The Night.

A man is hag-ridden, of course, by the fear that should
such opportunity ever present itself he will be either too
startled or too suspicious to take advantage. Fear of lurking
private detectives; of a muscled thug appearing in her room
at the moment of ultimate compromise; of V.D.; all might
quickly quench one's Drambuie induced passion. Even the
sudden suspicion she was really a feller sent by the Russian
secret police to set him up for a drugged night and some
terrifying negatives, to be exchanged only for a free look at
the Autumn sales figures, would push his companion's image
into a wild distortion of homosexual fantasy.

Yet in truth, the dangers of this latter blackmail paradoxically can be used by a philanderer to his own advantage. A

warning not long ago by the Foreign Office that Britons travelling abroad behind the Iron Curtain have often been lured into compromising situations by beautiful Russian women, photographed, and then blackmailed into surrendering state or technical secrets, can work both ways. Any businessman caught in any sexually compromising situation abroad in future can simply plead he was framed when the blackmailers threaten to tell his Mum.

Incapable of resistance, he can insist, his limp and flaccid body was arranged in a variety of grotesque positions in juxtaposition with a consenting male or female (or both) member of the KDV, exposed to the tell-tale camera at will, and offered as proof of the West's moral decadence.

He has but to claim, when the pictorial evidence is proffered in the Divorce Court, that he is the victim of an International Spy Ring to have indictment substituted by a wave of patriotic sympathy. What is more, there's no vinism like chauvinism; and the suggestion that he might be important enough to be in charge of national secrets should invest him with enough glamour to ensure he does well with the women at home too.

The average man's travellings, however, are generally less exotic and more inclined to the annual; and on holiday with money in your pocket and time on your hands there is only feminine companionship wanting. Unfortunately, it generally isn't wanting you.

Men in pairs are more likely to be lucky. A chum to laugh oafishly at your cheeky chaff and prod your drunken garrulity into even louder and bolder advances is an almost essential accessory to a basically shy man seeking the company of the opposite sex. Alone, a fellow must play his cards coolly and to planned purpose.

Confusingly, every woman does not react in the same way. National customs, national habits and environmental influences leave every girl with characteristics peculiar to her race or creed. And for a man seeking to spread his country's prestige abroad and bolster good will among less happier breeds, methods of bending women's receptive instincts can take on a nationalistic aspect.

Take the American lady, for example: The simplest

method of acquiring a girl from the U.S. has been widely publicised in the past but is perhaps worth briefly repeating for the purposes of this study.

Every beautiful and curvaceous American blonde is traditionally squired at the sea-shore by 120 pound weaklings. All that is required in order to insinuate yourself into her affections is kick sand in his face. According to time honoured ritual he will protest: 'Hey; quit kicking sand in my face,' but will shamefacedly avoid further action until such time as he has the opportunity to subject himself to the rigours of a body building course from Mr. C. Atlas. Meanwhile, you are off with the girl.

It is but fair to warn you that the traditional pattern of events in the past has led inevitably to a melancholy retribution when the 120 pound weakling catches up with his new muscles and his erstwhile antagonist. The only possible way of avoiding such circumstances is to find a new beach where he will be unlikely to trace you, or to take the same body building course as he does and maintain the differential.

Spanish girls are so starved of romance by the insistent propinquity of the inevitable chaperone, that it is necessary to attract them with heroism and break through the social obstacles by placing them and their family in your everlasting debt.

About the only way to meet a Spanish girl whilst you are on holiday, therefore, is to save her from drowning; but the possibilities of such coincidence are far removed and hardly conducive to affection if you find it necessary to chuck her in first. It is seldom, indeed, that the beach belle goes any where near the water. The Crash Plan is to wait for the water to come to her.

Once the incoming tide has swept to a few feet from where her lovely frame lies sunbathing, you can be forgiven for believing that this motionless figure has but recently been washed ashore by the waves. Fling yourself down upon her supine body and attempt to save her life by administering respiration by the mouth to mouth method. Until the protesting chaperone at last disengages you, the least any spirited girl can do is go along with the pretence.

It is never wise to admit to being an Englishman whilst

attempting to score with a French girl. National antagonisms between the two countries are as strong as ever they were. Better to take refuge in one of the traditional alliances against the Auld Enemy and pretend to be Scottish.

The French pride in your shared enmity for perfidious Albion will encourage her to drink a toast or two to your respective nations, and immediately you are on the road to good cheer. No more than a couple, though. Be warned: this girl has been brought up on wine-drinking since she was a baby and can probably drink you under the table. Not that under the table is a bad place to be with a French girl; but linoleum offers cold comfort to a man wearing the kilt.

Tea is very lightly regarded in France, of course, as is anything identified with an English kitchen. But the French girl's certain ignorance of Scottish *cuisine* could have her at your mercy in no time. Having wheedled your way into her confidence during several nights of the delights of her French cooking, you may very reasonably insist that you repay the compliment and prepare for her personally a fearful repast of salted porridge, jelly pieces, mutton pies, tattie scones and lightly boiled haggis. A sharp attack of nausea is the inevitable result, and you then have the right to insist that having upset her delicate constitution it is your responsibility that she be carefully nursed back to health.

This ensures (a) certain access to her bedroom, (b) certain access to her bedroom whilst she is in bed, and (c) certain access to her bedroom whilst she is in bed and feeling weak. With any luck it's a braw bricht moonlicht nicht the nicht.

Affinities are more naturally close between the English man and the Italian woman. The English image is still an 'aristocratic' one in Italy and has retained the pre-war belief that the majority of English travellers are unusually dressed but usually rich—especially when encountered at winter sports resorts.

In the Italian Alps, therefore, it is necessary only to attend the Nursery Slopes in an incongruous ensemble of home-knitted sweaters and baggy grey flannel trousers, and *après ski* functions in stiff collar and pin-striped suit, to be accorded instant attention.

The excessively maternal Italian girl is automatically attracted to the child-like and helpless novice and having her teach you to skate or ski whilst you loll helplessly in her arms is no bad way of spending an hour or two. And if ever you are in a position to drag her down backwards as you fall over your own feet, she could be painfully jolted in a sudden sitting position. And maybe you could get to rub the bruises.

Mittel European girls are unlikely to be deceived by the 'Mountain pass', but an unknowing girl from flat areas like Holland or Belgium or Norfolk may easily be impressed by your simulated knowledge of high ground in the area of a seaside holiday. Take her climbing in the sand hills just behind the beach, and extol the delights of the view from the summit. But once out of audible contact with the deck-chair man begin to scan the horizon anxiously. Tell her not to be fooled by the complete absence of cloud; when you suddenly see the sun coming from *that* direction (add authority to your information by pointing) visibility can clamp down in moments.

Better not chance the climb down. Safer—far—to spend the night in this hardy mountain chalet (you will have established previously that the Beach Life Guard vacates it each evening at five o'clock) than risk a certain plunge to death in the darkness.

There is small chance of a St. Bernard, tell her. The damned dogs are never around when they're needed. But by good chance you happen to have brought along a bottle of the Five Star with you ...

How to acquire a young lady on the way

IF TRAVELLING BY TRAIN project an air of prosperity by having a porter carry your single portmanteau to a point near where your quarry is standing. Then enquire in a loud voice as to whether this is the point at which the First Class compartments stop. Having established that it is not, have the porter shift your case to the right position on the platform.

Enter the train in the First Class section, and you may then make your way to the Second Class seat to which your ticket entitles you. But be back by one of the doors in the First Class corridor as the train reaches its destination.

Simulate a stumble as your quarry passes the door at which

you have been standing and fall out (case and all) aimed nicely to knock her off her feet. Due to the fine British class consciousness, she will show no antagonism at being knocked down by one of the Top People—and will guess from your simulated accent that you are a member of a noble family.

The gallantry you display in insisting that you take her in a taxi to the local hospital for a check up will be no surprise to her. She will take it for granted that you know the town well and are a respected visitor.

Leave her in the taxi whilst you go in to arrange things, and when you are in the Hospital simply enquire about visiting times. Back in the cab apologise profusely for the fact that all the emergency beds are filled—and insist that she returns with you to your hotel to rest up and recover from her shaking. Promise her that you will take her on to her hotel as soon as she feels better. Promise her anything, indeed. Offer her a drink strictly for medicinal purposes.

IF TRAVELLING BY AIR wait for the next load of package deal passengers when you arrive at your destination airport. Select the most attractive single girl emerging from Customs.

Whip on your Official Peaked Cap (as near a facsimile of a local policeman as you dare) and demand to see her passport. Study it with a frown and tell her 'Follow me, pleez.' She will follow (a) because she is frightened, and (b) because you have her passport. Lead her to the nippy little two-seater hire car you have arranged whilst waiting for her flight to arrive and instruct her to enter. Once she is seated, slam up through the gears and make straight for that darling old inn up in the hills where you can ply her with luxuries until she promises to be yours.

IF TRAVELLING BY SEA always insist that any assignation is in your cabin rather than in hers. It is only gentlemanly to try and persuade a guest against leaving, whereas it is merely churlish to remain somewhere when you have been ordered to go. Too, you don't have to walk back.

Explain knowledgeably that a half pint of rum has to be drunk daily at sea to avoid scurvy. Only as a last desperate trick resort to the revelation that the captain of a ship is empowered to marry couples at sea.

How to acquire your best friend's fiancée

Bearing in mind that it's an acquisitive world, it is as well to remember that friends are supposed to share and share alike— and if your Best Friend has a young lady of his own, then why not you? Why not, indeed, her?

As she circulates already in your own particular social circle, shares similar tastes with you (you're both fond of Oliver, aren't you?), and is reasonably easy of access, she seems about your best bet. After all, Oliver *is* your Best Friend and what's good enough for dear Oliver should be good enough for you.

The first thing to establish is an invented girl friend called, say, Hortense, who is clearly unreliable. Rather rueful mention of her occasionally will establish a sympathy for you in the kind heart of Oliver's girl; and if you treat that young lady with politeness, consideration and respect, she will begin to think that Hortense is hardly worth your trouble. Leave it at that.

A double date for the four of you should be easily arranged, and Hortense's failure to arrive (*again*—oh! She is so tiresome.) will produce the situation where you are cast together for an unequal evening with yourself as gooseberry.

Whilst you wait impatiently in the Lounge Bar for the missing Hortense, be charming to Oliver's girl only this side of smarm. Apply polite attention to her every word and, because you have mugged up on a favourite subject of hers which you know Oliver despises, engage her in intelligent conversation and wince with embarrassment when great, coarse Oliver shoves in his ignorant and dismissive two cent's worth. Smile sadly. Manage to impart the feeling that Hortense's non-arrival isn't spoiling your evening one bit; she can't hold a candle to Oliver's girl anyway.

Because he is out of the conversation, Oliver will be drinking more quickly than either of you, and this should be encouraged. Buy him rounds without including yourself, and give him every opportunity to get rosy. Check your own intake studiously and you will not only *look* soberer than Oliver—you will *be* soberer. Too, Oliver's bladder will begin to trouble him and will necessitate a trip to the Little Boys' Room. Fill up his glass surreptitiously, as he departs, and then drop a hint to his girl friend in the most sincere voice you can simulate.

'Look, Lovey; forgive what you might think is my inter-fering—but let's try and keep Oliver from going overboard on the booze tonight. I've known him longer than you and know most of his problems. Probably you know how he behaves, you poor darling . . .'

Probably she won't; but the seed of doubt is sown never-theless. Say a lot of things you don't like to say about Oliver. Drop an unspoken hint about the mad Grandfather, or that peculiar Oriental malady that Oliver picked up in Alexandria on the package deal holiday in 1972. It never really cleared up. Don't be specific. A girl can draw far worse conclusions than you dare utter in face of the Slander Laws. Tell her that if ever there's anything you can do to help . . .

When Oliver comes back, and finishes that Mickey, let his girl see you noticing his bad manners. Remonstrate with him gently about behaviour which normally wouldn't even be noticed were Oliver and you alone together. Project an image of loyal embarrassment. Embarrassed loyalty. When he calls for what he knows fairly to be his round, suggest he doesn't really *want* another yet, does he? Wait for her to start persuading him against more drinking. Whisper to her that you can handle this if she'll just disappear to the Powder Room for ten minutes.

When she goes, explain to Oliver (who is beginning to feel slightly persecuted) 'I had to take her part in common polite-ness, but now she's gone I'd like to warn you about that type. Look—old Buddy Boy—if I'm out of line then shoot me down; but I hate to see a right guy the victim of a takeover bid. Who gives *her* the right to ration your liquor? You can drink any-one I know right under the table . . .'

Oliver will now be anxious to *prove* he can drink anyone under the table the moment the girl returns. He will hit the happy juice even harder. Anxious suggestions on her part that he might ease up a bit will simply induce an urgent need for him to establish his masculine independence. The more she interferes, the more she will be faced with surly opposi-tion. By now she is disgusted with him, and he is utterly at loggerheads with her. The atmosphere is taut, they sit there glowering at one another and you. Exclaim that you are anxious not to intrude upon a scene which is hardly any of your business (where the Hell *is* Hortense. If she'd arrived on time you'd all be at the restaurant by now.).

The girl will suggest that it's hardly fair to blame Hortense because Oliver is acting like a pig. Surely people can get held up somewhere without other people having to drink themselves into a stupor. And please don't go and leave me with this bullying sot ...

That is Oliver's cue to threaten her, and you, being a gentleman caught up between two opposed affections, will have to take the lady's side in sweet and infuriating reasonableness. Already incensed by his fiancée's refusal to allow you to leave the two of them by themselves, Oliver will probably try to strike you—but as he is by now dead drunk you should be able to cope with him easily. Swing him over your shoulder, assure her you've been through this a dozen times before, and carry Oliver to the cab which you ordered with some foresight half an hour ago.

Push Oliver through his front door on to the floor of his hallway and leave him there. By the time he wakes up shivering at about two o'clock, you will be at a romantic all-night spot demonstrating how much more pleasant life is likely to be with you than with that disgusting, drunken, surly, coarse, uncouth Oliver. By now you will have lost your Best Friend of course; but with a new little girl to play with, who needs Oliver?

THE YOUNG LADY
AND VIOLENCE

THE FACT THAT A MAN HAS ACQUIRED AT LAST A YOUNG LADY of his very own in no way indicates that his troubles now are ended. In some ways, indeed, they are but beginning— for Possession may be nine tenths of the law, but Getting Possession is the tenth which really matters.

The march of industrial civilisation has changed the projection of the tournaments in which the achievement of a young lady's admiration is acquired—but the basis is still largely framed in mortal combat. Remember that for every man satisfied with a new young lady to himself there are some half dozen rogue males snorting on the periphery of the herd—each waiting to cut out a female for himself. That the one he eyes so covetously is yours will bother his conscience no more than your own conscience is bothered by the fact that before you got her she belonged to somebody else. It is seldom, in real life, that anybody *actually* marries a childhood sweetheart.

The urge for one man to beat up another man because he is accompanying a pretty young lady derives from two human male impulses: (a) to get her for himself, and (b) a jealous streak which disapproves of an enjoyment in which he cannot share.

The man in possession of the young lady is at once under a disadvantage for three reasons: one, he cannot too easily withdraw from any clear challenge without decreasing her admiration for him; two, the sexual enjoyment of recent nights, coupled with the rich living necessarily embarked upon in order to ensure it, has left him in no condition for physical violence; and, three, he is wearing his best clothes.

One's hesitation to spoil clothing upon which one has lavished considerable care and expense is largely responsible for the general belief that a concern with appearances is effeminate. Invariably reluctant to engage in fisticuffs which might tear or bloody his new suit, the temporary dandy is at once categorised as a coward and a cissy; often without justice. Indeed, when one considers that even the professional soldier is issued with one suit for walking out and another for engaging in the practicalities of combat, it seems at least

39

slightly illogical that the average lover does not carry with him a spare suit for punches-up.

The great boom in violence we have witnessed during recent years may well be traceable to the steady deformalisation of clothes into everyday acceptance of cheap garments like jeans and sweaters—for to be frank I have not entered into a brawl with any real enthusiasm since I realised that the basic prop in a young-lady-attracting projection is the perennial affecting of an expensive Savile Row suit.

In fine worsteds and fine linen, I react instinctively against the barbarian idea of blood letting if the blood is in any way likely to be mine. Blessed with a myriad of tolerant, philosophic and humanitarian attitudes, I couple them with an innate reasonableness and a love of life which together add up to being dead funky. Rolling about in dark alleys in a 100 Guinea suit is a form of indulgent extravagance in which I have never come to feel quite at ease. I suspect that achievement of really expensive elegance for *everybody* is the quickest way to cut down the incidence of violence, and confine controversy to the Courts.

But the trouble about being an instinctive peacemaker when one's antagonist doesn't care what happens to his clothes or yours, is the fact that in sudden bar-room contests the man who neglects to strike the first blow almost invariably comes in second.

If public-house punches-up all commenced fairly and squarely, with the officiating publican ringing his 'Time' bell, for another round, and the antagonists advancing slowly and warily—arms extended for a sporting touch of fists before settling down into classic Gentleman Jim stances—things might be bearable. One would even, in such a reasonable atmosphere, be allowed time to doff one's jacket neatly and roll one's sleeves up in that gentlemanly fashion which flattens the cuff neatly three times *below* the elbow (*not* in a great proletarian sausage around the biceps).

But turn away from your rival in actuality and—Clunk!— a light ale bottle makes contact with the back of your skull and the whole situation is suddenly No Contest. Simply begin to remove your coat in the interests of the sartorial proprieties, and the opposing thug will wait till it is halfway off and use it to pinion your arms whilst he nuts you circumspectly across the bridge of your nose.

Even reach up to your breast pocket for a white handkerchief to wave as a token of surrender, and your opponent will swiftly grab for his own coat pocket and produce a trusty razor with which he will monogram your face. 'Good-Night' too often begins with a Gillette.

Paradoxically enough, the gentle sex are far more likely to be responsible for the clash of male personalities than are the male personalities themselves.

'I wish you would speak to this man, Darling!' Even as you hear the words your blood runs cold. A semi-drunk has done nothing more than lightly jostle her as he reaches for his drink; but because you have not perhaps offered her all the attention this evening which she regards as her privilege, she decides his accidental brush is tantamount to a touch-up.

To a woman, involving her man in menace is the equivalent of the male enjoyment of a boxing match. It has blood, torture, fear, and pain—all enjoyed vicariously. Better still; if things work out perfectly and you are smashed to a pulp, she can extend her enjoyment via maternal instincts as she nurses you back to health, and via your knowledge that she will nurse for ever the vision of you at a disadvantage.

You have a chance of coming off best, but it is a slim one. If you are in luck, the third party may be a cheery drunk who will apologise with the readiness of a man who is enjoying life, offer you a cheery wave and a wink, and retire once more to his companions. You need then only catch her eye and nod sternly, to indicate silently, 'They don't mess about with me, Love.' In which case she will feel inwardly worsted and have recourse only to trying to involve you in an argument with a more belligerent bystander.

The belief that women find violence abhorrent is a very wide and general misconception. One only has to bear in mind the classic phrase: 'Are you going to let him talk to me like that?', and register consciously the number of times you have heard it said, to know that woman is born to trouble as her young sparks fall downward.

Men are basically more gentle creatures. Those cold-eyed, tight-lipped staring matches one encounters now and then in public houses are mainly a great sham. Two men of equal weight and substance take umbrage at a chance remark, an accidentally trodden-on foot, or the spilling of an inch of beer. Smiles fade, laughter dies away, and the silence spreads in circles like the widening ripples on a pond. Nothing but heavy breathing can be heard.

It is only the drink. The first protest is sheer bravado, the answering threat but empty pride. At once, both antagonists know they have gone too far this time—and a cold sweat of fear informs each in clammy confidence that he hasn't any confidence after all. Each realises he is about to have his face broken open. Both men's insides have turned to water, and they pray for the sudden and unlikely intervention of a policeman, their mothers, an urgent shout of 'Fire!', or the sudden shock of an earthquake.

Only a late arrival in the bar, pushing unknowingly through a knot of nervous spectators and up to the bar, breaks the tension of the suicidal denouement and—the spell broken—both heroes gladly turn away with simulated reluctance and hard-eyed mumblings; to face it out another day. Honour and cowardice have been satisfied.

Once a couple of men start chatting about doing one another up, there is little actual chance of the violence ever taking place. The real assassin wastes no time in threats but simply clunks you. The normal male is generally open to reason. Fighting to establish the sophistry of some point of academic disagreement—as I always point out to men bigger than I—is animalistic, contemptible, utterly without logic, and by way of proving nothing whatsoever. But as I usually point out to men smaller than I it is often the only way.

As a result, I have been given fat lips by more people than you can shake a stick at. And, indeed, any time I shake a stick at someone up he comes and gives me another fat lip. About the only advice I can offer as a result of a variety of brief encounters over the years is the practical tip that fresh blood stains are quickly removed from clothing by the simple process of moistening the area with a sodium perborate alkali solution.

If, however, you are anxious that a challenge should not go unaccepted whilst you are in the presence of a young lady whose admiration and respect you wish to retain, it is as well to take advantage of the simple fact that when you have been singled out for a thrashing it is a peculiar tradition among roughnecks that the physical humiliation is honour bound to take place in the open air:

'Come outside ...' is the inevitable invitation. There is a curious reluctance among the heavy mob to whack anyone with a roof over his head.

The moment words are spoken, even such menacing words as this, one can claim to be in the throes of negotiation—and time is always on your side. It takes but a second for him to die of a sudden coronary, to be spirited away by fairies, or to be overcome by a visitation as glorious as Paul's on the road to Damascus. Procrastinate.

One way to safety is to refuse point blank in the kind of jokey way which suggests to bystanders that you are really both old friends just larking it up for everybody's amusement.

'What? Go out there in the cold and pouring rain, Ducky, in my state of health? Give us a kiss in here ...' He may be shamed into a contemptuous refusal to hit a homosexual, and stand momentarily nonplussed. This gives you time to press a placatory £5 note into his hand, send the young lady for a policeman, reach for a defending bottle, or take such immediate action as seems advisable.

The bottle defence is not to be entirely trusted, despite its efficacy in cinematic bar-room brawls. There, the hero faces a quartet of knife-toting foreign devils, hastily grabs a bottle by the neck, and sharply smashes it against the counter. It shatters neatly into a pronged glass trident and the cowardly asiatics are out through the door in a trice. He, meantime, flings the remains of the bottle into a corner, lights two cigarettes at the same time, offers her one with that attractive lop-sided smile of his, and murmurs coolly: 'A Double Diamond works wonders ...'

In real life I have never found it quite like that. Twice I have had recourse to the ploy. The first time the neck of the bottle broke off absolutely flush with my fist and the beer in the bottle ruined my suede shoes. And the second time a glass splinter from the shattered fragments stuck in my hand and I had to hold up the action whilst I begged a piece of Elastoplast from my assailant.

If, on the contrary, you decide to see the thing through with quiet dignity when the hoodlum flexes his muscles at you, you may well decide that 'outside' gives you a much better chance. To the thinking man it can. It is necessary for you to decide simply who shall go first.

If you support the philosophy that first is best, you have two alternatives: (a) you can walk through the door with all that bustling haste which suggests to bystanders that you want to get at him and teach him his ultimate lesson as soon as possible—and then keep running like the wind the moment your feet hit the pavement. Or, (b), you can slip out smartly, dodging quickly to one side as you do so, stand out of vision behind the door jamb, and clobber him behind the ear immediately he emerges.

Going out second can have its advantages too. The really shameless coward can follow his antagonist to the door in the certain knowledge that since the fashion for fewer bars opened up the insides of most pubs, there are generally at least two doors to every bar. Once he has passed through one, you can slam it and make for the other—to be lost in the teeming West End crowd—or you can run upstairs and demand 'Sanctuary!' in the Ladies' Toilet.

If you are the bolder spirit whose pride demands the show of belligerence manifested in actually following him out, you must keep very close behind him in order to prevent his use of (b) above and, as he turns to square up to you, push him very smartly off the pavement and under the wheels of any passing heavy vehicle.

A broad and friendly smile, whilst it may seem an obviously placatory measure in controversy, has also to be criticised in the terms that it makes a clear target of your teeth—and teeth are a secondary armament you would not wish to be missing should the brawl reach really serious final stages. Every little helps.

Unfriendly Dissuasion is perhaps the best and safest way to steer through the shoals of bar-room menace. The fewer people you talk to, the less likelihood there is of getting in trouble. Simply looking perennially mean and bad tempered is enough to dissuade most people from approaching you—

but the lout looking for violence may well be incensed by such a visage, and even persuade himself that doing you up amounts to a service to society.

A 1946 type Drape-Shape jacket—with a couple of stones of padding in each shoulder and the simulated physique of a very hard boiled egg, or a roll-neck sweater with 'Golden Gloves Heavyweight Division 1968' emblazoned across the back (and the front and sides for wider advertisement) are traditional dissuaders.

More esoteric is a forged Olympic Gold Medal for Boxing on your watch chain, to be shown discreetly and in utter confidence to people who can be relied upon to blab the news about. This is strategic rather than tactical, though, for if you are in trouble with a man whose eye level is only up to your watch chain you should hardly be in need of any assistance at all—even though a straight left from a fellow that size is likely to be more painful than most.

With the currently wide appreciation of plastic surgery, I see no reason why the outright coward should not have his menace potential visually bolstered by a Broken Nose Job, or even the surgical addition of a pair of cauliflower ears. Each would suggest you've done a bit in your time, and can handle yourself—though their clear evidence that you have been to at least some degree a loser could the more encourage a bruiser who has so far managed to come through all his altercations unmarked.

Certainly you need not be afraid that a few interesting facial blemishes are likely to disenhance your attractions among the young ladies. The Butch projection is attractive to more than homosexuals. The sadistic impulses among the female sex too often merge with the masochistic. The virility image imparted by a lived-in face is emphasised to many women by the kinky promise of rough handling of herself. German students especially have explored this curious phenomenon via their extraordinary cult during Post War years for the duelling scar.

The sharply indented Prussian officer was a cliché of the First World War, but Hitler forbade the duelling tradition as wasteful of the military urge. Only in the late nineteen fifties did a resurrection of this curious blood sport spring again into a Germany looking to win back its pride in arms. In the German University 'duelling fraternities' each member had to undergo at least one compulsory duel, apart from any he might engage in on his own account via challenges to or from members of other fraternities—the main object being to induce what was oddly regarded as honourable disfigurement; badges of both social and sexual distinction.

Participants in the duels were actually wrapped up as thickly and heavily as ice-hockey goalkeepers, with eyes and all really vulnerable parts bandaged, padded and shielded so that there was no real danger of fatality—but with cheeks, chin and forehead areas all uncovered. They then faced one another and fought in a completely stationary position, each attended by his own Second—who watched to see no fouls were struck, and intervened with his own rapier in any such event.

The duel, called 'Mensur', was fought in the presence of friends of both parties, and a physician who attended the first blood by clamping the wound to stop the bleeding. To alleviate the pain of this rough treatment, the swordsman's second pressed and pulled hard on the victim's ears. It was all jolly good sport.

No plastic surgery was applied. On the contrary, the wound was deliberately kept open so as to encourage visible scar tissue. It was these resultant scars, indeed, which were the only trophies of such a curious pastime. Fraternally yours for life, they were seen as stamping their proud Teutonic owner as a man of University education, physical virility, admirable moral fibre, and superior fraternity. The ironical point to it of course was that, like the unmarked boxer, if you were a dab hand at the game you could presumably sail through the whole of your school days successfully carving out portions of your playmates and arrive yourself at graduation with a face as smooth as any of the morons who never aspired to your educational advantages. Not even the German Universities ever awarded a Blue for chopping off chums' ears—and only careless Hans could carry honourable marks into his post graduate days.

The duel originated initially in honest Trial By Combat, of course, an application which did not entirely support the principle of Might is Right because the rough idea was that the Almighty invariably favoured the more deserving party. Sometimes professional champions took the place of the actual litigants themselves (in much the same way as a skilled barrister is employed today to argue the case for a more inarticulate lay-man). Trial By Combat was sublimated in the Tournament during the Middle Ages, and then gradually into duels which as the Law became a more sophisticated and diversified factor of society, functioned only in controversies which had no recourse to it – like insult and romantic rivalry.

The first aerial duel, as a matter of fact, was over a woman. In 1808 two Frenchmen – a M. le Pique and a M. Grandpré —quarrelled over the affections of a beautiful prima donna of the Imperial Opera and agreed to settle the matter from balloons.

A then contemporary account ran: 'At nine o'clock the cords were cut and the balloons ascended majestically amidst the shouts of the spectators. When they had mounted to a height of some 800 metres M. le Pique fired his first piece without effect. Almost immediately afterwards, the fire was returned by M. Grandpré, and his ball penetrated his adversary's envelope: The consequence of which was its rapid descent, and M. le Pique and his second were dashed to pieces upon a house top on which their gondola forcefully alighted. The victorious Grandpré then mounted aloft in the grandest style and descended safely some seven leagues distant from the locality of his ascent ...'

But what should give a man more anxiety even than his susceptibility to the attacks of other men, is the growing trend for young ladies to arm themselves personally—not in defence *of* their male escorts but in defence *against* their male escorts. In recent years the tendency for handbags to carry ammonia sprays or mace distributors, even police whistles and alarm bells which will summon assistance should their companion's attentions become over urgent, is an added hazard to being an admirer of the opposite sex.

One of the most bizarre expressions of feminine self defence came a few years ago when one lingerie manufacturer disturbed by the rise in the incidence of mugging, invented a brassière with a holster and small pistol cunningly concealed in one of the cups. Market results were disappointing despite promotional assurances that it would be a certain draw. The dangers of disillusion doubtless played their part in the realisation that probably what you were admiring about a girl was merely her artillery; that her vital statistics in reality only added up to *Point* 45 : 32 : 40. And that whether she was flat chested or nicely rounded depended upon whether she was packing an automatic or a revolver. It was suggested at the time that a couple of hand grenades might have been more flattering armament in the position being utilised.

Cinema and Television must bear their portion of the blame for the seeming recent growth in feminine frightfulness. In the Bond movie *From Russia With Love* the villainess of the piece sported a pair of winkle picker shoes with automatically controlled flick-knife blades in the toes, just for kicks. And in *The Seventh Victim* the busty star Ursula Andress was called upon to wear a lethal 'killer bra'—a sex gun consisting of a metal brassière shooting two bullets, one from each breast. As with most automatic contrivances, all you had to do was press the tit and let the recoil look after itself. With such a weapon reaching the general market, there would be more young men than you could count with holes in their hands and pleading the *stigmata*.

But if the blame can be laid at a particular door, surely the cavalcade of heroines in *The Avengers* TV series (one recalls at once the forthright Honor Blackman and her successor Diana Rigg) come most readily to mind, with their spoil-sport ability to look so completely after themselves.

Not many years ago, the only defence a woman could muster against a man stronger than herself was strategic rather than tactical. Around the bush-telegraph went the message that a man was NSIT (Not Safe In Taxis), NSOD (Not Safe On Doorsteps), NSA (Not Safe Anywhere) or H (Help!). Diminutive and more cautious young ladies unprepared for a struggle simply asserted they were washing their hair that night.

At least a man knew where he stood in those times. The encouragement of female judo means that nowadays he doesn't even know where he is going to be lying. Too often, as one is firmly attempting to obtain one's just return for the considerable expense of a couple of tickets to the Ballet, dinner for two at The Tiberio, and a taxi to Tooting, one is as like as not to discover oneself flat on one's back on her crazy paving whilst she puts the kinky boot in. There is small consolation to your pride in your ultimate realisation that she has a Black Belt. Her black belt is clearly the last thing you are likely to see that night.

Where the examples of the Misses Blackman and Rigg have done so much harm is in the growing tendency among men to suspect athletic ju-jitsu proficiency even in a girl who hasn't enough coordination to tuck her skirt in her knickers for a game of netball without breaking the elastic. Every woman becomes a potential assassin, and there is a follow-up if unspoken suggestion that, with training, any woman is the physical equal of any man. There may still be only a minority capable of applying a Flying Mare, but the implied tendency among the Liberationists towards increased bellicosity needs a male primer on coping with women who are beginning to cope.

Properly considered, a woman has a variety of defensive accessories which can be brought into action at immediate notice—and in view of this fact it should be more widely realised why the Wine Waiter always brings the gentleman diner his cork after he has opened a bottle and decanted it for dinner. Later that evening you can thank Heaven for its efficacy as you adroitly place it in the *en garde* position as the young lady lunges with her hat pin.

Many protective ploys, indeed, are simply a matter of pre-planning. It is always wise, for example, surreptitiously to slide open the catch of a young lady's handbag before embarking in the taxi for the ride home. When she raises it to belabour you, she will not only be thoroughly unsettled by its contents suddenly falling about her ears, she will be incapable of attacking you further as she claws about on the taxi floor or the pavement for the motley grotto of rubbish without which she goes nowhere. If there *is* anything of value there, and you simulate penance for your behaviour by assisting in picking her gew-gaws up for her, you may well be able to pocket it.

A traditional trick of the young lady who wishes to resist

a pass is to start laughing. The psychology behind this move is to humiliate you into desistance via her clear contempt. Mothers have advised this method for centuries, in the belief that a normal man's arrogance can never stand the thought of himself as a figure of fun, and will urge him to quit the field in sulky silence.

If her eyes aren't laughing, then all you have to do to overcome the ploy is simulate a hearty guffaw or two on your own behalf. Assure her that there is nothing you admire so much as a girl with a sense of humour and that you are glad she doesn't take this sort of thing so seriously as other girls. 'Isn't it fun?' say, and carry on as you were. Indoors, fall about laughing—and drag her down with you as you fall.

More positive females require more positive counters, of course. But quite easily dealt with is the addict of TV and cinematic violence who has grown up to believe that a man can easily be rendered helpless and vulnerable through the simple method of slipping his jacket back over his shoulders and pinioning his arms to his sides inside his own sleeves (see above).

The answer here is found in the judo philosophy which uses a person's strength against itself by simply continuing the force exerted until the antagonist is completely unbalanced. So don't fight back as she pushes your jacket back over your shoulders. Continue this movement effortlessly until the garment is entirely discarded. Say, 'You little raver! Darrrrrling—this is madness; but who are we to fight it? ...' Then resolutely follow up what you see as her primary move by whipping her sweater up over her eyes, and whilst she is struggling to drag it blindly off her head unzip and swiftly step out of your trousers. She withdraws from such a situation only at the hazard of your spreading the word that she is nothing but *a Teaser*.

Perhaps the only defensive mechanism against which there seems to be no reasonable advice is the problem of the Biter. The hell-cat who surrenders far enough to allow your lips on hers, and then sinks her teeth into them, is carrying what I have always regarded in the light of competitive enterprise into the realms of vicious sadism at worst, blood sport at best. In my own defence, I must admit that my inability to suggest a counter attack derives from the fact that this is a problem of which I have absolutely no personal experience. By the time a woman is ready to go out with me, her teeth have generally long gone.

YOUNG LADIES
AND THEIR LITTLE WAYS

THE WAITRESS STOOD, PENCIL POISED, ACHIEVING A CONTRA-dictory projection of impassive impatience, and I relinquished all pretence of the customer's right by attempting to hurry my companion into instant decision.

'You'd better have at least a sandwich,' I said, 'the show's not going to finish until well after ten o'clock, and you had very little lunch. I'm having a sandwich. Have one with me.'

'Darling, I couldn't eat a *thing*,' she said. 'Not a *speck*. The coffee will be absolutely plenty for me. *Honestly*, darling.'

So I ordered two coffees and one cheese and asparagus sandwich on brown bread, and continued the conversation:

'Current theories postulate the initial formation of metal-loryl carbonates with subsequent rearrangement for the direct nuclear addition of carbon dioxide, or reaction of the same with an intermediately formed compound,' I said.

She said did they.

'The whole point is,' I continued, 'the alkali metal used has a significant orientating influence on the carboxylating reaction ...'

I noticed that her eyes had taken on that curious glaze I have often witnessed in women engaged in conversation, but a prompting to question it was interrupted by the return of the waitress with the two coffees and my sandwich. She shoved a shameless invoice beneath the rim of my saucer, stabbed her pencil stub back into her side-burns, and withdrew.

'As I was saying,' I went on, 'sodium phenoxide gives predominantly o-hydroxy benzoic acid, whilst potassium phenoxide favours the formation of p-hydroxy benzoic acid ...'

'Just that bit there,' she said suddenly.

'I beg your pardon?' I enquired politely.

'That corner bit, just there,' she said. 'The bit where the asparagus is sticking out. Just that little bit ...'

I picked up my fork and held it ready.

'Lay a hand on that sandwich,' I warned her, 'and I'll pin your engagement finger to the table.'

I pulled my plate closer by way of precaution. 'You could have had your *own* sandwich,' I said. 'I offered you one. This one is *mine*. I want a sandwich. Not eleven twelfths of a sandwich, nor even fifteen sixteenths of a sandwich. I want a whole and complete sandwich. Nothing less will satisfy me. Particularly I want that little corner bit where the asparagus sticks out. Just keep your hands flat on your side of the table and listen to me:

'Concerning the miscibility of some pyridine homologues in water, it has been suggested that ...'

It is a curious facet of the feminine mental process that the only thing which attracts it is something which belongs to somebody else. Peck, even distastefully, at a piece of unexciting steamed cod and any woman in sight will be instantly overcome by a gluttonous acquisitiveness. A piece of her own she wouldn't want. Yours, yes.

Her reaction to drink is identical. She 'simply couldn't pour down another drop, Darling,' until the waiter has deposited yours on the table in front of you, and then it's:

'P-l-e-e-e-ase. Just give me a tiny sip, Sweetie.'

You hand over your pint pot with gallantly concealed resentment and before you can say 'Chugalug' there are about two fingers left in the bottom. Furthermore, a smear of carmine goo all round the edge of the rim she drank from will now latticework the bridge of your nose with scarlet ferocity the moment you try to finish the dregs she so reluctantly returns.

A young lady's behaviour in terms of men in no way varies. Go to a party with a pretty girl who clearly admires you, and every female eye in the room will be flashing unspoken messages like a seductive Aldis. Lids will lower like drawbridged brothels. Busty vamps will sight you along their cigarette holders across the most crowded room. You will be ankle-deep in dropped hankies. Only your loyalty to the girl with whom you arrived will disbar you from an orgy of self indulgence.

It is a loyalty emphasising the essential difference between a young lady and a young man. For though open season on other young ladies' menfolk seems generally acknowledged among women as year round, an unspoken but widely accepted two-point tradition forbids a man trespassing upon the romantic rights of his fellows. The two points are (a) a rigorous and unswerving sense of honour, and, (b) the hazard of a mouthful of knuckles. A man will seek out women only where he has been offered seemingly uninvolved encouragement.

Having failed, therefore, to take advantage of the clear interest you evoked last time, you arrive at the next reception untrammelled by any companion; resolved to take full advantage of your single state and your clear attraction for the opposite sex.

Not a woman in the room gives you a second (even a first) glance. A man not clearly the property of somebody else has but minimal attractions for the predatory female.

Possibly the only thing not belonging to her which a woman demonstrates a strong reluctance to accept is a seat offered by a gentleman on a public conveyance. Sadistically sensing the embarrassment caused to the unthinking gallant, she rationalises her refusal by ducking behind Women's Lib and draws attention to the man's discomfort with a loud 'No thank you ... Please sit down ... I'm quite capable of standing ... Sit down ...' whilst the miserable wretch slinks back into his seat conscious that he looks foolish and conscious that the consensus of opinion of masculine churls on the bus who had made no such offer is that (a) good manners are effeminate or (b) he was simply trying to pick the woman up.

As the result of years of coaching by my Mummy and Daddy, I once leapt automatically to my feet on the Paris Metro and offered my seat to a mustachioed virago of some sixty winters with all the flourish of a denizen of international courtesy. She regarded me coldly for some three seconds or so and turned away without a word. Meanwhile the other occupants of the compartment rhubarbed sullenly beneath their garlic-laden breath and would doubtless have battered me to death with rolled up copies of *Le Figaro* but for want of a leader of real courage.

I have more sympathy for the young strumpet on the Bakerloo Line not long ago whose lack of a seat I had allowed to go unrectified due to my often reiterated experience of the independent ladies who refuse such an offer. My attention was suddenly distracted from my evening paper by her sharp kicking of my ankle and the querulous demand, 'Don't you generally give up your seat to a woman who is expecting a baby, young man?'

All blushing confusion—not least at the stretched necks and turned heads seeking a look at the thoughtless monster so castigated—I leapt to my feet mouthing shamed apologies. She sank into my seat in clear relief and I buried my scarlet face in the *Evening Standard*, glad to be out of the situation so easily.

Only after a couple of stations did I dare to peep round the pages and notice to my surprise a trim figured girl of not more than nineteen years and a waist measurement of hardly more inches. She sat with a half smile of contentment upon her face kindly regarding an advertisement for an employment agency displayed upon the half ceiling on the other side of the carriage. It seemed to me that she must be so tightly corseted as to hazard the early development of her embryo, or that it was going to be a very small child indeed.

Fascinated by the trimness of her figure, and encouraged to some degree by the fact that the compartment had more or less emptied at Regent's Park, I raised my hat at last and enquired with all the tact at my command: 'Excuse me please, Madam; but am I right in believing you to have informed me that you are expecting a baby?'

She turned her attention from the advertisement and nodded. As she did so, her jacket fell open and revealed a blouse only slightly distended by immature breasts hardly capable of filling her aspiring A Cup bra., and a stomach flat as a board. Unable to contain my amazement longer, I shook my head in admiration of her unaffected physique and paid her my clumsy male compliments:

'Incredible!' I said. 'Please tell me how long you've been pregnant.'

A smirk of smug nostalgia spread over her face as she contemplated momentarily the sensual triumph of conception, and then she looked down at her wrist watch. 'About twenty minutes now, I would think,' she replied. 'Doesn't it make your legs tired ...'

Trains, indeed, seem to be a guaranteed venue for finding women at their worst. In trains with a centralised corridor, watch to see who it is leaves the sliding doors open as they sweep through to the next compartment. Men of more than about twenty-three years of age will invariably pull each door across behind them as they progress along the train. Only young yobbos and women will leave a draughty hole to plague you once they have gone through. The women, as a matter of fact, will be sub-consciously incensed at the fact that they have to open the door in the first place, for they have been conditioned for years by a world which unfastens every latch as they approach it and pushes chairs underneath them as if by coincidence at the moment they decide to sit down.

Even before she boards a train a woman has already settled down to being impossible. Have you ever stood behind one in a ticket queue at a railway booking office? The existence of Enquiry offices is ignored as she engages the clerk in ceaseless conversation whilst you hear in the distance the 6.30 p.m. train for Tunbridge Wells slamming its doors in final warning of departure.

Apart from the price of her ticket, she must enquire regarding the time of her train's departure and the time of its arrival at her destination. Too, the ticket clerk must be badgered for the platform number at which she must embark. The inevitable argument regarding her right to use cheap day return tickets during the Rush Hour has to be experienced, and her suspicions regarding the clerk's personal involvement in the recent increase in fares established. Only then will she offer to pay, and only then will she reach for her handbag.

A man attends with the money ready in his hand. Not a woman. Only when all sources of conversation have finally been explored will she at last duck suddenly from the clerk's sight below the level of his pigeon hole whilst she reaches for the bag she has always left on the floor beside her. Where is it?

When after much panicky searching it is at last discovered in the position in which she placed it, the catch must be coaxed for several minutes before it will open. Then, she must dredge about in the tangled contents in search of her purse.

Unsuccessful, she usually tips the great tangled mess out on to the counter like the disgorged contents of a sick ostrich.

And when it is found at last, the purse too will refuse to open until the 6.30 is off with a cheery whistle and a derisive wave of the Guard's flag. Only the ingrained civilisation of centuries prevents you donning your heaviest boots and taking a running kick at her great fat bottom.

In a way, women supplement all those other little irritations which so easily accumlate over years of stress into a final coronary. Irritations so obvious and so general that no one ever seems to think they are worth rectifying. Irritations like the fact that publishers have never agreed on a general ruling to ensure that the titles and author's names on books' spines lie in the same direction as one another when a row of volumes stands upon a shelf. One passes along a library section cocking one's head from side to side like a puzzled Terrier, constantly adjusting from type which reads on its side from top to bottom to type which reads on its side from bottom to top.

Irritations like the fact that shops and buildings in busy main thoroughfares are not *compelled by law* to display the number of their premises on their front fascia. Put this to the test by measuring the spaces in Oxford Street, Piccadilly, Bond Street or Knightsbridge where you will have to walk uninformed until you arrive at one of the sparsely numbered shopfronts and then have to count backwards or onwards to the premises you are attempting to discover.

Irritations like the widely used tea-pot with the hollow handle full of scalding water. Irritations like the fact that every time you dial the telephone time clock the voice says '... and twenty seconds', necessitating your having to wait for the complete recitation in the unhurried enunciation before you are able to establish how late she is already for your appointment.

Such irritations are petty on the face of it, agreed. But those great love affairs which stumble at last into a sustained hatred of one party for the other—or a mutual hatred of both parties for each—seldom smack of the tragedy with which poets too often dignify the separation.

Seldom is the cause a passionate controversy, a schism in political principles, or a disagreement upon religious dogma. It is usually the cumulative effect of simple irritation and the inevitable boredom this induces.

Romantic admiration for a young lady can only be sustained provided you remove yourself from the subject often enough and long enough to return her image to its quite wrongful perspective. To a degree, the same applies with regard to the young lady's attitude towards yourself and is probably the basic reason why all the nice girls love a sailor and why travelling salesmen are invariably the subject of the sexiest jokes. Variety is the spice of life.

Two famous platitudes are usually produced as denials, or arguments against, the truth of one another—but it is *because* 'out of sight is out of mind' *that* 'absence makes the heart grow fonder'. Out of sight, you get a rest from her, a chance to diffuse your too specific concentration, a chance to revert to the attitude where your next meeting will allow a more generalised and consequently more idealised view. It is the basic reason why the most successful marriages are often those where the husband and wife are not constantly thrown into one another's company from the end of working hours on one day to the beginning of working hours on the next—but where contact is made irregularly, perhaps spasmodically, and certainly not too often. By extension, of course, it would be possible to say that the ideal marriage is that in which the two partners never meet under any circumstances whatsoever.

For boredom with the larger, diffused and generalised view will urge the viewer to examine the details more closely in the hope of rediscovering fascination therein. And it is the details of a woman that so often let her down.

Many years ago, I once broke off an engagement because of the shape of the girl's heels. The reason might seem paltry, my action almost melodramatic, but walking arm-in-arm with her became an absurdly jerky perambulation punctuated by her stopping every few paces to hitch up sling-back shoe-straps which could not be retained in place by a heel and Achilles tendon which merged without indentation. Court shoes, ankle straps and straps across the instep she assured me were *utterly* unfashionable at the time—and we would hiccup our way down Lovers Lane in a series of ludicrous little double hops as her sling back straps slipped with the vibration of every step and she kicked up her heels alternately high enough for her to reach out and adjust the strap to the position in which her lack of a prominent heel refused to maintain it.

In irritation, I finally chalked out an ironic Hop Scotch pitch on the pavement ahead of her, skipped into a passing cab, and have never seen her again to this day.

I recall with no more affection an ex-fiancée who drove me near to deafness with her collection of exotic slave bangles. In the way that I collect a marble egg from every foreign city I visit, she boasted a bangle in gold or silver from every Continental or Oriental holiday upon which she had embarked. At the time of our lives at which our romantic paths crossed she had amassed as many rings around her arm as would be revealed in the mature innards of a felled and ancient oaktree.

Each time she raised her elbow to transport another Martini to her lips, the bangles slid up her forearm to her elbow, one by one, in a clanking ritual as inevitable as the approach of Marley's ghost. Each time she put her glass back on the table for another drink (a ritual quite as inevitable as the former) the bangles slid down her forearm to her wrist, one by one, in the opposite direction. The noise was not unlike courting in a shunt-yard. Inevitably, we drifted apart.

It is a sad commentary upon the general slide into insensitivity that women seldom nowadays regard their speech as an important facet of their projected image. A gentle suggestion, once, to a beautiful girl, that her success in the commercial life might well be affected by her rigorous dropping of her aspirates, brought only an adenoidal retort that she didn't 'ave no wish to be all lardidar like wot I woz.

It shocked me to discover that I tork lardidar. Born in Scotland of a Scots/Irish ma and an English/Irish da, there is always some team to support loyally provided it is playing Wales. And I would have supposed that in my vocal delivery I would have compressed all the succinctness of the Scot, all the articulate charm of the Irishman, and all the verbal rectitude of the Anglo-Saxon. Brainwashed by a lifetime's contact with Italian and French waiters, Irish barmaids, Jewish tailors, Welsh dairymaids, and Cockney bookies' runners, any vocal projection I ever sought was simply that of a 'gentleman'—an unhurried, carefully expostulated firmness which would at once impart my superiority and induce at least the minimum of service. And I have always been led to believe that the upper-class accent which opens all social and commercial doors is that of the nation south of Oxford, north of Haywards Heath, east of Winchester and west of Whitechapel.

As with so much of the democratic levelling of recent years, the standard of the majority has not so much been improved as diffused. Accents which once upon a time had at least the authentic originality of specified localities are now quite disappeared in the home counties. Only men and women over the age of seventy or eighty years today project a Kentish accent, or a Sussex accent, or an Essex accent. Communication is too easy, and the merging of it is spreading regional talk thin and lifeless. Only Yorkshire and Lancashire, a dilute Brummie, Geordie, Welsh and Scottish accents persist in face of the verbal mergers. To the very practised ear there are still declensions *within* these regional voices, but on the whole we steadily drift into a great unattractive mid-Nothing; the speech of the lazy-lower-classes who have been offered the opportunity of education and improvement and, on the whole, decided to decline.

Where such issues from the studiously painted lips of an otherwise lovely girl, the inconsistency is difficult to defend.

How can she justify spending a half hour or so a day brushing her hair into glossy splendour, an extra twenty minutes enriching her face with the subtle shades of cosmetic skill, a tortuous time exercising her hips and stomach muscles into taut confinement of the slack flesh resulting from the disciplines of diet, and the main proportion of her weekly wage on lingerie, tights, pretty dresses and hairdressing bills, only to smash the whole fascinating projection via the nasal whine of an ill lubricated buzz-saw when she opens her mouth?

Speech is one of the main and most important facets of personality—and there is no reason in my book why as much care and artifice should not be lavished upon it as is lavished upon the application of false eyelashes, false lip-colouring, false complexion, or false falsies.

Curiously, speech is the only personality facet which has retained its 'don't try and get above yourself' accusations of a century and a half ago. In those days, even trying to look pretty was regarded as an inevitable path to a harlot's grave, and the attitude towards deliberately improved speech today —when the media affords everyone a chance of educated emulation—is as anachronistic as sumptuary laws which allowed fine clothes only to those in receipt of a certain stipulated annual income.

It is popular still, in reactionary circles, to consider the regional accents as part of Britain's traditional charm—like an extension of those 'Come to Britain' advertisements in the *New Yorker*, which represents us all as smocked Morris Dancers, playing croquet on the Vicarage lawn between interminable cups of tea and cucumber sandwiches. But they still brand a man or woman as a slightly rustic buffoon— however lip service to democracy may deny the fact.

There may, indeed, be some grain of truth in the evaluation. Certainly in the swopping of a thick and distinct regional accent for the idly slurred mumble of the age of cheap trains up the smoke, mid Atlantic cinema, and lower-class family entertainment on the Telly, I would incline to agree. For a girl who starts out as a *you-wozzer* and takes practical steps to rectify the matter is clearly more sensitive than she who begins badly and continues in the same vein. The first is at once a girl of horizons wider than those with which she is originally presented. The second is forever a vocal prisoner of her environment. And it is not the first who gives herself airs or could be accused of vanity and conceit. In an attempt to improve herself she shows only a personal acknowledgement of what she sees as her shortcomings. Here is no conceit, but humility. Only in the girl who thinks you may take her as you find her and you are still dead lucky, will you discover the unarguable vanity. She may leave the room, for my money, the moment she is able to squeeze her big head through the door, and the reasonably articulated young lady who fears that her adoption of an uninherited enunciation may brand her as a Snob, may console herself that it is immeasurably better to be a Snob than a Slob.

It has always seemed to me that a young lady who takes no trouble with her speech is likely to have dirty shoulder-straps—and surely the revelation of grubby underthings must be the kiss of death to any romance? Not quite so indictable, perhaps, but still a cause of embarrassed irritation to her escort, are those deep scarlet trenches in the girl's shoulders —unthinkingly engrained by the day's too tight brassière. unthinkingly revealed by the evening's off-the-shoulder gown. Not only does it unspokenly suggest that a date with you was hardly worth *planning* for (a bra-less day would be the correct preparation) it also suggests to every male in sight that denied the assistance of the most rigid suspension *your* girl's boobies would have no more uplift than a spaniel's ear.

Less general nowadays, but still a transparent giveaway of the gaol-bait nymphette who has temporarily fled parental observation into the dangerous promise of a swimming-pool Bikini, are those two red badges of courage—the knicker rings. These are the result of having to wear elasticated closed-at-the-knee knickers whilst still subject to the strict sartorial rulings of a convent education. Any young lady displaying such should be told to 'come back in about two years time'. Three to be safe.

In the nineteen thirties, when the wearing of closed-at-the-knee knickers was a more general phenomenon, I recall that my own first venture upon mixed bathing disturbed my stirring puberty with a realisation that girls and women of all ages were naturally marked with two curious rings around their legs—about halfway between hips and knees. I accepted the fact without demur. Only experiment in later years brought the realisation that the Almighty, in His Wisdom, had decided to clear up the condition in a number of older young ladies at least.

My confusion was indirectly dissolved by the Chief of the Armed Forces when he ordered at the end of World War Two that fraternisation with German women would be regarded as an offence punishable by death. I had read a report in a trade paper that a very high percentage of fraus and fräuleins had remained staunchly loyal to the *directoire* style of knicker, and coupled with a popular but possibly apocryphal story that summary justice had been carried out on a Lance Corporal who had been discovered with a red ring around his wrist, the curious tattoo marks were at last explained. The confinement of their fashion to only the very young nowadays should be regarded not so much as an irritation at their

spoiling an otherwise attractive area of the female anatomy
as a handy reference point when trying to establish whether
or not the young person concerned is beyond the age of
consent.

What is too little realised by the young ladies of older age
brackets is the fact that whilst a woman delights in a man
who is imperfect, in that it offers the opportunity of making
him over completely in the image of perfection to which all
her dreams subscribe, a man has other things to build—
bridges, businesses, a reputation—and he needs his romantic
images ready-made. His young lady should be already as
near to perfection as possible on first acquaintanceship; for
that is how he will learn to love her. Imagination, in the male
sex, projects itself beyond the footling process of making for
himself something he regards as an adjunct to which he
is naturally entitled by *droit de seigneur*. In a man's world,
the only excuse for a woman is that she be feminine—and
once she does it badly she is begging for rejection.

Women should realise, therefore, that make-up should be
repaired the instant it becomes chewed off, smeared, or
dissipated—even if productivity in office or factory declines
the meantime. There is nothing quite so grisly as the girl with
a two-tone complexion and her mouth on sideways. The
coiffure, too, is a basis for the female Rejection Projection.
Up-swept hair-do's should be avoided at all costs. Arresting as
it may seem for as long as it takes to walk from Guiseppe's
cash desk to the swinging floors of the salon, one step outside
will have it pinging out from the twine of bobby-pins and
hanging like octopoid arms of non-conformist spaghetti at
the nape of a neck dandruff-speckled by cornflakes of displaced
lacquer. It is almost as unforgivable as the hair of the blonde
who has seen blonder days.

Desperately forcing fairness back into her implacably
darkening parting, she ends up with a wig like candy floss—
so bleached brittle you can practically snap it. Indeed, snap
it does, sooner or later—falling in tell-tale whisps on the blue
serge shoulders of her married lovers, and weaving in tatty
tentacles along the collar of the little black dress she studiously
affects to emphasise her phoney Nordic albinoism.

Too often women fail to score through their inability to

realise how much good-will is engendered by simply doing their best. They are too often unattractive because they forget that their attraction does not depend on natural attractiveness so much as an obvious attempt to achieve it.

A man's ego urges him to believe that a girl striving to improve herself is so striving in order to attract his attention. He concludes, therefore, that she admires him. And nothing is so attractive as the belief that someone finds you attractive. Easily flattered, a man accepts a girl who has tried to look nice as a personal compliment.

What a man does not want, on the whole, is a hearty, scruffy, female companion trying to be one of the boys. His insecurities are ingrained enough without a monstrous regiment of women threatening him with their male impersonations. He does not mind a woman using a certain kind of strong language— because it bespeaks a relaxed and progressive attitude which might be more easily acquiescent to the liberal principles of free love. But he does not want her to use the four letter words which concern themselves with the bodily functions. These are obscene, ungenteel, and therefore disrupt the respect syndrome which seeps into his admiration out of his inevitable Oedipus complex. Yet the majority of women attempt to be a sister rather than a mother—when in effect the man is looking for neither. Indeed, he probably has both already. What he is looking for is someone to go to bed with, and the convolutions of incest are far beyond the ken or aspiration of the normal fellow.

If women would only keep the idea of going to bed in mind, indeed, they might assist themselves in clearing up another of their curious little illogicalities—that of believing that sex is enjoyed only after ten o'clock in the evening. Even their Mothers and Fathers fall into the trap of insisting their young daughters be in by ten o'clock at night—quite ignoring the fact that a girl can get up to anything that pleases her at any hour that pleases her, if that is her inclination.

The curious attitude, though, is cause of the fact that in more adult and sociable circles there is all the difference in the world between asking a girl to have lunch with you and asking her to have dinner with you. The former is an Honest Jack, straightforward, reliable, pipe-smoking compliment.

The latter, to a young lady, is the first step in an attempt at seduction.

It is difficult to decide why women should beware of companionship in direct proportion to the lateness of the hour—unless it be via the simple instinct which tells them that bedtime is getting nearer every minute. For your average man is probably at his most virile and vital at about eight o'clock in the morning—provided he is free of hangover. His cells restored by eight hours sleep and a hearty dish of the Sunshine Breakfast, it is only business appointments which urge him away from the lascivious warmth of a bedtime companion. Come ten o'clock at night—after a hard fourteen hours' breadwinning—the possibility of inflaming him with a surge of impassioned concupiscence will be considerably decreased by the demands upon brain and physique made by his working day. Yet the average British woman believes implicitly that it is impossible for a man to become emotionally involved before about 6 p.m.

Not long ago, the French novelist Francoise Sagan debunked the sexy projections of Paris by protesting that nowadays everybody in Paris is too tired to find time for romance in the evening, and it could be because those pioneers of fornication —the French—are just too tired from shacking up all afternoon. For a sociological traffic report emanating from Paris at about the same time as the Sagan pronouncement insisted that where it has long been the masculine tradition for an executive husband to visit his mistress each evening on his way from the office to his wife and family, the growing jam of outgoing vehicles has produced a situation where Paris is grinding to a halt.

Faced by a home-going journey of lengthening duration with every new car released upon the roads, French business men have necessarily been obliged to shift their amorous dalliance back a couple of hours to between two and four in the afternoon.

In terms of commercial organisation and industrial production—with the wisest brains of Paris unavailable at key hours following upon traditionally prolonged lunch times—it is easy to see that the French economists could soon have on their hands as ominous an industrial problem as has been occasioned in British working circles by the sanctity of the tea break.

To a degree, of course, we might all take a lesson from the French—though a qualified one. Clearly, an arrangement most calculated to lead to more widely enjoyed sexual liaisons would be a national agreement to turn over all industrial and commercial work to the night hours. Leisure time, boy and girl assignations, social dates, romantic meals, the sex act itself, could then all be brought out into the bright and respectable sunlight. The stigma of furtiveness with which the female Grundies have so long besmirched the thing that makes the world go round would at last be swept away. With London traffic beginning to congeal as solidly as Paris, it might be the only way.

HOW TO GET THE BETTER
OF A YOUNG LADY

THE TITLE OF THIS CHAPTER IS NOT STRICTLY HONEST. IT IS relatively impossible to get the better of something which is wholly bad. In a woman's psyche there is no 'better'. Generations of evil and perversity have gone into the development of a female character of consistent outrage and the uncomplicated mind of a man is unequipped to deal with its instinctive machination. All that can be done is emphasise, possibly, the illogicality of their attitude and of the social system that supports them in it.

For example, women are widely acknowledged as irrational, eccentric, neurotic, exaggerating, misunderstanding liars—yet they are inevitably believed. Offer conflicting stories, one from a male and the other from a female; and it is the latter which a jury, a magistrate, or the general public will be more inclined to believe. It is like applying the handicap to the one who is already crippled and invests the simple fact of being born male with a considerable hazard.

A woman has but to stand up and scream in a darkened cinema and the poor devil sitting in the next seat to her is for it. He may have simply brushed against her as he reached over to flick his cigarette at the ash-tray. He may have shifted his knee involuntarily as the result of a sudden cramp, relieved his pins and needles by rolling from one buttock to the other, or reached down to undo the pain of shoelaces biting into swollen insteps. Or he may have done nothing more provoking than inflame her frustrations with his complete disregard of her proximity. But however he may protest his innocence, that one shrill scream will have marked him for ever in police records as a potential sex-maniac.

For the real trouble lies in the fact that as well as being given the benefit of the doubt, all women are obsessed by the belief that every passing male smoulders with the hardly controlled desire to fling her to the ground and have his obscene will of her. Even the most grotesquely mustachioed viragos hoard their sad bodies to themselves like lesbians on a battleship. And the simplest, male, anti-hero, bent only on getting home as soon as possible to his fretwork and his stamp collection, runs the danger of ending up in the assault cellar any time he ventures on the shortest journey.

I speak here from sad experience—a trauma at whose memory I wake up screaming to this night; even though it took place so long ago as during my nineteenth year, and so far away as the outskirts of Durban, South Africa, during the Second World War.

A studious and sensitive soul, I had wandered far from the shore-going delights of the steak egg and chips which supplied the major satisfaction of my materialistic shipmates, and in a laudable determination to see more of the real Natal than was offered in the amusement arcades of the dockyard environs, had finally lost track of the route home somewhere in the outer suburbs. Feeling that any honest South African citizen would savour a reflected war effort in aiming a loveable Jack Tar back at his headquarters, I donned my disarming smile and approached a middle-aged matron on the losing side of fifty who stood with an air of resolute virginity at a nearby bus-stop.

That my lonely explorations of the evening had been punctuated by an occasional beer in an occasional bar I would be the last to deny. But some three light ales is hardly likely to engender in an eighteen-year-old youngster an inflamed concupiscence which might urge him to fling himself upon the body of a portly mother-figure some three times his age.

Do not expect logic to intrude. I had not progressed in my polite approach further than the introductory 'Excuse me ...' when the lady in question took a rapid defensive step backwards and whacked me sharply across the face with her rolled up evening newspaper—abruptly cutting off all communication and sending my little round hat spinning across the pavement like an errant hub-cap.

The sudden surprise of her quite unwarranted attack dazed me momentarily, and I came-to to realise that the danger of my situation no longer depended upon the muscular matron alone. The brittle slap of her newspaper across my face had focussed upon me the attention of a few neighbouring citizens until that time largely unaware of my presence; and convinced that a respectable female member of their community was being beset by a transient maritime rapist they hurried to her support—converging upon me in menacing phalanxes of outraged suburban decency and murmuring 'Rhubarb, rhubarb', darkly the while. The instinctive reflexes of a man of action came to my aid at once, and I took to my heels like a startled fawn.

As I ran, I began to understand for the first time in my life what it is that motivates an entirely innocent man to flee his accusers. The empty assurance that if a man has done no wrong he need fear no indictment carries little weight when the hue and cry is in full hue and cry and you are intent only on increasing your lead. Heroines of Hollywood epics who traditionally advise weak younger brothers that, 'You can't run away for ever, Joe ...' could never have convinced me that night that it wasn't worth at least a try. My desperate flight was blind and instinctive. I can thank only God and the patron saint of coincidence that when I had finally shaken off the vigilantes my feet stumbled to a halt practically opposite the dockyard gates. How I would have got back otherwise, I cannot guess. Certain it is that I would never have dared ask a Policeman. Policemen are always on the woman's side.

Any sensible man will decide early on in life that it is practically impossible to get the better of a woman, and the more normally spiteful will settle simply for getting his own back as often as possible. In the direct confrontation this is not often possible, but a certain satisfaction may be found in the fact that a woman is always vulnerable in terms of her reputation. And it is a prime example of the paradoxes which crowd upon the war of the sexes that a man is regarded as a bit of a bounder and a rotter if he announces his intention of dating a busty, luscious, sex symbol, whereas it is in reality the man who dates the homely and plain young lady who has better chance of resolving his sexual frustration before the night is over.

Announce that you are that evening squiring the torrid Suzy Laverne—or whoever may be the local temptress—and all your men friends will begin winking grotesquely, tapping the sides of their noses, wriggling seductively and bruising each other's ribs with nudges in depth.

'Aye aye aye,' they will leer, clenching their fists, slapping their biceps, and bringing up their forearms sharply in the traditional gesture of expectant vulgarity. 'Good Luck!' they snigger; 'Get a bit for me . . .'

Inevitably you will find that the really luscious looking peach is not to be plucked so easily. So experienced is she in the consciousness of her beauty's market value that she is seldom prepared to surrender herself in return for a casual evening's entertainment.

The beautiful girl is inevitably the accomplished brusher off, the warm-hand-shaker, the it's-too-late-to-ask-you-in-for-a-final-drink-er. In the last resort she can even become the foot-in-the-door-crusher, the steely-eyed-hat-pin-stabber, or even the suddenly-revealed-Black-Belt-Third-Dan.

She will remain chaste, and never caught. You will both emerge from the evening in much the same state as you entered upon it—except that she will be fractionally fatter and you will be considerably poorer. Only in terms of reputation can you hope to get your own back.

For it is easy to destroy a woman's reputation by the simple process of seeming to defend it, at the same time elevating your own reputation as both a successful bounder and yet a nevertheless ethical gentleman. You have but to refuse to answer questions from your male friends regarding the denouement of the evening, insist upon being smilingly non-committal on the grounds of gallantry, simulate a nostalgic expression akin to the cat who got the cream, and her whole social reputation is gone for good. And serve her right.

'All right, then?' they all enquire the next morning as you arrive at work. They grin, and nod at one another, and stick their quizzical thumbs up in lecherous inquisition.

She left you the night before with casual thanks immediately after the last strains of *God Save The Queen* faded from behind the cinema screen. You shook hands, she side-stepped your proffered taxi-ride home with an insistence that the Tube would take her practically to her door and it was well out of your way, and parried your offer of a meeting next night on the assurance she needed to wash her hair. She left you and melted into the train ticket queue with never a backward glance, the bitch.

But if you recite such entirely truthful anti-climaxes with

the faintest ghost of a smile playing at the corners of your mouth, and a touch of a twinkle in eyes that refuse to meet theirs, they will conclude at once that before your two torrid bodies squirmed sweatily in last night's tempestuous congress, love-making had been in its infancy.

'*What* a liar you are,' they will giggle in rare delight, living vicariously the wild embraces of abandoned intimacy existing only in their dirty minds. 'Come on, then, tell us ...'

Your refusal to acknowledge culpability will simply sharpen their belief that you are honouring that old aphorism that a gentleman does not screw and tell. The less you say, the more you assure them with a private smile that you went to bed only with a beaker of Ovaltine, a *Playboy* gatefold and your strong right arm, the more they will imaginatively rip the clothes from your companion and her respectability to pieces. Hundreds of thousands of women every week lose their public reputation for private virtue through their erstwhile escorts verbally maintaining its absolute unassailability. Yet had those escorts regaled their friends with morning-after inventions of elaborate seduction, their natural scepticism would have dismissed him as a frustrated flanneller.

The way to get back at a beautiful young lady who has refused you is to relate the fact with a self-conscious smirk, and achieve the release of your sexual frustrations by taking out the girls who aren't much to look at.

The dedicated seducer dates the plain girls, because he is unencumbered by the simple vanity which urges a man to be seen only with pretty women. The plain girl never pretends to be washing her hair. This is the first time she's been asked out for months and is getting hungry. Unable to pick and choose her appointments, she will accept at random with naïvely obvious gratitude; and the fear of not being asked again will inevitably lure her to indiscretion on the first night. And, as any vile seducer knows only too well, a pretty face is hardly pertinent once the lights are out.

Unlike beautiful young ladies, plain ones seldom have bad reputations because few men are interested enough to enquire; and if the beautiful ones regard this as some kind of injustice they may console themselves with the resigned acknowledgement that you can't have everything. In the pursuit of love it is not simply making the most of your own situation that matters. It is quite as important to make the most of the situation of your potential quarry, and often these personal reactions to male-female relationships reflect their own wild paradox.

For example, I remember reading in my teens an article in *The Picturegoer* which only the paucity of my pocket money prevented my rectifying with an instantaneous decamping to Hollywood. Hedy Lamarr revealed how she would often sit wistfully at home of an evening, lonely as a cloud, because her transcendental beauty discouraged people from summoning up the nerve to ask her out.

I am prepared to believe it. Beauty in a woman inclines to emphasise a man's inferiority complex. Basically insecure, and inevitably modest as a result, a man is inclined to suspect any show of interest by a woman on the grounds that she is (a) sending him up, (b) seeking companionship barred to her in the circles of her intimate friends through their knowledge of her venereal disease, (c) acting as an *agent provocateurse* for his wife's private detective, or (d) seeking a fall guy for a paternity suit whose actual progenitor she is not *quite* able to put the finger on.

One of the main problems a man has to face is that standards of attractiveness in the male are not so simple as the basic aesthetic standards by which the attractiveness of women is judged. Most people of the same age, race and general education will agree on what is a beautiful woman. But it is difficult to establish in such basic terms what makes a man attractive to girls. Those perfectly built curiosities who illustrate the heavily muscled pages of the fitness magazines are regarded as grotesque jokes by most women, yet if standards of masculine attractiveness were based, as are standards of feminine attractiveness, on generous and proportionate physical development, they would have to beat the women off with sticks.

But they don't. Women find attractive such diverse projections as Henry Kissinger, Michael Parkinson, Yul Brynner, Mick Jagger and Dudley Moore, none of whom could be categorised sincerely as facially 'good looking', except possibly the last—whose almost comically diminutive proportions one would have expected to relegate him to outside the sexually exciting class.

The two sexes incline to judge their opposites in their own terms. Women seem fascinated in men by qualities which other men would admire. *Not* looks, but talent, character, personality, wit and equanimity. Women admire prettiness, grace, a good figure, elegance and good cooking in other women; and so do men. Clever women, busy women, strong women, independent women, intolerant women, and arrogant women are heartily disliked by both sexes.

The man without good looks may therefore be encouraged with the realisation that the ammunition one needs is Charm rather than Handsomeness. The importance of over-emphasised courtesy cannot be over-emphasised. A slight bow as you open the door for her, a kissing of hands, tenacious solicitude; all these act upon a woman's senses in much the same way as the sight of deep cleavage works upon a man's. And a lop-sided smile to project in conjunction with the sad eyes which bespeak a romantic tragedy somewhere in the past —these are basic essentials to the really smooth male operator. The sudden change of countenance from disciplined sorrow to the splendid smile which bespeaks your joy at being beside her, like sunshine suddenly breaking from behind a cloud— is an essential ploy for the man who doesn't have the looks.

I have tried it. I can recall a dozen girls who have said: 'Darling—when you suddenly smile, your whole face lights up,' as they pressed my hat firmly down to ear level, pinned the tails of my woolly muffler behind my back, and pushed me out into the cold passageway. For it is essential that the suggestion that you are a failure with women be basically phoney. A woman is not interested in your tragedy if it is true, only in romantic connotations she may weave around its invention. Women have an instinct for recognising *really* unlucky men and are not prepared for (a) sharing their dinners with your bitter and chagrined memories of failure, or (b) wasting time adding to them. For behind and beyond all her easy sympathy lies her realisation that in the alleviation of your problems she has only one thing to offer—and that, as her mother has so often pointed out—is the only thing a man is after.

This is the basic obstacle from which all feminine suspicion derives—suspicion which ultimately ignores all charm, rejects all sincerity, and even refutes all logic.

If one has a talent for the neatly turned compliment, for example, female suspicion will see it as dissembling insincerity. All your most beautiful verbal approaches will be met with the insistence that you really are altogether *too smooth*, and not therefore to be trusted.

Useless to point out that your very professionalism, education, and literary talents have sharpened your articulate expression to a point where you are thus equipped to pay her proper verbal homage. She will scorn the retort as untrustworthy repartee.

But stand before her like a great, glum *shmoe*, making nothing but glucking noises with your adam's apple and she will nevertheless not be constrained to cry—'There is a man who *really* adores me!' More likely she will insist: 'If you honestly loved me, you'd find a way to say it ...'

In an attempt to overcome both these diametrically opposing parries, I once simply poured my heart out on paper in a hastily hand-written note and pressed it upon the young lady concerned. She studied the manuscript with tense concentration for a moment and informed me: 'Hand writing that slopes backwards indicates a deceitful nature.'

What this chapter really amounts to, therefore, is a warning that there is no great point in pushing your luck. The more urgent you become, the greater does a young lady's suspicion expand. Like fortunes, women are made most often by the man in the right place at the right time. So stand ready, and let her make the behest of it.

YOUNG LADIES
AND HOW TO ENTERTAIN
THEM AT DINNER

IF YOU SEEK A WILD AND PARADOXICAL INJUSTICE, STUDY THE fact that whilst businessmen are disallowed from claiming luncheon and entertainment expenses against their income tax, the Productivity Council insists that it would be dangerous to industry to attenuate the tea-break.

If the second, why not the first? As one who long ago sacrificed the efficiency of his liver and duodenum to the bitch goddess, I can suggest an even more realistic attitude towards the Business Lunch—it should not only be allowed as deductible; it should be fully recompensated as Overtime. Any man who has left one of those culinary crucifixions with that muscular cramp just back of the ears (surely the derivation of 'pain in the neck'?) from the fixed sycophantic grin which such occasions demand, will know the lack of justice in expecting a man to suffer such during the mid-day period of *his own time*.

What lathe operator would suffer the boredom of being quizzed on production figures as he crouches over his pie and beans in the works canteen? What counter hand would readily substitute a conversation with a haberdashery customer for that precious respite when he hazards his weekly guess upon the Football Pools or submerges himself in the escapist delights of *Men Only*? The Business Luncheon is an impertinent infringement on a private period of the day when a man might reasonably expect to be left in peace.

That the actual *cost* of the meal would be a perquisite of certain strata of business hardly puts the operation beyond the pale; any more than there is a grisly immorality in miners getting cheap coal or transport workers being allowed cut price train fares. Are colliers expected to pay personally for the luxury facility of their pit-head baths? Is getting dirty any more a personal inconvenience than getting fat? If we are to believe the medical profession it is at least less of a health hazard. Might not the business executive be partly compensated for plunging onwards towards a coronary in the cause of duty?

Carried to its logical conclusion there seems no reason, if our taxation system is to accept as a deductible Allowance

83

the expense of maintaining a wife once you have acquired one, why a benign state should not regard the initial expense of acquiring her as a Capital Investment. For in some cases at least, a good cook/housekeeper/lover/mother/servant/chauffeuse might be regarded as a capital investment.

Unfortunately, the possibilities of an income tax allowance for petty cash slips declaiming, 'To luncheon for Miss Makepiece concerning projected possibility of matrimony':

Taxis to and from Rugantino Restaurant	£1	25
Aperitif	£2	15
Meals	£12	25
Tips	£2	00
	£17	65

is hardly likely to be regarded by the Inspector with any proper sympathy. Real economy can come only from a study of exigencies in the actual field.

That a meal need never cost as much as a woman is expecting was a lesson I learned early in life when it was my Mother's habit every Thursday to attend a lunchtime whist-drive. As I was but nine years of age at the time and at a day-school, it was necessary in consequence to make other arrangements about my own mid-day meal—and I was regularly presented with a Florin and instructed to stock myself up at the Lyon's's (next door to Boots's's) in Streatham High Road. There, a plate of cream of tomato soup, roast beef and two vegetables, a roll and butter, and a piece of apple pie and custard, were easily covered by two entire shillings—leaving a couple of pennies over for emergencies.

The bill may seem absurd in these days of inflation, but I recall the menu clearly to this day because it was necessary for me to learn it pat in order to recite it with some plausibility when quizzed as to what I had bought for lunch. But my actual order was regular and unfailing: One Small Baked Beans on Toast (Twopence ha'penny, then), One small portion of Baked Jam Roll (Twopence ha'penny, then), and a Draught Board and counters (free) for a spirited game with a school companion whilst we awaited the arrival of our refreshment. A total expenditure of Fivepence thus left me with One shilling and sevenpence for Chocolate.

Though this constituted my first essay into the fiddling of expenses, it also emphasised the fact that no woman really cares how the money is spent as long as it goes. The more realistic male philosophy should be based upon the proposition that the amount of money expended does not matter so long as it isn't much, and the achievement of this target demands serious and deeply researched study.

Though the flexibilities of which restaurants are 'in' and which are 'out' differ with each passing season, it should be remembered that there are basically only four types of restaurant:

(a) Restaurants with waiters;
(b) Restaurants with waitresses;
(c) Restaurants with waitresses where complete strangers come over and sit down at your table with you;
(d) Restaurants with waitresses where complete strangers come over and sit down at your table with you with their hats and coats on.

Generally speaking, one would not expect to entertain a young lady one holds in any esteem at any level other than (a), but these can themselves be sub-divided by nationality.

Paramount in status terms, and therefore the venue for a luncheon or dinner for a very seriously considered target, are the *haute cuisine* French restaurants such as the *Coq d'Or*, *Pruniers*, *L'Ecu de France* etc; the uppercrust English restaurants such as *Rules*, *Stones*, *Hunting Lodge*, *Simpsons*, *Wheelers* (Old Compton St. particularly); and perhaps three hotels—*The Savoy*, *The Connaught*, and *The Dorchester*.

At secondary level for the *initial* meal (or *entrée*) but particularly suited for providing 'our special place' restaurants for a romance once it is embarked upon, are the Italian restaurants. These abound in Soho and Chelsea, where a variety of swarthy entrepreneurs have amassed fortunes via the simple processes of painting cellars white, and though the food is no more than thoroughly palatable, the atmosphere is invariably romantic and the wine is relatively inexpensive.

Tertiary level finds the Greek, Cypriot, and Kosher restaurants; and Chinese restaurants divide their status between the Pekinese (I often suspect) tradition and the Chop Suey joints which are cheap, cheerful and suited only to the least sophisticated of your young lady acquaintances. Somewhere below all this comes Tandoori—which shamelessly flaunts its lack of social significance by being open at almost any time of the day or night. The least socially acceptable restaurants in terms of status, it will be revealed by a look at the list above, are those restaurants such as Chinese, Indian, Tandoori, etc., where wine is not regarded as a natural supplement to the meal.

The wine is often the basic indication, indeed, as to how you *really* feel about the girl—for once you have arrived at the level of expensive eating the chance to show off is confined by the fact that the room is full of people apparently spending as much money as *you are* on food. Choice of wine is the ultimate ploy provided you are dining with a young lady sophisticated enough to understand what your chateau bottled choice is likely to cost. Otherwise, a wine with a shipper's label will see you through normal levels of appreciation; the carafe is for secretaries and last-minute, address-book girl friends; and the scrubber must be content with a glass of beer.

One of the main reasons for the expensiveness of modern dining *à deux* is the acceptance of a long and varied menu from which the guest is regarded as being at liberty to choose. This has replaced the old-fashioned tradition where, if one was planning a dinner party, one contacted the restaurant previously and planned the meal beforehand. This allowed complete control on what your guests would be given—in much the same way as one would offer a guest at one's dinner party *at home* a meal to which there would be hardly more than possible alternatives for first course, sweets or cheese. It is a sensible and practical arrangement which disappeared with the going of that other delightful, sensible and practical arrangement—the private dining room with the *chaise longue* and the key on the inside of the door.

The long and varied menu, with its parallel variety of prices, is your main enemy in arranging that your retreat from the meal will leave you with at least enough small change for the taxi home. It is the menu which must be defeated.

Female emancipation has seen the advent of a minor irritation in the disappearance of the tradition where a man ordered for the young lady—a reflection, then, of the female projection of helplessness which had a number of merits. It gave control, again, and if a young lady nowadays too idle, too myopic, or too dead drunk to study the *carte* coyly requests you to order for her, do exactly that. But first take the menu from her so that she is unable to check on the prices as you suggest some dishes. Remember—you have eaten *here* before. Suggest only dishes whose price you are prepared to consider. It is then only necessary to disguise your parsimony with an air of expertise and wise consideration.

The serious, bald approach is to put on your spectacles with deliberation, regard the waiter thoughtfully for a moment, and say, 'Nothing for me to start with. I always think they relegate the main course to a sense of anti-climax.' Turn to her. 'What would *you* like, my hungry little darling?'

If it is your first meal together, or one of the early ones, she is practically guaranteed to follow suit and refuse the first course along with you. Not only will she be anxious not to seem ill-mannered at this stage of the courtship by choosing to eat alone—she will not like to be thought a pig, even if she is. And when she goes along with your sophisticated and ascetic decision reward her with an approving nod. Just tell her, 'I'm so glad you feel as I do that appetisers paradoxically destroy the appetite. Especially at expensive restaurants such as this one where everything is cooked to order and one can wait between courses sometimes long enough to close up the hunger pangs if you aren't someone who eats an enormous amount ...' In this sentence you have established that it is an expensive restaurant you are taking her to, you have suggested to her that she is not a glutton, and you have established unspoken agreement to a future policy of never having 'starters'. You are doing well.

Once the *hors d'oeuvres* trolley has been shoved off resignedly it is time to push the basket of bread rolls and *griscini* at her. Realise that she *wanted* the 'starters' because she is ravenous, but was simply outfumbled by your superior technique. Carbohydrate dangled before her, and emphasised by that crisp snap as you break open your own roll, could tempt her unresistibly in the several minutes you must endure before the arrival of your main dish. She could be blown out to a point where she can hardly finish it (given enough *saute* potatoes) and will have to settle for just a coffee afterwards. No sweet or cheese is the saviour of another quid, at least.

Your average cheap-skate might be satisfied with the triumph which getting off with only one full course represents; but the really professional economist will wish to scale down the potential charges on even that single dish. A flattering imputation like: 'I can see with a figure and complexion like yours you're a salad and fruit girl,' can be worth two or three pounds (*avoirdupois*) to her and two or three pounds (*Sterling*) to you; but where she resolutely refutes any fear of the calories, switch your appeal to the eccentric. Go for a Fun time. Appeal to her maternal instincts with Small Boy type experiment. Persuade her that you both indulge yourselves in *haute cuisine* constantly as a natural concomitant of your social and financial status. Say, 'Let's go for some soul food tonight, eh? Let's go mad—and have a fry up. You know—like those marvellous British Railway breakfasts ...' Or, 'What I really feel like tonight is Bangers and Mash. My dear friend Peter Sellers first introduced me to them—and I've wished ever since that I was poor, so I could have them every night. I'm sure you've never tried them—and you *must*!' She *has* tried them, of course; and never thought much of them compared with the *Homard a l'Americaine* (£4.20)—but is she going to admit it? Say, 'Isn't this fun?' when they arrive. And reflect to yourself silently that the enormous advantage of a really good and expensive restaurant or hotel is that they will serve practically anything— whereas a self-conscious establishment halfway down the scale would be affronted even by your suggestion that they had such a thing as a sausage on the premises.

Where the eccentric approach might be pushing your luck, the, 'Knowing what kind of a girl you are, I'd better go over and have a word with the *maître d*. Don't want anything to go wrong, do we?' The *maître d*. reference is largely superfluous (except to establish that you know him well. He has been—remember—eternally grateful to you since you carried him in over your shoulders after that brief brush with the enemy just outside Tobruk/Seoul/Dien Bien Phu/ Manchester United's ground), but no girl can resist asking you what kind of a girl you know her to be.

Oh! Of course you know. The wildly expensive, rightfully spoiled, inescapably pampered, beautiful, sophisticated, experienced type of girl who is out at some different high-spot every night with alternating peers of the realm. She'll adore the image, and love you for it inwardly; but modestly insist upon its coy disclaimer. Not her, she'll say. She's the quiet home-body, who tires of ultra lucullan dishes easily, and really enjoys only very simple pleasures.

'Well, how about that,' you register stunned admiration, a small lump working in your throat as you act through your eyes the question: *'Could this be her—she—at last?'*

'In which case,' (this out loud) 'they have an excellent steak and kidney pudding you might like; or perhaps just the lamb cutlets and a few new potatoes ...' She could bite her tongue—and reflects that she may have to before this meal is long over, but can hardly go back on her simple projection by demanding the Beluga.

The new rash of restaurants which seek to neutralise embarrassment by excluding from the menu handed to your guest any reference to the prices, can actually work in your favour if you insist on control of the ordering. The idea, basically, is that a pure choice may be influenced by the knowledge that what is instinctively chosen happens to be extortionately costly, and a thoughtful guest will have second thoughts as a result. But the majority of women ordering a meal simply study the right hand column for the biggest price before they run their eyes across the page to check up on what that means they're going to be eating. The priceless menu foils such consummate greed, and actually gives you the upper hand.

With the prices there for you to study on your own *carte,* you have the information at your fingertips should she by sheer chance happen to hit on something you are ill prepared to pay for. Here you simply need to say, quite bluntly, 'Actually, Darling, this place isn't too good for Fish/Sea-Food/Pasta/Meat/Oysters/Game/Poultry/*et al.* Can I recommend the *Omelette Fromage* and one of their superb, crisp, morning-picked, green salads?'

Where the feeding of young ladies has to a degree become confused in recent years is in the aspect of female emancipation which has brought them into the executive level and now often occasions the situation where you are the guest of a female (or her organisation, to be precise) and where it is necessary for her to play hostess. Particularly have women made themselves executively independent in the profession of Public Relations; and writers and journalists increasingly find themselves invited out to eat apparently at a woman's expense (more correctly—on a woman's expenses).

A few years ago only, this newly emergent situation prompted many of them to sidestep their new responsibility by shoving an envelope full of used oncers at you under the table rather than call for the cheque themselves and stigmatise you publicly as a ponce; but in the latter day permissive society such an appellation has achieved a status akin to a compliment—and represents no longer any reputational hazard. Beware only the instinctive masculine gallantry which urges you to return her invitation simply because she is a woman.

It is easy to convince yourself that she has bought you the meal because she is personally interested in you and wishes desperately for you to have your carnal will of her. The truth is that she no more aches to be twined in lustful congress with you than you ache to be twined in lustful congress with that male business contact you suffered for two and a half hours in the hope of landing his office cleaning contract, though she will not mind your believing as much if she thinks it will get her your business, your advice or your assistance. Remember that a young lady's emotional ambitions seldom parallel her commercial aspirations, and one can often encounter the paradox of a sophisticated female accounts executive whose romantic life is inextricably intertwined with Fred who works down the local garage. The *rognons de veau flambès fine champagne* she winkles out of you at lunchtime—or even buys for you if the business soliciting is on her side—is not a hot-knickered come-on but simply a gastronomic stoke-up to balance the fact that her dinner will be composed of an individual fruit pie, a cup of tea, and Fred—roughly in that order. Bear the insurmountable shadow of Fred clearly in mind, therefore, before you speculate good money on a woman whose contact is purely a business one. She is not worth the expense. There will be a billing but no cooing.

I was once asked by an affronted female why I thought paying out for a crummy evening entitled me to a hot embrace on the doorstep or an ambition for even more intimate possibility, and if one puts real consideration to work the answer is plain enough. Just calculate the price of a meal in the West End for two (say, conservatively, £8—£10); two stalls at the theatre (at least a Fiver); taxis, tips and aperitifs (at least another Fiver); and regard it as taxed income. About Forty Pounds is involved, dear readers, and it seems a relatively inflated price for a limp warm handshake. I explained this to my interlocuter at some length and enquired—if she considered £40 expenditure as being rather less than worth a brief show of her affection, what she might regard as a fair price. She hotly demanded whether I thought she was a whore, and I pointed out that in consideration of the fact that she had been the first to evaluate her embrace in terms of what the evening had cost me such a conclusion might not be deemed unreasonable.

There are young ladies, however, who are either innocent enough or practical enough not to be eternally on the *qui vivre*; and the pleasure of coolly observing the steady decline in the resistance of such may be numbered among the more esoterically satisfying.

That gradual development from aloof formality on the other side of the table to steadily giggling; the encroachment of a warming glaze above the hitherto gimlet pupils; that cynical sudden revelation of an intimate confidence regarding a mutual acquaintance—all these are welcome manifestations of the fact that you are at the beginning of a beautiful friendship.

It is not so much an indictment of his lack of originality as a clear proof of the method's efficaciousness that a man still largely resorts to liquor to effect a transition; and it is worth realising that because women will invariably trust the sweet tasting drinks which agree with their sticky palates rather than the fiery jolt of basic spirits, that liqueurs are the readiest and most disarming trap.

Half a pint of Advocaat slopped over her trifle and explained as your Mother's own recipe for custard has all the respectability of maternal sponsorship and all the advantages of quite extraordinary effect. A tumbler or two of Orange Curacao has the disarming ring of a fruit cordial—and it is worth referring, indeed, to liqueurs always as 'cordials' in order to allay suspicion.

Already the very sweetness of the drink inclines a woman to trust it—though actually the sugary drink, especially if it uses cream or eggs in its recipe gives not only a suggestion of mildness but also delays the effects of the alcohol. Thus there is time for two or three more before she begins actually to feel anything and is warned thereby.

Creme de Cacao is another good example: made in France from Cocoa beans and other wild ingredients, it not only tastes like Cadbury's but, being a rich dark brown in colour, it looks like Cadbury's. Try slipping her a mug of this at chocolate time.

Creme de Cassis is made in Dijon from crushed blackcurrants and, served in a normal liqueur glass resembles nothing so much as a mean helping of Ribena and must be absolutely crawling with Vitamin C. You only have her health in mind as you feed her another bottle. And as for Benedictine—isn't it made by monks? And doesn't it have a dedication to God on every label? How could any girl come to harm by putting away a pint of the beverage brewed by holy men? *Pax vobiscum.*

It is a physiological fact, anyway, that women are affected by drink quicker than are men—due apparently to a missing kidney enzyme—and the drinks to use to accelerate inebriety are fizzy drinks or drinks with a ten to twenty per cent solution of water additive. The air and the water introduce the alcohol into the system more rapidly, so that whisky and soda acts more quickly than neaters (to paraphrase Ogden Nash one might suggest that Shandy is dandy, and quicker than raw liquor), and undiluted gin, rum, brandy, etc., are too strong for quick absorption. As warm alcohol also takes effect more rapidly than cold, the quickest way to instant drunkenness is probably gluh-wein, whisky toddy or a strong hot rum punch. But more on Spirits in a later chapter.

It is to be admitted that there is little sophistication in a plying of the young lady with strong, warm, sticky, disguised alcohol until you can assert your *droit de seigneur*. To give that fifty/fifty chance atmosphere to the chase, and to acknowledge that your ultimate goal of sex is considered in the light of *shared* experience rather than as simple exploitation, there must be a delicate appreciation of the meal and of the drink which accompanies it. There is no doubt that a shared bottle or two of Burgundy brings that touch of Togetherness which marks the mutual respect for one another of the man who is the hunter and the young lady he hopes will be game.

The trick in wine drinking, therefore, is to ensure always that the man drinks slightly less than the woman, and this may be effected by the simple process of filling up her glass as soon as she has emptied it. Brought up unswervingly on her Nanny's insistence that she 'finish that up now, or you'll get it for your tea,' the reflex action of reaching automatically for a full plate or a full glass will be on your side. All you need do to ensure an attractive image the meanwhile, is bring to your own drinking the positive and sophisticated rituals of wine imbibing which have so long elaborated and spun out the simple swallow.

In the pursuit of such an image, one can hardly improve upon going straight to the top—and the French National Committee for Wine Publicity have produced an approved ritual for the drinking of a glass of wine which male readers may care to study in private before they embark upon an alcoholic seduction via the vulgar process of simply pouring one bottle after another.

'Tasting wine,' it says here, 'is a sacred rite to be carried out with gravity and serious attention.

'First the sense of taste should be neutralised and the palate cleared with a little bread. Take neither water, cigarettes nor sweets.

'Fill the glass but half full, that the fragrance shall not disperse. Hold the wine up to the light to judge of its colour, clarity and brilliance, and then revolve the glass gently so that the wine swirls around and releases its fragrance. Insert the nose into the mouth of the glass and inhale the released bouquet fully.

'Only then, taste the wine in small breathtaking sips ...'

It is clear that such a pantomime, carried out by yourself prior to every glass of wine you drink, will waste enough time to ensure that she gets at least two thirds of the bottle; with all the erosions of her suspicions and self-disciplines which such self-indulgence induces.

How susceptible one can be without the assistance of the natural rationing imparted through a strict observance of the wine-taster's ritual, was proven to me many years ago at my first Wine Tasting—which I embarked upon without the forewarning of the French National Committee's injunction to circumspection.

I arrived at a candle-lit cellar somewhere in the region of Holborn Viaduct armed with no other qualification than my invitation, and was confronted with what in later years has become the familiar sight of a cavalcade of small naperied tables stacked high with bottles, disciplined squads of up-turned empty goblets, and small spartan dishes of hard dry biscuits. Without the advantages of instruction into the 'sacred rites' of the Publicity Committee's ritual, it seemed that all one did was pass as rapidly as possible from one table to the next getting down as much of the happy juice as the ruminative press of aficionados allowed. I entered into the spirit of things with an enthusiasm which mounted at each bibulous experiment.

A sense of increased relaxation was to some degree diminished through embarrassment occasioned by the behaviour of several of my fellow guests. Manifesting their critical faculties in a manner hardly less than churlish, wine of which they apparently disapproved was offered public opprobrium by the ill-mannered reaction of spitting it into a handy bucket of sawdust. Motivated partly by a sincere desire to assuage the wounded professional pride of the shipper (and my host) and partly by a determination not to look a gift horse in the mouth, I felt it only expedient to swallow all that came my way with a polite smile of appreciation.

Confidence grew with each induction, and as others around

me were acting out an esoteric little ritual of holding their glasses up to the light and studying its colour with appreciative comment I decided that the duties of a grateful guest demanded I should follow suit.

Looking into the glare of naked light bulbs at a brimming wine glass held high above an unsteady head is feasible provided only that a couple of litres of the vino has not already produced a latent vertigo. It needed but an unsteady pace backwards and an involuntary shift of grip upon the glass's stem to find the wine coursing down my centre parting.

The sharpened sense of humour of a man already three parts smashed assisted me in treating the catastrophe as a matter of noisy hilarity against the mounting silence of my fellow guests' disapproval, but a wilful tenacity urged me to recharge my glass and try again; this time elaborating the performance with a parallel demonstration of deft glass twirling.

The basic idea here, as the French National Wine Committee for Wine Publicity will readily explain, is to rock the stem of the glass through an even orbital axis—thus swooshing the liquid around the inside of the goblet and containing it therein via sheer momentum. A notable parallel to this anti-gravity process may be witnessed in the performance of those intrepid motor-cycle riders who ride horizontally around the confined annulus of a Wall of Death but, as with the motor-cycle, an uncontrolled momentum can shoot the wine clear over the edge of its container and straight into the faces of the onlookers.

I sponged the shirt-fronts of fellow guests with my pocket handkerchief wringing it out into the buckets of sawdust, and conscious of a mounting general antagonism decided it might be more popular to confine further demonstration to the surely manageable ritual of the aroma appreciating.

I bent my head forward towards my wine glass, and sniffed delicately in the manner of those about me—only to discover to my sharp disappointment that it smelled of little other than wine, really.

Persevering, I lowered my nose closer, and inhaled once more with the assertive suction of a deep chest and a passionate nature.

It was unfortunate that in my polite enthusiasm for my host's hospitality I had filled my glass rather fuller than the mandatory half measure. My nostrils submerged themselves in the wine and the glass went down like a butt of Malmsey trunked dry by an elephant with a drink problem.

My hair plastered to my scalp, my shirt front soaked, my nose running scarlet as a chastised cruiser-weight's, I was at last no longer oblivious to the ill-will of those around me. I shook the wet hand of a thin-lipped host and repaired to The Cloaks, where I managed with no undue effort to insert both arms down the same sleeve of my raincoat.

As I turned to leave, the attendant who had extricated me from the strait-jacket of my own making touched his forelock with a fine humility and purposefully pushed towards me a saucerful of what were clearly (I being the first to leave) his own half-crowns.

I accepted one with thanks, pushed through the swing-doors, and assuming all the circumspect dignity of the dreadfully drunk, made off in all directions.

YOUNG LADIES
AND DRINK

I HAVE A YOUNG LADY FRIEND WHO SEES ONE ASPECT OF Women's Liberation as a studied embrace of all those gadgets which offer to simplify the domestic chores. From the whistling kettle to the electric back-scratcher, she has surrounded her life—and the lives of her guests—with a myriad of inconvenient little mechanical conveniences which not only supplant the comforting familiarity of normal household arrangements but which refuse to work.

Recently, during one of those evenings towards the end of the month when I find it economically advisable to have dinner at a friend's place, she wheeled on to the table after dinner a small trolley device supporting what seemed to be the lower sections of a Bunsen burner, and enquired whether I would like my brandy glass warmed.

As is my wont, I had been preparing the goblet for its measure of *armagnac* with the simple process of fondling it lovingly with my small hot hands—but she rescued it resolutely from my grasp, placed it upside down in the trolley so that the mouthpiece was inverted, and applied a lighted match to a wick encased in the base.

We sat back and regarded the pretty blue flame as it licked its subtle warmth around the thin glass of the brandy balloon. Whilst waiting for the brandy there was little else to do.

'It should be done now,' she said after a few minutes. I said yes I thought it probably was.

She put out her hand to retrieve the goblet, withdrew it with a small curse, stifled as she stuffed her fingers into her mouth, and finally placed the glass in front of me after wrapping the stem in a piece of Kleenex dredged from her handbag and already revealing signs of considerable duty. Then she poured me a shot of the *armagnac*.

There was a succulent and sibilant sizzle and a brief puff of blue vapour. But no brandy.

Slightly cooled by the first draught, the glass accepted a second measure without evaporating it entirely, and the brandy lay there invisibly boiling as I raised it gratefully to my lips.

The skin on my tongue will grow again soon, of course,

99

but spoiled brandy is lost forever. It is a pertinent allegory to point the way to the importance of living every moment fully and correctly, ensuring that a romantic moment is not lost through ignorance of its essential inducements, and assuring you that a French Kiss is agony with a scalded mouth.

My brush with the Brandy-glass warmer was to a degree a warning that a man should not deliver up to a woman the responsibilities for how their drinks should be drunk. Only in barmaids do we find females who can be to a minor degree trusted with the dispensing of liquor, and here the achievement is the result only of much training and practice.

Barmaids are worth short observation in a volume such as this, indeed, as they are at once a regular background feature of the life of any normal man, and are at once a primer to the behaviourisms of women at their best and their worst.

Barmaids, as any man who has got gradually drunk throughout the course of a succession of rounds will know already, get steadily more and more attractive as the evening goes on. And to the male reader who may be afraid to go home alone in the dark after closing time, it is of interest to speculate upon them as a source of enjoyment and a companion of lonely hours.

My Uncle Hubert insisted to his dying day that the way to be popular with women was to treat barmaids like duchesses and duchesses like barmaids. The philosophy had a certain lack of authority in that he never met any duchesses, but barmaids he knew by the hundreds, and they all loved him with that deep affection afforded by any member of the retail services to a customer who promises to keep the till ringing almost incessantly.

For full appreciation of barmaids, however, it is necessary to realise that profitable observation of them is to a degree dependent upon current fashion in terms of female dress. What we might call for the purposes of this study Positional Drinking, is a facet of public house usage which alters out of recognition over the years—and the erogenous or erotic zone of the female licensed victualler's assistant can shift from top to bottom according to the decline or ascent of popularity of the *decolletage* dress, or the acceptance or rejection of the Mini-Skirt or the Hot Pants.

In *decolletage* periods Prime Positioning involves a hunched stance at right angles to the bar counter and flatly facing the position of the barmaid herself. Only then may the eyes be opportunely cast downwards as she bends over to secure a bottle of Light Ale from the lowest shelf.

During Mini or Hot Pants periods, with the exposure concentrated more thoroughly at hip and thigh level, Prime Positioning will involve a seat at the far end of a curving bar counter where the view is *enfilade* and the young lady's bent posture is observed from the rear.

Taking advantage of a barmaid in this way is perfectly ethical as she is all the time practising upon you certain esoteric techniques calculated to bolster the bar takings at the expense of your susceptibility. Note, for example, how the position at which the low-necklined, large bosomed barmaid regularly bends to reach for bottled beer is invariably situated near the Black-Sausage Hot Plate—a piece of equipment of relatively recent utility in public houses which is the barmaid's equivalent of turning up the cinema thermostat to sell more ice cream. Grouping as many male customers as possible in the propinquity of one of these radiating electrical accessories has been proved to induce a body-fluid loss of some seven fluid ounces per man per half hour period— with all the extra expense the fluid's replacement is bound to involve.

It is never clear what percentage of those counter bottles purporting to contain pure Highland water for mixing with your Scotch were in reality simply re-filled at the municipal tap that morning by the young lady who pushes them at you (always approximately half empty, to excuse the broken seal), but because they are offered free, one suspects the generosity. Particularly when one considers the initiative established by so many barmaids of punctuating their counters with a selection of siphons which, when their levers are depressed, emit nothing but a damp hawking noise. Supplemented with a good stock of bottles of soda which can be sold for a realistic charge of a shilling (there she goes—bobbing down to the lower shelf to give you *something* for your money) the soda *jerk* turns out to be you.

An interesting facet of a study of barmaids is that any wholesale criticism of them could possibly evoke legislation in terms of the Race Relations Act, the profession having become almost entirely a monopoly of immigrant citizens of the Republic of Ireland. Expatriates of the West Indies are confined almost exclusively to the utterly cheerless establishments of the British Railways catering section, and I suspect that the latter fail the needs of the normal hostelry through their colourful linguistic refusal to confine their conversation to the official listings of that essential stock-in-trade—the Barmaid's Cliché.

'No—you can't have the same again, Darlin'. You can have similar ...'

'That'll be forty pence *to you*, Darlin' ...'

'Goo'nite, Darlin'. Don't do anything I wouldn't do ...'

'Ta-ta, Luv. If you can't be good be careful ...'

'I'll have it later, if you don't mind, Dear ...'

'Large or Small, Sir?'

This last demand is possibly the only really pernicious example of the Barmaid's Cliché. It is directed at you only if you are a non-regular, in the certain knowledge that you will feel intensely mean at making a vocal assertion regarding the smaller measures and will thus be tricked into ordering twice as much drink as you require and spending twice as much money.

It relies, too, upon the fact that when buying drinks for a woman your man-about-town image cannot afford to suffer the stigma of tight-wad, and that in round-for-round drinking with another man your companion will be forced to reflect your generosity when his turn arrives.

It can only be dealt with boldly. Experiencing it, you must repeat over and over again, 'Two Scotches, please' every time she enquires, 'Large or Small, Sir?' An experienced barmaid will know finally that she has encountered a parallel professional and will at last reluctantly turn to a single dispensation from the optic. Only occasionally will you encounter a virago so brash you will finally have to fix her with your snide appraisal and explain: 'I asked for *two* Scotches, my dear. Not *four* Scotches, my dear. Will you please give me *two* Scotches, my dear. That means you work the optic *twice*, not *four* times. Now do your best, because I'm a big tipper.'

It will not cure her for ever, but may cure her *for you*, because barmaids react in a cliché way and she will be switched from her normal channel of thought by the realisation that you are an individual, albeit a troublesome one.

Barmaids think in clichés, and deal in clichés, because they are constantly serving clichés, and regard a customer they have never seen before as a possible Dupe Cliché. Other categories, into which you may fit yourself only through regular custom are The Hearty Laugher, The Space Gazing Scot, The Inveterate Tapper, The Circle Infiltrator, The Periphery Smirker, The Trouble Looker For, The Tiddley Lunchtime Housewife, The Groper-when-she-comes-round-the-bar-to-collect-the-glasses, and The Major. She has no cliché category for The Handsome/Gallant/Generous/Charming/Man-I-Would-Like-To-Take-Home-To-Bed-With-Me, so never try to fool yourself that you have the slightest chance with a barmaid. Anyway, she probably sleeps upstairs on the third floor of the pub, and a fat chance you have of getting past the fat landlord.

That a spark of real humanity lurks somewhere underneath it all seems proven, though, by reports a few years ago that experiments were being carried out to produce a public house which is fully automated and therefore barmaidless. The attempts seem to have ended in utter negation.

Coin operated dispensers, we were promised at the time, would serve any attendant customer with every possible requirement from iced beer and cigarettes to brandy and cigars. Adjacent mechanisms, meanwhile, would be dispensing traditionally burned sausages, Scotch Eggs, packets of Crisps, and even selections of Spillers' Shapes for the Landlord's Retriever.

Having acquired the food and refreshment from equipment impersonally void of the possibility of human error, the customer would seat himself at an automatically cleared table where his behaviour could doubtless be observed through closed-circuit TV by a licensed victualler's Eviction Operative. The Landlord, if such a responsibility should continue under such systems, would be required simply to oil and maintain his robot equipment and possibly to adjust it to ensure its giving the usual change for a Pound when proffered a Fiver.

The Automatic Barmaid never arrived at general acceptance, probably because it didn't have breasts, and it is a feature of the Permissive Society and of the Women's Liberation movement which has ridden upon its back, that in recent years barmaids have come to be regarded as fair game —a situation which no real gentleman would have considered in days when society was ruled by unspoken expressions of *noblesse oblige*.

A reminder of such attitudes is recorded for every sociological student in *Naval Occasions*, a stirring book (by 'Bartimeus') of Royal Naval short stories first published in 1915 and read by myself some fifteen years later, when I was still enough of a little boy to be moulded and influenced by its intransigent moralities.

One of its tales relates the adventures in Portsmouth of two young Naval officers enjoying their last night ashore prior to sailing for a long spell of service on the China Station. At one point during the evening the younger is seen to linger behind in a bar as his companion begins to leave; to wish goodbye to a young, pretty, poor (but honest) barmaid, and to press into her hand a brooch purchased that evening by way of farewell present. His friend is understandably disturbed at this shattering of the social conventions, and Jerry feels ...

... a vague hint of disapproval as they fell into step.

'That girl,' Peter ventured presently, 'isn't she a bit fond of you, Old Thing?'

Jerry paused to light his pipe. 'I—I don't think, Peter. Not more so than of half a dozen others.' He glanced at his companion, reddening. 'You don't think I've been up to any rotten games, do you?' ...

The other shook his head with quick protest.

'... I like her awfully, and she's a jolly good little sport.

'It's a rotten life cooped in that beastly atmosphere, being made love to by half tight fools. The only refuge from it is marriage if she cares to take advantage of some young ass, but she has refused half a dozen Naval officers. Prefers to wait 'til some scallywag in her own class can afford to take her away from it. Yet I've heard her talking like a Mother to some rorty Midshipman—a silly young ass wasting his money and health pub-crawling. She shook him to the core. Lord knows I don't want to idealise bar-maids—p'raps I'd be a better man if I'd seen less of them myself, but—'

Peter gripped his arm, soothingly. 'I know, I know, Old Son. Don't get in a stew. Unless a man knows people ashore, and is prepared to pay asinine calls when he might be playing golf or cricket, where else is he to speak to a woman all the days of his life ...?'

The extract served to establish for me at a very early age that though all the nice girls love a sailor there are certain social declensions standing in the way of widespread recipro-cation, and that most barmaids would rather wait for 'some scallywag in her own class to take her away from it all' rather than some scallywag in any other class, up or down. So it is usually advisable to leave the barmaid as you would wish to find her. She is something else; and though you may have similar you cannot have the same.

Furthermore, a man is transparently revealed not only by the behaviour of *vino veritas* but inevitably by the kind of drink he orders. Cross study applies the categorisation in both sexes, indeed.

Brown Ale is the lout of drinks. One might even say it is the drink of louts. In masculine connotations it conjures teenage football-fans ripping railway upholstery; in female circles it is the drink of an unsophisticated woman who is determined to get tiddley but likes something with a sweetish taste. Women turn to it inevitably after they have discovered that Mackesons does not taste of Blackcurrant as they expected.

Light Ale is an acceptable drink for men—especially in its stronger categories, but makes a young lady sound slightly 'common' unless she insists upon the relative expense but cooling practicalities of Lager. Lager is 'all right', mainly because of its Continental (and therefore 'imported') image. One suspects that a lady who drinks Light Ale might belch when she goes to the Ladies'.

Gin and admixtures are untrustworthy in the male (never buy a second-hand car from a gin-and-tonic drinker). The only serious Gin drinker is a Pink Gin drinker. Therefore a woman who drinks Pink Gin is probably a lush. The Gin and Bitter Lemon or Gin and Tonic woman is sophisticated but of little depth. She is a good timer, a gold-digger, the kind of girl who will go into a pub by herself but will avoid standing her round once she's there. Women who drink Gin and It read about it in a book.

Bitter, over the years, has superceded Mild and Bitter as the immature people's drink. It is drunk by young people on Saturday mornings—late teenage boys in cravats and the Second Position and their girl friends who are all called Susan and have Mummies and Daddies—and by older men who have never managed to grow out of it. Older women who drink Bitter are slightly camp followers of Rugby Football clubs, or lesbians, or both.

Whisky drinkers are on the whole a superior race. The men are mostly professional, generally trustworthy, generous in their hospitality. Women Scotch drinkers are usually career girls of experience who have adopted Whisky as another proof of their essential liberation. They are the best type of female drinkers, usually steady in the head, and never unconscious of the fact that it's their turn to pay, though a woman who drinks Ginger Ale with her whisky is really little superior to a Gin drinker.

It is difficult to categorise many other drinks with their female devotees. The more exotic aperitifs are indicative of nothing more than a package holiday in Spain, Italy or France, the more usual aperitifs indicative of nothing more than a susceptibility to television advertising. Champagne is difficult to attach to certain kinds of women because its very expense establishes that it is generally ordered voluntarily by the man as a gambit. A woman who would ask for it when invited to have a drink is simply an inveterate taker of liberties and should be warily treated.

Whatever a woman drinks, though, she is as subject as are men to the hazards of the hangover—in many cases, indeed, she is even more susceptible. In the way that people of general good health are normally the worst patients, women are inclined to suffer more from hangovers because they are not so used to them, and are therefore the more startled by the symptoms.

At the same time, a man often evens up the torment because he invariably bolsters his post alcoholic remorse with the post sexual remorse which follows upon a realisation of what his (and her) drunkenness finally led to last night. Women never blame *themselves* for that.

As is pointed out in our chapter of Young Ladies and Pregnancy, Women's Lib has not liberated the female sex from an absolute conviction that when the sexual act occurs it is inescapably and individually *the man's fault*. Generations of brainwashing have left the man with the similar conclusion, and guilt complexes feed upon the physiological, psychological and psychosomatic consequences of hyper-acidity, acute irritation of the membranes of the intestinal tract, catarrhal provocation and reactional depression.

The tragedy of the situation is that nobody can really help except Old Father Time. The hair of the dog that has savaged you lurks bristling in the distant kennel of Opening Time, and even a desperate visit to a doctor draws small sympathy and less antidote. After ordering you to show him your tongue he will simply push it back in with a gesture of distaste and remark that it is no wonder you feel sick with that thing in your mouth.

Where you may win medals from the young lady for your solicitude is in advising her as to how to ward off the hangover the second time she partakes of your hospitality. Let her suffer the first time round. It is all a part of life's rich pattern, and she will be the more grateful in future for knowing what you are saving her from. For, like all drinkers male or female—she will not really keep the promise she makes to herself of never drinking again. If, by your kindly intervention, you can offer a good time and seem to minimise the retribution, you are on the way to becoming her best friend; with all the rewards such a position involves.

One of the great problems of drinking is that not only does one drink lead to another, but another drink leads inevitably to another cigarette. Smoking rate inevitably climbs because the social atmosphere encourages extra indulgence and camaraderie induces the hand-them-round feeling of false generosity.

Dire effects result from the combination of heavy smoking and heavy drinking—for the human system is then being dragged in diametrically opposing directions. A woman's blood vessels are expanded by drinking, but contracted by smoking; so she is being subjected to a parallel situation of that where a victim is pulled apart by wild horses. As she gulps down the alcohol and sucks in the smoke at the same time, she is elasticating her blood vessels like a rubber band. From thick to thin they go, up and down like a yo-yo and never satisfied with a drawn game, they are steadily contributing to the mourning after.

Alcohol is a stimulant which increases the rapidity of the blood's circulation and thus rushes its own poison to all points of her system more quickly than it would were she still sober. So the more she drinks, the quicker she gets drunker; a situation further confused by the relative idleness of her liver.

The kidneys are no answer. Dodging off to the Little Girls' Room after every drink will not only induce in your friends the embarrassing suspicion that your party is suffering a sharp attack of bladder trouble, but it does not even assist in arresting drunkenness. She may be slightly thinner through fluid rejection, but only about five per cent of the alcohol she consumes is accounted for by immediate transit through the system.

About another ten per cent is accounted for by vaporisation in the lungs through the simple process of breathing in and out, and to get rid of the other eighty-five per cent, she must wait for the normal process of oxydisation which is the function of her liver. And Nature, originally not banking on such over indulgence, has arranged for a young lady's liver to be able to handle the oxydisation of approximately a single Gin or Scotch in about one hour. More than that amount has the surplus slopping around inside her, eating through her stomach walls and expanding her blood vessels to the size of sausage balloons. No wonder she hates you in the morning.

The dainty expertise of drinking with a woman is keeping

her largely sober, therefore, with enough to brighten her eyes but too much to brighten her brain. And it is worth considering, too, the fact that a man's own performance can be mightily affected by over indulgence. Men who drink heavily for years risk impotence, according to Dr. James Smith of the Seattle Shadel Hospital for Alcoholics. Research suggests that one in ten of more than 14,000 alcoholics studied over a 37 year period suffered total impotence.

Even Shakespeare noted the link. His Porter in Macbeth makes the point that drink 'provokes the desire and takes away the performance'. Whilst any man will know that a little of what you fancy makes you fancy other things, he will probably have also experienced somewhere in his life the fearful consequences of what has been vulgarly entitled 'Brewer's Droop'. And the American *Journal of Psychiatry* claims that alcohol can cause a fault in the mechanics of erection. The dangerous amounts are difficult to measure, but one doctor in the U.S. defined it as starting at a level approximating half a bottle of Bourbon daily for five to ten years—the U.S. bottle being slightly larger than the British equivalent. As one sad sufferer wryly put it: 'I used to drink "Early Times"—but the result was only "Old Grandad".'

It can be seen that for a man's own sake he should be solicitous regarding his young lady's alcohol intake as well as his own, and prepare her if possible for the way ahead. A stomach wall lined with the wherewithal to combat the attacks of the alcohol helps—so that a spoonful of olive oil before beginning the evening's drinking assists in repelling some of the worse damage. Little benefit, other than a kind of faith cure, can be derived from the traditional picker-uppers, for a hangover is only mild alcohol poisoning, and no poison exists which can act as its own antidote.

Eating well, before a party, is helpful because when the alcohol reaches the stomach it is partly absorbed by the food itself and may not come in direct contact with the stomach walls, where the real trouble is done. The best foods for this are proteins, lean meat, milk and eggs. Starches help very little, and sugar actually intensifies the alcohol's effects (see above).

Drink as much water as you can get down you before going to bed and keep a jug of the stuff handy at the bedside. Curiously enough, excessive drinking has a de-hydrating effect, and if you can keep your non-alcoholic fluid level nearer a fair balance you will feel better in the morning than you deserve. Certain resultant pressures may ensure a slightly wakeful night, of course; but if she is there beside you it isn't a bad idea to wake up a couple of times anyway.

COMMUNICATING WITH YOUNG LADIES

DESPITE THE INVALUABLE APHORISM 'WRONG NO MAN—AND write no woman', research claims that one out of every ten letters posted anywhere in the world is a love letter. Frankly, I am surprised. Certainly none of them is mine, and I would have concluded that given reasonable efficiency in the telephone service the sloppy habit would have been reduced by now to an incidence of about one in a million.

With so much more immediate methods of communication in modern times, the only real use of the postal service lies in the intransigence of its recorded evidence in terms of certain offers, statements or misguided propositions. And when you are communicating with the female sex, the last thing you wish to place on ineradicable record is the specific phraseology which seemed a good idea at the time.

Thus, the telephone has taken over at a sensible level of romantic protestation—and one need then beware only of a sharp click and faint whirring when one commences a conversation with the traditional 'Hello, Darling ...' The tape recorder has got more men into trouble than President Nixon.

An extra reason for reluctance to commit anything to paper and ink is the sad fact that in the cold light of a breach of promise action the words are not only condemning; they are ludicrous. Projected with the venom of the prosecuting attorney, you are made to look not only a monster but rather soppy. Irresponsible romantic outpourings, however sincere at the time, have a transient charm long gone before they have embraced the spite of being mouthed by a professional specifically employed to project your image at a vast disadvantage.

Even men acknowledged as great lovers and great writers cannot face up to the reiteration of their private prose in later years. As eminent a man of letters as Victor Hugo cannot come through the test without avoiding a decision on the reader's part that he would have been better off 'phoning. Take, for example, this purple portion from a love letter written by him to a contemporary young lady he imagined had favoured him by accepting his proposal of marriage:

'I tremble lest brusquely I be awakened from this beautiful

divine dream. Oh, thus thou art mine! Thus thou art mine! Thus I am destined to enjoy on Earth a heavenly felicity. I see thee young wife, then young mother—and always the same ...'

Put yourself in Hugo's position had such indulgent brainstorming been read out in a court of law. Imagine the smirks of the other chaps at the office, or the club, or down at the local, as they spelled it out for one another from page three of *The Sun* or *The People*—especially the married ones. How Hugo himself must later have regretted the banal outpourings.

'Always the same,' he writes—utterly ignoring, as all men embarking upon matrimony do, the inevitable fact that wives invariably grow into their mothers; fat, waspish, mustachioed, and implacably antagonistic. How often did the shrew of his later years drag out that sickly epistle and throw it back in his teeth as retribution for some minor matrimonial forgetfulness?

See how other great men are reduced to slobbering idiots when the target of their pens is some chit of a girl rather than political injustice, national pride or the dramatic verities:

Honoré de Balzac to the Countess Hanska: 'Dear Star, far and near, count on me like yourself. Neither I nor my devotion will fail you any more than Life will fail your body ...'

Napoleon to the Empress Josephine: 'Are you not the soul of my life and the sentiment of my heart? Are you vexed? Are you ill at ease? My soul is then broken with grief, and there is no rest for your lover ...'

You get the picture? Had any of these rash hot-bloods realised that his camp slush would have been published in the years to come, would he have left himself open so plainly to derision? Would he not, rather, have just sent an expensive present with a plainly worded addendum: 'Regards, Honoré.', or 'All the best, yours Vic.', or 'Looking forward to meeting you again when I'm on leave. Nap.' The fearful prospect of such indulgence being publicly recited, whilst the embarrassed writer stood there with egg on his face, would bring second thoughts to any great man reaching for his quill.

Especially nowadays is the love letter an anachronism—when the exigencies of inevitable postal delay mean that you've probably fallen in love with someone entirely different by the time the postman screws up your letter to shove it through her letter box.

And can one suddenly descend from such spirited phraseology as is recorded above to add the banality of FIRST CLASS MAIL to the outside of the envelope? Far preferable in these days of intensified litigation to send merely the envelope and the simple legend FIRST CLASS MALE typed above your name and address on a card contained therein. This makes a claim—but no rash promises.

But those of you whose hearts dictate the compulsion of an occasional rash promise, if only as a kind of safety valve for pre-relations frustration, should embrace your foolhardiness within the insurance of one or two ploys designed to render identification difficult should second thoughts ever bring you, via courting, to court.

Type the letter—for a start. And type it on a machine which cannot easily or at all be traced to yourself. Stay late at the office and use the typewriter of a lesbian member of the secretarial pool, or of a male clerk for whom you have a personal antipathy. Wear gloves to avoid leaving your dabs on either the typewriter keys or the letter itself, and moisten the gum on the envelope at the tap in case of a saliva test.

Post the letter from a central area which has no immediate personal connection with your own domestic or working venue, and always sign it (typed or left-handed) in the pet-name which any man of sense will establish as his and the young lady's confidential personal secret before ever putting pen to paper. *Poochy-woochy, cuddie-bubs* or *chuchie-face* may well actually be you—but in a court of law it will take some proving if you hotly deny it. If both of you have respected the embarrassing pseudonym as deeply confidential (*Our* secret, Darling!) then the case will resolve itself into your word against hers—and it is a basic facet of our great legal system that every man is innocent until *proven* a rotten, lying, double crossing, sonofabitch.

In communicating with a young lady, the business of nominal endearment has a considerable importance, of course. That affection is a shared experience prompts women to identify it specifically—and no ordinary christian name is private enough to manifest the magic of being in love; for (to a woman) *nothing like this has ever happened before.* Calling you Herbert, or Fred, or Jim or any name shared by a million others, simply degrades a beautiful relationship into something quite commonplace, and any feminine ego would perish the thought.

Even terms of endearment suffer from the changing fashion, however. 'Love', for example (even 'Luv'), which during the nineteen thirties and forties was regarded as palpably proletarian, has returned to favour in recent years and shares favour especially in the more flippant levels of upper-class love affairs.

'Darling' has become slightly devalued through quite general use, and 'dear' is so widely applied to waitresses, conductresses, shop-girls, and transient contacts with whom one has no sexual connection whatsoever, as to be as unmeaning and impersonal as Mrs. or Miss.

'Sweetie' had a run of popularity following soon upon the Second World War, as did 'Poppet'—which largely replaced the largely Americanised 'Honey'. Others come and go constantly—mainly as a result of the *blasé* cynicism of whatever happens to be the currently 'swinging' society set; which calls *everybody* by an overstated endearment.

'Daaaaaaaahleeng!' gushes the upper-class young lady to her feminine contemporary in a ritualistic greeting, empty of truth, 'How I envy you your quite *Heavenly* hat ...' This can mean anything from 'Christ! Surely ten generations of in-breeding can produce better taste than *that*!' to 'Keep your blood-shot eyes off my man, you bitch!', and does tend to cheapen and blur the meaning of companionable terminologies originally invented to project affection and sincerity.

The trend has been further complicated and diffused, oddly enough, by a tendency in recent years for certain classes of sophisticated menfolk (particularly those involved in Show Biz) to apply similarly honeyed phrases to the paradoxical images of their working male colleagues:

'Fred, baby doll,' intones the gargantuanly obese producer, lighting himself a monster Havana and flicking the ash into the open mouth of a handy Yes-man, 'your script stinks, darling.'

'And what would an uneducated, inarticulate crumb like you know about a work of art, sweetie?' retorts the writer furiously. 'For two million dollars I would ram it up your fat ass, dear heart.'

Such devaluation in no way adds to the dignity of forms of affectionate address which the ordinary man will apply to a young lady acquaintance only after the experiment of several expensive dates, considerable soul searching and a great screwing up of courage. It is not only the advantages of nominal camouflage (see above) which therefore advises a man of initiative to invent some form of endearment of his own. 'Kupkake'—an endearment used by Pat O'Brien in the nineteen thirties—has always seemed to me to be worth wider application, as have 'Tiger', 'Bundle' and 'Peachie'. Anything of originality is acceptable provided it does not dive into the bathos of baby talk.

Fully examined, indeed, the more traditional endearments reveal themselves as either inadequate or as basically unrealistic. 'Darling', for example, is simply a corruption of the much earlier 'Dearling' or 'little dear'. Applied by a young lady to a great, thick, muscle-man from the Second Row, it takes on a rare absurdity once you know the meaning. Other basic definitions hardly help.

'Dear' has a cynical verity when applied to most young ladies—as any man who ever footed the bill for an evening *a deux* will readily recognise. And 'Sweetheart' according to *Chambers's Twentieth Century Dictionary* is defined as a 'lover or mistress'. That both these connotations nowadays insist upon a shared sexual relationship to establish their accepted general meaning, changes utterly the old-fashioned image of 'sweetheart' as being the object of a quite innocent and juvenile affection.

The problem of *what* you call her, though, is somewhat seconded to the problem of *how* you call her, in view of the fact that we are subjected to a telephone system much on a par with the efficiency standards of the letter service. I admit without shame to not knowing who the Postmaster General is as we go to press, but I defy anyone to justify the rank. Postmaster Lance-Corporal would be more in line with the kind of service we obtain. I never know whether to regard the

GPO's suggestion that Somebody, Somewhere, would like to hear from me as an invitation or a challenge. Obstacles the technical system lays in the path of direct communication are generally too implacable for the defiance of an ordinary mortal.

Repairing to a telephone box to ring a young lady and suggest an assignation for that evening perhaps, inevitably faces the caller with one of several insuperable problems:

(a) the instrument and/or the box have/has been torn bodily from the wall;

(b) an apparently unmolested instrument offers nothing but roaring silence to the most continued patience and the most circumspect depressing and releasing of the receiver cradle; or,

(c) a steady and studied rectitude in dialling procedure produces only a steady and studied reiteration of the dialling tone.

At Charing Cross Station where GPO engineers have developed the Non-Phone to a degree of extraordinary inefficiency it has often been possible to find only one booth in a row of half a dozen in any kind of working order. It is a comfort to know that here at Charing Cross, if you are misogynistically sick of the whole monstrous regiment of women, you have only to pick up a telephone to be immediately cut off from the entire human race.

Indeed, with regard to (a) above, there can be no doubt that the wrecking of telephone booths is far too often unfairly attributed to a relatively innocent indigenous population of juvenile delinquents. I suspect that in nine cases out of ten the wreckage is simply the result of the exploding fury of some completely normal citizen frustrated beyond his tether during his attempts to contact another human soul on the telephone.

For it is the disembodied spirit of the telephone which is at once the most frustrating and infuriating of all. A surly cab-driver can have his tip witheld. A churlish waiter can be similarly treated, reported to the *maître d.*, or even offered a mouthful of knuckles. A saucy secretary can be sacked. But you cannot reach out to throttle the telephone operator, and if you cuss her she simply unplugs. Submitted to the cavalier treatment generally offered by the official switchboard, one realises at last the mephistophelian cunning behind the decision to equip telephone booths with small mirrors at head height.

The ploy is a shameless dodge behind human vanity. The chance to stand and look at himself is perhaps the one thing in the world for which a man will put up with an otherwise quite inexcusable delay; particularly where this is coupled with the inescapable chance to hear nothing but his own voice for long minutes at a time.

'Hello, hello ...' you say with mounting irritation as the line remains lonely. And as you catch sight of yourself in the mirror, you hastily wipe away the small smut beneath your eye and suck into semblance of whiteness the teeth stained at lunch time by the *carafino rosso*. 'Hello,' you repeat automatically to the stern visage regarding you from the glass. 'Hellooo, there,' you continue as drifting whimsy turns it into your Gary Cooper face ...

'... so you sit here with your regiment while your son dies by inches—well I won't! I'm going after him whether you like it or not ...'

You rattle the receiver in desultory fashion again and regard the twisted cynical smile of John Wayne as it peers back at you from the wall of the booth ...

'... get back to the reservation, Running Dog,' you advise in a voice of tempered steel, 'or the tepis of the Sioux will burn like signal fires and the blood of many braves will stain the forests ...'

Returning to the present temporarily, you give passing consideration to the young lady you are vainly trying to contact and as the hissing emptiness of your unanswered line ignores your urgent calling, the face changes to Boyer and your voice to the throaty insistence of the gallic charmer:

''ullo; 'ullo, may darleeng.' The words trickle treacly over your jutting lower lip as you light a Gauloise left handed. The dark sardonic features regard you mockingly from the mirror. 'Whatevvair Pepe le Moko wants, 'e taiks ...'

'Do you want Continental?' asks the switchboard at last. 'If you'll repeat the number, I'll change the line ...'

Yet it is undeniable that this frustrating invention was once upon a time a clear generator of pleasure—a handy mechanical contrivance upon which an earlier generation relied entirely for its initial contact between the sexes, its arrangements of romantic assignation, its vocal assurances of undying affection, and its indirect responsibility for the ultimate procreation of the human race.

For imagine to yourself the problems of an empty evening, a full address book, but the social handicap that the telephone system (for all its faults) has not yet been invented.

With time to spare, a man turns to the pages of his little red book and muses through the alphabetical sequences until the kind of company he feels inclined to keep slides into view.

Turn to A—and there is Angela AArdvark's name and number staring up coyly from the page to remind me that she may be readily contacted at CHIswick mind-your-own-business. A few drinks with Angela will not be amiss, I muse, for Angela is certainly a miss, and a miss is not only as good as but considerably better than a male. I must speak to Angela.

What would I have done without the telephone? What I would have done is have to go all the way over to CHIswick is what I would have to have done. And by the time I have got there, Angela has long ago despaired of the arrival of a sudden Prince Charming that evening and has gone off to the cinema with her spotty friend Mavis. With the doorbell still ringing in my ears I sit on Angela's doorstep and carry on through the As.

Audrey Anstruther is a great little sport, but lives in CROydon. With the telephone as yet uninvented there is nothing for it but to start hiking. Audrey emigrated to New Zealand only last Tuesday, her Mother reveals tearfully, would I like a cup of tea?

Desperation persuades me to weigh up the potential of Audrey's Mum for a fleeting moment, but the sight of Mr. Anstruther hovering in the background discourages the acceptance of her hospitality. Back to the Book.

Ann Arbuthnot (next on the page) lives over in BALham and I can get there in three quarters of an hour if I get a reasonable bus connection at St. Leonard's Church in STReatham. It is at present only twenty past nine and the 133 bus is already in sight.

But the Arbuthnots are on holiday in Middlesbrough, the night is no longer young, and we're only half way down the A's.

How did a man fix up a last minute date in those days before we had the telephone to help? Was every randy assignation preceded by a cheerless succession of back and forward copperplate letterheads, hearts beating madly with every delivery and the heavy footfall of a GPO emissary in his frock coat and high beaver hat? And was the relative respectability of the Victorians due simply to the fact it was then too hazardous ever to contact a woman you ought not to be contacting? Nowadays, if a man answers you can just hang up or, more imaginatively, simulate a Glaswegian accent and enquire if that's Joe's Pie Shop and do they do Pudden Suppers?

As a negation of the protective parent, too, the 'phone has its uses. The mother who is averse to her eighteen-year-old daughter exposing herself to the questionable company of an ageing roué of some thirty odd summers cannot be overcome —but she can at least be avoided.

When your call is answered by a voice that shatters the glass in the telephone booth, you have only to breathe steadily into the mouthpiece for a few minutes to reduce the old harpy to screaming hysterics at the thought of a sex maniac on the end of the line.

I discovered this quite by accident some years ago when a determined mother insisted on answering the 'phone personally in order to protect her daughter from contact with myself. Faced with the problem of explaining who I was and the inevitable snub which would follow, I would stand nonplussed for minutes at a time, my mind desperately churning over possibilities of what to do or what to say. All the matronly virago would hear would be the reiterative breathing of my undecided considerations. Then, at a loss, I would simply hang up and the receiver would click mysteriously back into place. The mother went into a nursing home, quite to my surprise, and I used to pick her daughter up in my blondebait M.G. Midget every evening at the end of visiting time.

But the days of the dirty 'phone caller seem to be numbered, now that we are all looking forward to the days when telephonic communication will be accompanied by a visual screening of the caller. It is unlikely that even the sickest of loonies is going to mouth out his wretched obscenities whilst his victim is in a 'telly-'phone' position to study up on him for an eventual Identikit picture.

Another tradition likely to disappear with the advent of visual 'phoning will be the blind date. 'Can you bring along a friend for my friend?' amounted to a considerable gamble when the only clue to the attractions of Mavis, the spotty friend, was the nicely modulated voice she projected when her girl companion introduced her over the line.

The rejoinder 'You've got to be joking!' may dent a number of female egos in the more honest and revealing future, but it will save a deal of dull, grey evenings too. And, talking of dull, grey evenings, why is it that obscene and suggestive telephone calls only ever seem to be made to women by men? What is the Women's Lib explanation of *that* phenomeon?

Is it that women suspect that a man might accept the implied invitation? Or does it mean that the whole thing is an enormous sham—and that if only the contacted woman had the sense to answer: 'What a marvellous idea! I'm feeling randy as all-get-out myself! Give me your address and I'll be round in just a few minutes ...', the sad wretch on the other end of the 'phone would be frightened out of his life and not stop running until he was back at home having tea with his Mum? It's worth a try surely? Whether the woman, once she has the address, passes it over to the police or retains it against the need of long lonely evenings to come, is her own decision. All I know is that I have sat expectantly by the 'phone for many a long evening on the chance that some frustrated young lady will see fit to stick a pin in my directory number and contact me with some random suggestions aimed at making me hers. I am not ex-directory.

A useful if incidental tip in terms of speaking to a young lady on the telephone—especially if you have achieved any degree of intimacy—is never to reveal your identity when 'phoning, but simply to announce yourself by saying, 'Hello, Darling ...'

To her reply, 'Who is that?' you simply demand in outraged terms, 'How many damned men call you "Darling", for Heaven's sake?' The rest of the evening has you in the psychological ascendency whilst she wheedlingly attempts to prove to you that she isn't some sort of an Anybody's. Even should a fit of pique at your suspicions urge her to hang up on you, a swift click and a purring sound puts you back in touch with the operator, and maybe she isn't doing anything tonight either.

One telephone habit which should be strongly discouraged in women, but which has been clearly growing since the advent of emancipation cleared the way for the female business executive, is the Delegated Telephone Contact. I have found it particularly rife among female public relations executives—who seem to be acquiring all the bad manners of their male equivalents without necessarily emulating their efficiency.

Delegated Telephone Contact is where the Executive instructs the Secretary to instruct *her* secretary to instruct *their* switchboard to instruct *your* switchboard to instruct *your* secretary that *you* are required to speak on the telephone.

Whilst apparently admitting you have your uses (*you* are being contacted, after all) the true Executive refuses to mix with the *hoi polloi* on the way to your ear, but wants you, personally, on the line hot and ready for conversation.

Each of a succession of minions, therefore, contacts you in person—passing you back along the line only once a stern inquisition has established that you really are you. At first you readily concede your identity, whilst deftly doodling bunnies on your blotter and attempting to extract a match and a cigarette from their boxes with only your left hand. Only as a third, and then a fourth, voice suspiciously demands verification of your telephone credentials does your exasperation mount to the level of beginning to spit blood. You almost expect the last link in the chain to order you to place a square of gauze over your mouth before you breathe down the line at Little Miss Big-Shot.

Have no fear: By this time she has gone to lunch already or has surrendered herself to the hour long ritual in the Ladies' loo which inevitably precedes that foray. Will you hang on for a couple of hours, or will *you* call *her* back?

Should the time lapse be long enough to catch her back in the office before you have even been connected, it will certainly be too long for her to remember having booked the call. 'Yes?' she will demand in the irascible tone of a woman who has not made her way in life by suffering fools gladly.

At this point, the best thing to do is shout into the mouthpiece: 'Your house is on fire! Hurry in the name of God!' and hang up at once.

She can always 'phone home if she wishes to check. There is always a chance she will get through. A slim one, but a chance.

A more rewarding method of communicating during the courting procedures might emerge from a deeper study of what has been scientifically dubbed Kinetics—or Body Talk. It is a new study in sociological terms, but it is a very old practise. For example, that fascinating, rippling, side-to-side shift of avoirdupois which rotates her sweet little buttocks in a symphonic dance reminiscent of two young puppies struggling under a silk sheet, is simply saying, 'Follow me ...' And a girl who draws her hand back sharply and then brings its flat area swiftly in contact with the side of your head is saying, 'Keep your hands to yourself.'

We begin these unspoken projections very early in life. Throwing your Teddy out of the pram every time an indulgent adult shoved the damned thing back in was simply an inarticulate attempt to get across to someone responsible the news that it was time your nappy was changed; and if a red-faced small boy suddenly throws his Porrage all over his Mother's head he does not do it because he does not love his Mummy, nor even because he is not especially fond of Porrage. He does it because he feels the deep need of feminine affection and instinctively realises that the first step towards achieving it is getting a little attention.

Later in life, our body talk can become more explicit. As august a body as the Shirt, Collar and Tie Manufacturers' Federation revealed some years ago that when a girl reaches out to straighten a man's necktie she is simply indulging in a safe and moral substitute for a sexual caress.

The claim may seem far fetched, but it could well explain why head waiters are reluctant to allow a man inside a restaurant unless he is wearing a tie. A restaurant full of young ladies deprived of these simple and harmless alternatives to ripping off their escorts' trousers might be a swinging spot in terms of the tourist trade but is hardly likely to get in the Good Food Guide.

Where Body Talk—or indeed any kind of internationally recognised sign language—would be useful would be in circumstances where willing parties to a temporary affair might find their romantic inclinations obstructed by a language barrier.

It is not too widely appreciated that sign languages of one kind or another have been quite widely and successfully employed by a variety of cultures in the past, and to great advantage. When Natchez, Chief of the red indian Piute tribe, and representative of all the Far West Indians, was summoned to Washington to agree a treaty, the consultation between himself and the paleface delegates took place entirely in sign language—the dumb-show discussions were recorded in official volumes, and marginal notations were drawn up to indicate all the signs used.

It has long been established that the Deaf and Dumb Alphabet is not a replacement of the age-old sign talk of deaf mutes, but simply a tidying up and organising of its ancient traditions. To get closer to the subject of our book, indeed, Cornelius Haga, an Ambassador to the Turks in the 17th. Century, discovered upon his arrival in Constantinople that the mutes serving in the Sultan's seraglio had long ago established a sign language for easy conversation between themselves. It was because of this sign language that the Turks finally abandoned the practice of cutting out the tongues of harem minions in order to ensure their discretion. The alternative physical amendments they turned to were pretty unspeakable too.

But certainly with the growing popularity of the Continental summer holiday a fund of simple internationally acknowledged gestures would ease the path of the exiled romantic, such as are readily recognised as meaning:

'Are you married?'

'Is your husband in the country at present?'

'When is he likely to return?'

'Shall we take a taxi or do you live close enough for us to walk?'

'Where is the bedroom?'

'Who's that at the door for God's sake?'

'Where can I hide?'

And even, 'Good evening, Sir. You may well be wondering what I am doing standing in your cupboard without any clothes on, but I can assure you I have a perfectly rational explanation ...'

One has wasted enough time in the past drumming into an already crowded brain the translations of such unessential phrases as, 'My postillion has been struck by lightning', 'I have just landed by parachute', and 'The man has drunk the milk behind the door of the church'.

Let's get down to business, I say. My problem is that I can't say it in anything other than English.

YOUNG LADIES
AND PARTIES

THE SIGNIFICANCE OF A YOUNG LADY AT A PARTY BECOMES diminished in direct proportion to her age. It is a curious paradox that on the whole the things we used to do at children's parties are the kind of thing which we then regarded as bothersomely 'soppy' but which now we would enter upon with a great and warm willingness.

'Sardines', 'Winking', 'Postman's Knock'—all these are all wasted on children and presumably foisted upon them by frustrated parents trying to live their sex-lives vicariously. That wicked, wicked pastime, where we sat in couples in a darkened room and the boy with a torchlight had to illuminate a kissing couple in order to change places with the young male discovered *in flagrante*, could be enormous fun at the age of forty with a couple of gins under your belts. But as soon as we get old enough really to enjoy kissing games we chicken out—standing about in bored little knots with our feet in the Second Position telling each other how sad it is about Oliver and Jill but anyone with any sense could see it would never last they were so *wrong* for each other.

The only way to emerge from such gatherings with advantage is to make a mental note about Jill. Now that Oliver is no longer on the scene it might be worth while getting in touch with her privately and exploring *a deux* the games people play when they aren't at parties.

Why don't we play Postman's Knock at those Sunday lunch-time routines when we reluctantly pose ourselves against the uncut moquette, devote ourselves to the hopeful damnation of Socialism/Conservatism, and are expected to hold on to a small measure of Cypriot Sherry until it comes practically to the boil? How often have I stood there swallowing yawn after yawn, contemplating the female guests, and speculating as to how much more enjoyable it would be to be giving Four to Number 27.

For the unitiated, 'Postman's Knock' was a party game, organised for children by their parents presumably with the hope of easing them gradually and without trauma through the shifting sands of puberty. One of the boys was designated as 'Doorman' and a second was sent out into the hall as 'Postman', whilst each of the little girls left in the room was numbered consecutively. The Doorman—a relative non-participant—would then quiz the Postman as to whether he had any deliveries to make.

Off the top of his head, generally, the reluctant martyr outside would declare 'Three for Number 14', or (bolder spirits) 'Six for Number 8', and the little girl so identified would be pushed wriggling and squealing through the door-way to a fate worse than death for the little lad who was ex-pected to deliver. Having bumped his lips reluctantly against her cheek the required number of times, he would then be allowed to return, blushing, to the front room—leaving his brief encounter with her pinny up over her face and her turn to choose from among the consecutively numbered boys.

The trick among the more precocious young males, as I recall, was to bribe the Doorman into a *sotto voce* revelation of the more fancied numbers, and one could embrace the ritual with an expectation of at least passing tolerance. Other-wise, you could get that dog Millicent Buggins with the ginger pigtails and the brace on her teeth. In such a case there would be no danger that anxious parents might need to resort to the hall to force your lustful little bodies asunder.

The whole affair, indeed, was practically without hazard in days when kissing offered no greater danger than trans-ferring from one face to another the faint traces of the morning's breakfast egg. Children had not discovered the delights of the 'French Kiss', a far more intimate osculation where the tonsils play almost as important a role as the lips. Indeed, in those far off days before the Permissive Society it is doubtful whether many adults had, outside of France.

But nowadays, with Puberty arriving at about the age of Eight years, the return of the 'Postman' from the hall would be awaited in vain—and after about half an hour you would probably have to go outside and throw a bucket of water over the little darlings.

Parental anxieties must all be tremendously sharpened today against a variety of childish pastimes regarded as utterly harmless thirty or forty years ago: 'We've been down in the shed playing Mothers and Fathers ...' could bring instant whiteness to the hair of any Daddy. Asking a small boy found loitering in the hall what he is up to, and being told, 'I'm waiting to give One to Number Seven', would bring at least a dry throat to any parent versed in the current vernacular of permissiveness.

As loosened sexual moralities percolate down through the age groups, indeed, it is pertinent to realise that the basic difference between children's parties and grown-up parties is that at children's parties all the children *already know one another pretty well*—invitations are invariably issued around among a closed shop of local and family intimates. On the other hand, one of the basic functions of grown-up parties is to bring people together. At most of these functions, the chances are that most of the people present, apart from the host and hostess, will know only a small percentage of the other guests.

The contradictions in such an arrangement are at once apparent. That the little girls and boys already know one another well surely suggests that serious extensions of intimacy may be encouraged by forcing them into practice sex games in an age when carnal knowledge is hardly longer regarded as unworthy. Conversely, if you really wish to bring adults together, and engender in your various friends a long lasting affection between them, what better than to shove them out into the hall in couples of opposing sexes, and switch the lights out?

The great problem about meeting a young lady at a party is mainly concerned with the fact that you have probably met her before, some months or years ago, at the last party given by this particular host and hostess, and with no contact in the intervening period, have forgotten her. Even if you have not forgotten *her*, it is highly likely that you have forgotten her name. An unmemorable young lady is automatically eradicated from a male memory trained to remember the names only of people who can be of use to its owner in business. And a memorable young lady will be remembered for physical appurtenances, because that is how a man remembers a girl. Names have little place in the male recall after the age of about Forty years. At that time, a man's mind is inclined to say '*That* is enough people ...' and thereafter only prolonged acquaintance, closely shared interests or reiterated meetings will bring people's names readily to mind.

Inevitable as is this situation, it evokes no sympathy in the female—who regards the forgetting of her name as the ultimate insult. To her there is no excuse in the fact that those who number among their occupational hazards the necessity of meeting steady waves of the human race daily finally evolve a mental block against almost all relatively new name retention. This manifests itself in a subconscious defence-mechanism decision by the young lady to be one of two kinds of hand-shaker: (a) the I-take-it-for-granted-you-know-who-I-am type, and (b) the let's-be-coy-about-it type.

The former is perhaps the more conceited but on the whole infinitely the more preferable. She will descend upon you out of the blue, chat to you like a close relation on matters of some intimacy, and move on with never a moment's acknowledgement of the fact that you obviously haven't any idea who the Hell she is. By ignoring your obvious ignorance she avoids the inherent insult to which its revelation would submit her. She will never talk to you again, but that's alright.

A worse genus of the human nuisance is the girl who realises almost before you have spoken that you have not an idea in the world as to who, what, or even why, she is. Wishing to punish you for the offence she cloaks her revenge beneath a simulated effort to jog your memory—and assists your efforts of recall with enough delicacy to stun a Hippo.

'Har, har,' she interpolates coyly. 'You don't remember me, do you?' She knows the question to be utterly rhetorical but makes no effort to simplify the situation via a reiteration of her name, address, husband, clubs, etc. She thinks you hateful for forgetting her—but will not be satisfied until you *feel* hateful.

'Darling, of course I remember you!' you insist with unconvincing insincerity, determined your chivalry shall not be found wanting by this clearly spoken challenge. You embrace her in a great loony grin, slide your arm around her shoulder, and follow on with a red herring: 'How *are* you, sweetie?' you demand solicitously. 'You look absolutely divine. I *love* your dress/hat/shoes/dog/new nose ...'

She is not to be sidetracked.

'Oh, no you don't,' she says kittenishly, showing her claws. 'Come on, now. Who *am* I, eh?'

You avoid the obvious retort. 'If *you* don't know, how the Hell do you expect me to?' and flounder about in her sadistic pleasure until she reveals that she is your Managing Director's wife. Next morning you may as well begin studying the *Sits Vac* columns. She will never forgive you. Nor will she ever speak to you again, but that's alright too. Because for abysmal insensitivity the 'go-on-who-am-I-then'-er is one of the most distastefully embarrassing categories of social nuisance extant. She is a nasty mixture of the masochistic and the sadistic; firstly because she is resolutely seeking out her own humiliation via insistence on your confession of forgetfulness, and, secondly, because she is deliberately drawing to your own and public attention the ineffectuality of your re-call. No one who is less than sick would approach a cripple and elaborate vocally upon the uselessness of his truncated limb—yet brash revelation of a withered memory is cruelly dragged into conversation without female demur.

For some reason, personal criticism is regarded by women as perfectly excusable if directed at men; and parties—because they bring together people who have not met since the last one, and have changed in the interim, are especially susceptible to such outrage. A woman will seize upon a man's increasing Baldness for comment because she is relatively certain of her own sex's immunity from the hazard. Too, like a spent memory, Fatness is generally regarded as fair game.

Suffering as I do myself from an easy obesity, I have been subjected often to the unthinkingly churlish observations of people who seem to believe that nobody can be fat and sensitive at the same time. Though they would not dream of laughing at a hunchback's hump, a surgical boot, a pair of squinting eyes, or a strawberry mark, they will declaim hilariously upon the shameful bulk of people who are certainly not fat because they wish to be. I have in recent years taken to a perhaps unforgivable form of defence which I would recommend to none, but whose adoption I would understand completely. When badgered in bantering style regarding the increase in my waistline, I retort with similar bantering pleasantry:

'How clever of you to match up your blue eye shadow to your varicose veins,' I laugh gaily. Or, 'Darling; your breasts have all the uplift of a brace of hot water bottles,' I giggle. Or, 'What a pretty yellow your teeth have become,' I suggest. Or, 'I *love* that Mexicali mustache, dear.' They are hurt, of course. It is inexcusable. But it is only retaliation.

In terms of introductions at parties, the woman's instinctive belief that everybody knows who she is, is at its worst when you are in the plight of having to introduce one woman to another. Mothers should be taught to instruct their young lady daughters that on encountering a man they have not seen for some time they should state their name clearly even before he can. No man will be offended by the assistance, though he may gallantly insist that his memory needed no such prompt. At the same time, both man and woman will be relieved of any possible embarrassment.

But faced with the need to introduce one young lady to another young lady, the man is also faced with a reluctance on the part of either young lady to admit that she might be the unforgettable one. Both will remain dumb—waiting.

'You both know each other, of course,' you say hopelessly. 'Let me get you both a drink?' Whilst you are at the bar, their instinctive antagonisms for each other may settle into at least an uneasy truce, you pray.

'I'm afraid not,' they say in one voice. 'Do introduce me ...' They stare malevolently at one another, their great shiny teeth bared in wary simulations of the smile, limp hands extended in a damp ritual of phoney camaraderie.

What do you do?

I don't know what you do. Run is what you do I suppose. I've tried everything else.

'Darling,' I've said before now, not knowing either's name. 'This is a very dear friend of mine,' and have edged off before they can decide which is which. 'Well, I'd have been certain you'd met,' I said on another occasion, suddenly looking off into the far distance. 'Good God! I think that curtain's on fire.' Failing such ploys, the only thing to do is faint dead away and hope you will be passed out over the heads of the crowd. No way are you ever going to arrive at that apex of male courage where you can state without fear or favour: 'I haven't a clue about the pair of you. You must do something to sharpen up your personalities, my dears. Clearly, you are both far too easily forgettable.'

Deliberate arrogance, indeed, is excusable in that it is the only way for you to emerge with your dignity intact. Attempting to cherish the feelings of a brace of dummies utterly insensitive to your personal predicament is wasted effort. It is a person's own fault if she is forgotten. She is forgotten because she never did anything to be memorable for. That is hardly *your* fault.

That the predicament is universally, and timelessly, experienced is proven by the gems of extrication handed down in the collections, of course. 'I never forget a face—but in your case I'll make an exception,' is possibly the most generally quoted squelch for use against the Brash Party Claimer, though I have always personally preferred the slightly subtler brush: 'I don't recall your face; but your manners are familiar ...'

Even nicer, perhaps, is the story told of author Douglas Jerrold. Striding purposefully down The Strand one day, late for an appointment, he was accosted by a celebrity-hunter of faint acquaintance who decided to use Jerrold's urgent air as an excuse to buttonhole him.

'Hullo, hullo,' gushed the interloper, catching Jerrold by the sleeve as he essayed to hurry past. 'What's going on?'

Jerrold regarded the nonentity with quizzical irritation for a moment, and deftly removed the hand from his sleeve with an expression of faint distaste.

'I am,' he said, and disappeared into the crowd.

It is because they want to know what is going on, of course, that women will approach any man with a claim of acquaintanceship. It is because they *must* know what is going on that they attend parties—of which basically they disapprove—but to be truthful there is no point in their presence there once they have attained the age of about eighteen years (see above). Only the emancipation of women has allowed them to attend at functions where they have nothing to offer but conversation. Only their social elevation has allowed them to change The Party to a function entirely couched in their own terms.

A party, after all, is a celebration—or should be. Only over-civilisation of the event, mainly due to 'the presence of ladies' has rendered it down to the point where we fidget idly from foot to foot enthralling one another with exciting local discussions about the recent rise in the Water Rates. Is it simply that I am older? Or has the whole world gone sane?

God knows I try to liven the proceedings at parties to which I am invited. My imitation of Billy Eckstein singing *I Apologise*, for example, is widely acknowledged among my friends to be utterly uncanny in its verisimilitude. Even if a snide minority are sometimes heard to remark upon the outstanding appropriateness of the title. Bird imitations, too, are a noisy but individualised talent which once enthralled many a fellow guest at War-time gatherings, before the strangling garotte of female respectability reduced parties to nothing but chat. My bird imitations might have been traced, sub-consciously, to the lack of birds in those days; but half-way through the evening I would be enlivening the proceedings with my Wise Old Owl, stirring their curiosity with my mating call of the Curlew, riveting them against the bar with a vocal facsimile of the Wood Pigeon said to be so true to life as to be vaguely creepy.

To some degree, of course, I was merely the Warm-Up man. My act was regarded as simply the *hors d'oeuvres* to the greater feast of male madness to come—the Human Defiance of Gravity, for example.

The Great Human Defiance of Gravity was a great favourite in most officers' messes (those havens of barred femininity) during the Second World War; when under the collective influence of drink one drunken entrepreneur was held in position—sideways on and upside down—by all the other drunken entrepreneurs whilst he made impressions of his footprints in ink or mud (as the mood took us) up one side of the wall, across the ceiling, and down the other side. Visiting WRNS and WAAFS were encouraged to join in the fun if wearing skirts; but few were prepared to submit their Passion Killers to the light of day, and the Great Human Defiance of Gravity became unswervingly identified with male party-goers only. As did most of the bases for a wild time in those days.

In the still undisciplined days of early demobilisation, I remember a good party man who had lost an eye in a fracas just outside Mersa Matruh, but who managed to bring a spirit of true celebration to the handicap of the glass accessory with which a grateful government presented him by way of alternative. He was sought after widely by successful hosts of the time due to his highly personalised knack of prizing the orb from its socket almost exactly on the stroke of 2 o'clock in the morning and executing an elaborate juggling act with it and four or five stuffed olives. Widely regarded as the excruciating facet of this nightly ritual was that during the rest of the party you were never really sure what you had in your Martini.

And what has happened in these days of female-controlled parties to all the Tumbler Eaters? In my young days, one of the reasons that party conversations never took place was simply because you couldn't hear yourself speak above the sound of masticated glass.

The death wish was on us, I suppose; but any young fighter pilot worth his salt hardly ever bothered with the salt. Having revived himself from the previous night's party via a healthy inhalation from his oxygen mask, he was back to have another drink and assuage the possible retribution of heartburn with a bite out of his glass—munching it up to a salivary powder until nothing remained but the stem.

It must have been in those days—and in scenes such as I witnessed again and again during the War—that that hoary old joke originated where the First Tumbler-Eater regarded the throwing away of a glass stem by the Second Tumbler-Eater and told him: 'I say, Old Boy, you're leaving the best part ...' It got to the point where every time a pilot went to the toilet is sounded like someone had dropped a set of dishes.

The last time I witnessed a new ex-pilot essay to chew up a wine glass, he was expressly forbidden to do so by the young lady who was now his wife but who, some ten years previously, had not dared do other than simply bask in the reflected glory of his sublime idiocy. *Sic transit gloria mundi.* In such ways has the influence of young ladies relegated the Party to an occasion of nothing but idle chatter.

Why do we never see the Cowboy Confrontation enacted nowadays, if I am wrong? Always the subject of wildly shared hilarity but now conducive of nothing but anxious silence from guests not in the know, the ritual of the Cowboy Confrontation called for one party drinker suddenly to throw the door open and stand glaring hotly at his prearranged antagonist. Then, for as long as their vocabularies could sustain unreiterated imprecation, each would revile the other with a string of passionately worded insult.

This introductory period terminated by a contraction of scurrilous originality, the two key phrases of 'Make Your Play,' and 'Draw!' were then introduced into the confrontation. Whichever antagonist felt his vocabulary was beginning to feel the strain could then initiate the next stage of the contest by the simple recital of the words 'Make Your Play'. By now, both men would be facing one another with every simulation of deathless hostility, hands hovering over hips in the traditional stance of Dodge City mayhem.

The first antagonist having introduced the next stage of the duel via his key phrase 'Make Your Play', the initiative now passed to his rival—who was immediately at liberty to shout the closing key phrase 'DRAW!'.

At which point, each would dive his hand into a side pocket of his jacket, produce a box of Bryant and May, and whip out and light a single match as rapidly as possible. The last to hold up his flaming splinter was reckoned to be shot plumb in the stomach and was required to fall screaming to the ground clutching his belly in simulated agony and roll about the floor in hideously moaning contortions of grisly death.

As you can see, it was all simple fun; but the last time I tried it out at an unsuitably respectable party at Tunbridge Wells—with the only like spirit for miles around—a white-faced hostess tugged at my sleeve, before we were halfway through the Vile Imprecations stage of the game, and protested: 'This has gone far enough. You're supposed to be decently behaved adults. Let's go into the next room away from the other guests and cool off ...'

Sheepishly we followed her, and attempted to explain that it was all an elaborate joke—an explanation which, in face of the fact that absolutely nobody had been laughing, she clearly found difficult to accept. To this day the word is around the neighbourhood that my friendly antagonist and myself (dear friends as it so happens and the only sympathetic spirits towards each other within a radius of some fifteen women-dominated miles) are social poison if invited to the same place on the same evening.

To a degree, we both welcome the fact—which assures us only alternate invitations to at least one boring evening per annum; and I tend to think sometimes that a really terrible black is about the best thing a man can put up if his life is not to be crucified to a succession of unendingly respectable parties dedicated to the discussion of the merits of local preparatory schools.

I wonder, indeed, if there might not be room in the commercial scene somewhere for a How To Be The Life Of The Party correspondence course couched in mephistophelian connotations aimed truly at being the death of party. Other social graces such as Learning To Play The Piano In Twenty Minutes Flat, or How To Prepare Weak Punch For Thirty Guests For Thirty New Pence, or How To Feed People On The Cheap, have evidently been circulating in book and pamphlet form for a number of years now, if experience is anything to judge by. Why not a comprehensive primer on How To Be An Unwelcome Guest?

This I see as instructing a man in essential little party tricks like Ventriloquial Cussing When The Vicar Is Present, Priceless Spode China Juggling, Stamping Out Cigarettes In Cashmere Carpets, Pouring Punch Into Petunias, How To Upset A Jug Of Water Into The Piano, Indiscriminate Bottom Pinching, and Accidentally Tipping Your Drink Down Your Hostess's Decolletage.

It would need only a volume of Vulgar Innuendoes, and the basic back-up of such necessary props as the False Runny Nose, the Electric Hand Shaker, and the Rude Cushion— and a man's social life would soon be immensely simplified.

The steady flow of those dreary, Cypriot Sherry *conversaziones* would dry up before the month was out; and you could settle down at home with your own bottle of Scotch and watch the rest of the world go hang.

HOW TO KISS A
YOUNG LADY

THREE PSYCHIATRISTS WORKING TOGETHER AT THE Pennsylvania School of Medicine not long ago published findings which suggest that the main desire of a woman when she responds to a male embrace is simply to be hugged or held securely in a state of protectedness. Fear of pregnancy subconsciously discourages her from desiring a more intimate relationship—but she is often actually prepared to risk the ultimate sex act in order to satisfy her psychological desire for nothing more than a simple cuddle. Surrendering to you is no more than a kind of bribe.

Particularly during times of economic, political or personal stress, a woman has a compulsive need for a man's protective arms around her. According to the three good doctors, a normal woman cannot be satisfied with the embrace of another woman because of the stigma of lesbian suggestion inherent in the juxtaposition. This despite the fact that the retreat into another man's arms is tantamount to a wish to return to the womb.

It has also been established that women encounter great difficulty in finding men prepared to stand there all evening with their arms and legs stiffening up and no apparent hope of any escalation into proper (or improper) intimacy—and this is to a large degree understandable. Squeezing herself against a man, snuggling into his arms, exposing him to the warm soft pressures of her body, stirring his heart with the thumping of her own, burning his ear with her hot breath; this is no way to concentrate a man's thoughts on a sympathetic respect for a woman's vulnerability—only on a deep gratitude for it.

And breaking off at last from a prolonged and yielding embrace, with a satisfied little sigh and a cheery suggestion of 'How about a game of Gin Rummy?' is like allowing a starving man to swallow a piece of steak on a string—and then pulling it back up out of him before he gets the real flavour.

The doctors at the Pennsylvania School of Medicine conclude that this most unsatisfactory balance of sexual desires between the male and the female is the most likely factor in urging her into reluctant surrender, promiscuity, and even prostitution. In defence of the male attitude, it might also be seen as the motivating force for all those Rape cases which indict some wretched, confused male defendant who had been encouraged 90 per cent of this way to the womb—only to find the denouements he and she had had in mind were two entirely different matters.

To complete the injustice of the male position, it has also been medically suggested that a woman's arms are full of hazard for any man whose heart is unsound. In his report on the death of a 23-year-old man who died in the arms of his sweetheart, Dr. H. A. Heggtveit of the University of Ottawa described the great physiological stresses induced in the male system as a result of making love.

These are said to be as rugged as the equivalent of playing six sets of Tennis against an equally fit opponent and without rest between sets. It seems a curious but apt coincidence that you court a girl before winning a love game, and the net result rests upon how well you serve.

As a matter of substantiation, Dr. George Trimble, writing in *Journal of the American Medical Association* claims that far more men expire in The Act than is generally believed or ever reported. The women concerned are all naturally reluctant to reveal the reason for death as anything other than natural causes—even though most men might be prepared to suggest that when their time comes that's the way they want to go.

Dr. Trimble reveals also that he has never ever experienced a case where the woman has suffered a heart attack in similar circumstances, so this might fairly balance the male hazard against the female dangers encountered in childbirth. The whole of the operation might fairly be considered henceforward as a parlous undertaking in which both participants share the peril.

A curious connection between the female heart and childbearing, however, is established by the researches of Professor Salk of Cornell University. He has discovered that a mother instinctively holds her baby on her (the mother's) left side. Apparently, says the Professor, the sound of the mother's heartbeats are comforting to the child, and babies exposed to recordings of heartbeats cry less and put on more weight in consequence. The sound of the heartbeat reminds them of, again, the womb—where it was all warm, cosy, sheltered and tension free, like in the old days.

It would seem a good idea—in light of the average woman's contrary maternal instincts—that a man sharing a settee or sofa with a young lady should therefore sit on her left hand side and keep her on his right; with his right arm around her shoulders or waist.

Not only does this satisfy her instinct to clasp a loved one to her heart, it also avoids too obvious evidence of the pounding of his own heart (now on the far side)—a manifestation which any young lady is trained to recognise as a danger signal.

Furthermore, the juxtaposition of the two bodies is thus controlled by his right—and stronger—arm. And should she favour double-breasted styling, her buttons are on the nearer side to his free left hand—should she become uncomfortably warm as a result of his protective embrace and he be gallantly constrained to assist in removing her blouse.

It should be realised, too, that the shoulder of the normally right-handed male is inevitably longer, fuller and deeper than the other—as a result of the simple processes of physical development. Thus is afforded a roomier and more comfortable surface for the resting of the female head. It all clicks naturally into place.

Victorian etiquette, appropriately enough, ruled that at a meal table the lady should if possible be placed to sit on the right hand side of her partner, as might befit a guest of honour. That such a placement renders it more difficult for a right-handed woman to pick a man's pocket or defend herself with her hat-pin lends the arrangement an extra logic.

A man's *left* hand, therefore, should be regarded as his operative courting hand. The right hand, with its right arm, remains tensed about the young lady's waist in a state of firm, rigorous and unmoving control—something akin to the lower unit of a pair of chopsticks. The left hand must be trained to pinch, squeeze, stroke and reconnoitre with delicacy whilst remaining forceful enough to operate a cigarette lighter, switch off the light, or wrest itself free from the restraining grasp of both her free hands at the same time.

There is one natural scientific phenomenon which might quite easily be encountered whilst a man is in close juxtaposition with a young lady in a darkened room, and which should be suspected as highly irrelevant despite its dramatic manifestation.

This is the phenomenon of the Whenever-I-Kiss-Her-Sparks-Fly-And-The-Whole-Room-Lights-Up syndrome. Many besotted young men have been drawn towards the dear octopus of matrimony through an ignorant belief that some kind of miracle is urging them together.

The fact is that some man-made fibre materials used for the fashioning of women's shirts and underwear (and some men's shirts and suits too) incline to accumulate small charges of static electricity—and the drawing together of the man and woman acts as two plates of a condenser, discharging a pretty blue spark across the gap. Not long ago it was reported in a scientific paper that the build up of static electricity in the man-made fibre bras. and pants of female operators was throwing certain computers out of phase; sometimes even bringing them completely to a halt. The information is whimsical in sociological terms, even fascinating in scientific terms, but in romantic terms it has little bearing other than to advise against conducting yourself in this fashion in a gas-filled room.

The menace inherent in a simple kiss is more versatile than as represented in the simple field of physics, however. Research has shown how a quite ordinary embrace between two people of differing sexes can send a normal man's pulse rate up from the usual 72 into the 90s. And kisses of a more exploratory and determined category can send it soaring to 110 or 120 (the pulse rate registered by Neil Armstrong as he took off for the Moon).

What is more, a normal grade kiss exerts a normal grade pressure on the faces of the kisser and the kissee of about 10 pounds; and in the ecstatic levels this power can soar to a pressure of 25 pounds—evaluations established by the great make-up artist Max Factor, in an effort to decide the kind of attacks his cosmetics would have to withstand during the normal day of a normal woman.

Outside of normalcy the hazards increase in direct proportion to the engendered enthusiasm. There are medical reports of quite a few embraces where the boy or girl concerned has come up for air with a dislocated jawbone, a snapped collar bone, or badly bruised ribs. In the early nineteen sixties in America, a passionate couple in the back row of a New York cinema took their cue from the screen so wildly that when the lights went up an usherette had to enquire as to whether there was a doctor in the house. The young lady concerned had broken her arm.

As a result of the pressures physically, and the emotional disturbances involved, it has been estimated as a result that every really serious, get-down-to-it kiss affects a man to the extent of shortening his life by the equivalent of three minutes. Every 500th kiss in these terms, therefore, has witnessed the departure of a day in the life of.

Official medical recognition of the hazards of the practice came as long ago as in 1952, when the December 27th issue of the *British Medical Journal* announced with a straight face:

'The dangers of kissing depend very much upon the technique. The dutiful kiss involving application of the lips to the forehead or lateral part of the cheek may resolve in the contamination of the lips by bacteria causing a *dermatitis* or *furuncles* ...' (So there's danger in it—even fur uncles) ... 'but the full blooded passionate kiss in which lips are applied to lips with a varying degree of pressure for a varying length of time, necessarily involves some exchange of salivary bacteria. How far this involves the risk of transmitting throat infection it is difficult to say. It is, of course, worse to be coughed or sneezed at, and the probability is—though there is no experimental data on this point—that a kiss would be preferable to either of these experiences.'

There is a compelling attraction to the last sentence, but it has certainly been medically estimated that during the course of a single kiss some 800,000 individual microbes can emigrate from one dear friend to another—an exchange which one would be hard put to it to categorise as a welcome aspect of affection. One of those curious nuts who invariably appear at moments of national emergency to fulfill their peculiar destinies, did indeed produce what he promoted as a prophylactic Kissing Veil—designed to prevent the transmission of these germ hordes—some years ago. It seems to have achieved no great commercial success, being at the time dismissed by one happy philosopher as tantamount to 'eating a toffee with the paper still on it.'

Clearly the medical hazards of kissing could be behind the official Italian view of public embrace—which threatens its exponents with legal action. There is some irony to the attitude, as Cato has revealed that the mouth to mouth greeting in Ancient Rome originally derived from suspicious returning husbands tasting the breath of their wives to establish that the lady of the house had remained sober during the master's absence. In its discouragement of alcoholic indulgence, the Kiss might originally have been regarded as a kind of equivalent to the chastity belt.

If the Roman Kiss has its hazards, though, how much more menacing must be the potential of the French Kiss— where the tongue and tonsils play a larger role in the anatomical juxtaposition than do the relatively relegated lips. And the physical dangers of the American Kiss were widely reported upon in the late 1960s when medical science drew attention to the rising incidence among dedicated courting couples of the dreaded *Mononeucleosis*.

This unexplained malady was officially embraced within that handy if vague diagnosis with which a baffled medical profession identifies any condition of which it has no certain knowledge—a virus infection. It manifests itself in glandular swellings, temperature fluctuations, and even temporary local muscular paralysis; and the two latter symptoms would seem perfectly natural and traditional reactions to any practised devotee of the *osculatory syzygy* (Look it up). Going all hot and cold and even seemingly to temporarily lose the power of one's arms and legs are by no means unusual results of passionate kissing. Only the swollen glands surprise. Perhaps we have stumbled, at last, upon a logical reason for referring to the practice as 'Necking'.

Apparently, the malady *Mononeucleosis* is not to be regarded as a new disease, but simply as an old one which has at last been isolated. Doctors believe that the human race has been subject to it for some time—but has in the past been attributing its symptoms to other and unknown causes.

In the United States, by all accounts *Mononeucleosis* puts some 10,000 college students on the sick list every year— ironic result of a practice where at least the male participant of the triggering ritual might be *hoping* to end up in bed— and it appears that the harder and more often a man kisses the more likely he is to be struck down.

Adult males are believed to be more susceptible to the attack than are small boys; and this seems hardly surprising in view of the fact that adult males submit to female embrace without protest, whereas a small boy is honour bound to wriggle out of the embarrassment of soppy demonstrations of affection until the arrival of puberty begins to suggest that girl cousins have uses other than standing obediently still and acting as goal-posts. But from the moment of that realisation, the medical researchers would have us believe, he is a sitting duck for the virus contamination of any passing *Mononeucleosis* carrier Fate throws across his path.

With Britain constantly anxious regarding her industrial productivity, man hours lost through *Mononucleosis* could throw our whole economic future into the hazard. Just rheumatism accounts for more than 10,000,000 working days lost each year to this country; the common cold adds up to another 4,000,000, and sciatica alone is responsible for another 700,000. Add countless more for hangovers and grandmothers' funerals, and the plague of the kissing bug could bring the whole national effort to naught.

The only answer which the Government so far seems to have considered is a labour force which can deputise at will for sick employees—but the degree of specialisation essential to the peopling of a modern industrial plant renders haphazard substitution a danger to overall efficiency.

Far wiser, surely, to engage specialist substitutes at an earlier stage of the proceedings, inoculate them against *Mononucleosis*, and allow them to carry out all necessary intimate social relations on behalf of the artisan classes—thus ensuring the latter's continued good health, the maintenance of a low national level of absenteeism, and the maintenance of a high level of industrial production. I am prepared to give all my time to the job.

To be frank, what might seem a bold sacrifice on my part is little more than an evens gamble—for the advantages may well neutralise the disadvantages. Another medical report suggests that people who kiss a lot are better able to resist cardiovascular, respiratory, gastro-intestinal and endocrinal diseases. A TV and cinema orientated society is far readier, I am sure, to accept the good news rather than the bad.

Not that the simple kiss plays much of a part in the modern cinema—where *dramatis personae* scarcely bother with the preliminaries of love-making in the permissive spectaculars which call for no more than a casual grope and the ability to tell the Stork from a half pound of butter. But the coyer years of the nineteen twenties, thirties and forties, relied entirely on the kiss for sensual suggestion—and only lengthened the duration of such in order to inflame the audience participation in the back stalls.

So important became the length of time given to the sexually exciting exhibition of two people of opposite sexes pressing their faces together that the censors began to become anxious. The time seemed fast approaching when all that might be required for a eight reeler was a cast of two and a neat job of editing when either paused for breath.

Finally, following on the first screening of *No Orchids for Miss Blandish*, the censors officially rejected a 45 second long kiss and insisted it be cut back to 25 seconds. And though 45 seconds may not seem over long in cold print, it is astonishing how long it may seem to live through in hot circumstances. And you may test it for yourself.

Take a young lady, preferably under the age of forty, and place your left arm tightly around her neck so that your wrist falls in such a position that when your face is flush with hers you may study your watch by opening your right eye. Next—fasten your right arm firmly around her waist, drawing her closely to you and, placing your lips upon hers, kiss her warmly and passionately for exactly 45 seconds according to the second hand of your watch.

Now: Take up an identical stance—but this time kiss the young lady for exactly 25 seconds. Purely for research

purposes, of course, note the difference. I think you will find
it to be exactly 20 seconds.

Why the witnessing of two people kissing should be deemed
possibly morally corrupting to the people watching is difficult
to decide. One can understand why officialdom should forbid
it in public, of course, because there are always minorities
who wish to prevent others from enjoying themselves; but
whilst we consider the origins of kissing—and whilst we
are also noting their effects upon the modern cinema—it
might be worth considering a possible scenario to record
the very first kiss of all time. Its conception can hardly be
less ridiculous than the initial explanation by Sir Walter
Raleigh of the habit of smoking cigarettes:

'How about a kiss, Darling?' offered Ugg the Inventive
Neanderthal, one cosy prehistoric evening by the embers of
the glowing cave-fire.

'A what?' enquired his busy mate, shoving another dino-
saur steak down into the glacial deep-freeze. 'What's a kiss,
then? What is it *exactly*? You know I never had your
schooling ...'

'A Kiss is a thing I just invented while I was sitting here
thinking,' said Ugg with the pleasurable pride of one who
brings good news. 'What we have to do to do it, is press our
faces together ever so hard—so that our noses sort of slide
sideways past each other's and our lips come one lot on top
of the other, all sort of moist and smacky. It's what you might
describe as an anatomical juxtaposition of contracted obicu-
laris orisis muscles, but the name's a bit long for popular
acceptance. I think I'll call it a "Kiss" for short. How about
one?'

The Ice-Age wife regarded his flat, Mongoloid features—
with their thirty-five years of matted fuzz and uncombed
dandruff; his gritty, sweaty forehead; his mouth greasy and
slimy from the fat of their evening meal; and the nose with
the untended evidence of a heavy head cold, and replied:

'You've got to be out of your palaeolithic mind ...'

It seems her prehistoric instincts extend into the anxious
suspicions of young ladies—even to this day—but a persuasive
man might finally dispel the fears of infection by quoting
the transience of real hazard as is suggested in George Mere-

dith's glum but medically encouraging dictum: 'Kissing don't last. Cookery do.' What escaped the appreciation of Meredith's culinary cynicism, of course, was that kissing don't have to last, Thank God; you can always have some more.

THE YOUNG LADY
AND SOMEWHERE TO GO,
OR HER PLACE

LOVE MAKES THE WORLD GO ROUND. AND ROUND AND ROUND and round and round looking for somewhere to be alone. Since the advent of the open-plan decor system, there is practically nowhere a young man and young lady may go to be in relative privacy. The Night Club—with its semi-darkness and often cubicled tables—offered for a few years as near to intimacy as the then relatively moral courtship could wish. A shy nuzzle and an evening of clasped hands seemed sufficient in those days. With the advent of the permissive society, the normal suburban household is useless unless your potential father-in-law is a *voyeur*; and the night club's shift into relative respectability is already showing public reaction in falling gates.

In the nineteen thirties, the semi-det. mod. chalet-type, bijou residence generally comprised at least two down and two up, and the courting couple could be left in the parlour in peace whilst Mum and Dad listened to the 'wireless' in the back dining room. Though even this was hardly fool proof. Likely as not you would be warming to the ultimate intimacy of a sly suck at her ear lobe when in would come Mr. Glum with his collar off, his brass stud staring at you like the great eye of Polyphemus, and his yellowing snapshots of the Gallipoli campaign.

If you are not too high bred to be associated with the retail trade, the shop doorway is about your only cheap alternative, though here the hazard is that no sooner has your embrace begun to develop in more urgent directions but a member of the constabulary is shining his bull's eye all over your back and reaching between your throbbing bodies to try the shop's doorhandle.

How many desperate courting couples are further frustrated by the policeman's absurd nocturnal duty of testing tradesmen's entrances would be hard to assess—but it is clear that a Constable can be your best friend if you can only persuade him to arrest you. Knock off his helmet together and the chances are you may be locked up in a windowless cell for the night. At worst your parade before the Beak in the morning will cost you in fines rather less than a room at a reasonable hotel.

155

Furthermore, there is no need to dress the part—and I must point out to the tyro lover that clothing gives considerable assistance to plans which need more for their completion than the simple acquiescence of the lady in question.

To conform with the fashionable hyperbole traditionally applied to invest a questionable situation with verbal dignity, I shall not refer to it as a dirty weekend, but as a sexual sabbatical. A frequency of seven days hardly seems too much to expect in terms of a red-blooded young man and a permissive society. What is too much to expect is any assistance from the army of spoilsports dedicated to keeping yourself and your dear friend apart.

For all the world does not love a lover. Certain sections of it—hotel managers and desk clerks to name but two—are as implacably set upon frustrating your knavish tricks as would be her parents if they but knew she was not playing away with the Hockey Team this weekend.

I mentioned the need to dress the part when attempting to enter an hotel because hotel hierarchies are notoriously snobbish, having been weaned on a tradition of sycophancy to The Toffs—who largely ensured their income for many past generations. So the clearer your arrogance, the more obtrusive your education, and the more expensively restrained your clothing, the less chance there is of a marble eye at Reception.

Your sartorial ploys are all subtlety: a Savile Row suit, an obvious Old School or Regimental tie, a waistcoat with a Stock Exchange watch chain carefully threaded across the front, black leather shoes with discreet broguing, a plain white (rolled-edge) breast pocket handkerchief and a supplementary companion to it peeping from your sleeve-cuff—these are the psychological tricks with which you allay a reception clerk's suspicions before they are even prompted.

For it is a curious belief of the *bourgeoisie*—unsupported by the faintest shred of historical evidence—that the Upper Classes are infinitely more moral in their treatment of women than any other section of society.

But your clothes must, of course, be supported by expensive and high-class travelling accessories and by parallel behaviourisms. There is no point, for example, in arriving at the hotel with a selection of impressively elegant solid-leather portmanteaux emblazoned with the initials G.St.J. McD-P. whilst you are signing in as Fred Jones Esq. Particularly if you are forced to ask the clerk how to spell Jones.

Your treatment of your companion is important, too, at this stage. Licking her ear; breathing heavily on her; running your left hand up and down her spine whilst you are signing-in with your right; treating her with hardly restrained sexual anticipation; none of these is calculated to project an image of the old married couple which you need to get as far as the lift.

Neither should she be treated with any of that deference which departs in matrimony even before the honeymoon has ended. Speak to her casually—even curtly. Or disregard her altogether. Her squeaky nervousness will immediately betray you should she attempt to answer questions, and it is safer to bar her from the conversation—especially as any solicitous enquiry from the clerk to 'Mrs. Jones?' is going to need a hearty kick in the ankle before she offers reply. Better to ignore her and simply take it for granted—as any *real* husband would—that she ought to be off helping the bellhop with the heavier luggage.

But warn the girl of the situation beforehand. Unexpected discourtesy, even if only simulated, can lead to the disaster of her sudden outraged outburst: 'If you think I got off early from the shop on a Friday—our busiest day—just to come down here and be treated like dirt George Sinjun McDonald-Pollard you've got another think coming ...' Try explaining *that* to the desk clerk as the Porter politely shoves the swing door around to accommodate her imperious exit.

Of course, it is only the rashest adulterers who will duck behind the camouflage of matrimony. More usually the embarrassment of the Reception Desk can be simply over-come by booking two single rooms and accepting the welcome and intimate propinquity which two in a narrow bed involves. Here your only verbal ploy is the simple additional in-struction: '... er—not necessarily adjoining.' The con-trariness of hotel clerks is such that you are not only bound to get two adjoining rooms—they will with luck have a communicating door.

Without a communicating door, two single rooms can be at least slightly irritating. And if you feel in deference to the lady's reputation or as a foresight against the hazards of private detection that you must each be alone in your separate rooms to lend respectability to the delivery of the early-morning tea, it is wiser to book your own room 'without Bath'.

This has the logic of necessitating an early morning stroll along the corridor to the bathroom. You can leave from one door with a cheery swing of your sponge bag, and return to the other in time to rumple up the bedclothes before the chamber-maid arrives. No casual observer is likely to note the difference between two adjoining doorways.

The ultimate demand, in establishing the respectability of your weekend at Reception is to pointedly send 'Miss Jones' away to make some secretarial telephone calls whilst you are registering, and ask the clerk to ensure that for the requirements of expenses the two bills are made up separately. This places your relationship at once on a sound business footing. What is more, it can save you a considerable proportion of the cost of the weekend if you conveniently neglect to recall that you should have paid her back her half in the car on the way home.

Bedclothes are important, of course, (see above). Any experienced chambermaid who finds one set of bed linen crushed into sweaty unrecognition and the other merely gently dented where you sat down momentarily to take off your boots, will have her report buzzing down to the front office before you can say as much as 'Can we have breakfast in our rooms, please?'. Even should the manager stay his hand, it is going to be difficult to get in the same hotel again next weekend.

Bed*clothing* is even more important; particularly in terms of the image you wish to project. Pyjamas with Union Jacks on the breast pockets—suggesting that you have done this sort of thing for England—can be categorised as so naive as to hardly warrant inclusion in a work of this seriousness. But the inclusion of some form of pyjama suit within your weekend luggage not only ensures reasonable respectability to a short morning trot along the landing, but also suggests a sophisticated fastidiousness which will allow the young lady to invest your unpacking with a certain dignity. Too, the respective nakedness neuroses are vastly different between the sexes. Men are generally loath to be seen completely unclothed, whilst most women delight in it.

Personal experience, indeed, emphasises this fact in my own case: The only recurring dream from which I ever suffer (I suffer it at least once a year) consists of my finding myself some half a mile from my London flat dressed in nothing but a short Winnie-the-Pooh vest which just fails to cover my privates.

Fate, having lured me as far as Oxford Street in one direction or the British Museum in the other, suddenly fills the streets with hurrying hordes of puritans and such disapproving spectators as the Chairman of my Board of Directors, my maiden aunt Cecilia, Mrs. Mary Whitehouse and the Archbishop of Canterbury. I wake in a muck sweat of shame.

The 'nakedness in a compromising situation' dream is by no means uncommon amongst males, I have been told, and is widely regarded by psychiatrists and dream translators as a manifestation of waking insecurity. And it is certain that the Great Dream Arranger—wherever he may be—would hardly choose the display of a woman's naked body as a means of manifesting *her* insecurity. A woman only becomes insecure when nobody wants to look. It might be said, indeed, that a woman only really achieves a feeling of superiority and the security which such involves when she has taken all her clothes off and is busily enmeshing some newly acquired slave in the initial stages of that ritual which is widely credited with making the world go round.

The difference in these diverse attitudes towards nudity, between the male and the female sexes, may well have been established not by the resulting revelations when both have their clothes off, but by the progressive stages through which each has to go before arriving at that delicate situation.

She peels off her dress, and still looks marvellous in pants and a lacy bra. Reaching back over her shoulder to unclasp the bra. has the momentary advantage of inducing unusual uplift via the involuntary muscle flexing involved, and the sinuous wiggle necessary to divest herself of her pants is at once exciting, dignified, aesthetic, and calculated to send the blood pounding through any man's temples.

But how about the man? Unplanned, his undressing can do nothing but project him as a target of hilarity:

How many would divest themselves of their jackets. and promptly surrender all panache to a revelation of their braces? And if one's trousers are attended by braces, it is necessary to remove one's trousers before one can remove one's shirt. And a man without trousers, standing in shirt-tails, sock suspenders and a pair of brogues is guaranteed to destroy any romantic connotations in the mind of even the most enthusiastic adulteress.

During the 1930s, indeed, a complete theatrical tradition was conceived by the Alfred Drayton–Robertson Hare team which based itself entirely on the principle that nothing in this world is quite so funny as a man who is not wearing his trousers. Devoid of your slacks, therefore, it is as well for you to remember that you do not look sexy so much as farcically vulnerable. And even the final desperate strip-down to one's jockeys is hardly conducive of dignity—with the commercial projections of an elastic waist-band spelling out the name of the manufacturer in bold capital letters in the region of your navel.

Forward planning for seduction, therefore, should always reject braces in favour of a belt and rehearse undressing in the order least likely to induce a sense of the ridiculous. A man will look less foolish if he removes first his jacket to reveal belted trousers; then takes off his shirt; and then removes his shoes and socks. There is at least an image of peasant virility about the bare feet and bare chest—particularly if he has had the sense to fix his chest-wig into position prior to arrival at the hotel. Removing the shoes first, also negates the possibility of jamming your boot in your trouser leg and having to hop about on one foot knocking over the bedside lamps and the patent electric trouser-press.

Certainly in recent years the advent of the Y-front has gone far to take the pain out of undressing in front of a young lady. The long coms. of Edwardian and immediate post-war years allowed trouserless farces to be staged in complete decorum—because shirt-tails were voluminous and the baggy confinement of Long Johns necessitated no adjustment other than an occasional fork lift. As he shot through one of the ever-opening and ever-closing doors in urgent retreat from the booming summons of the Dowager Duchess (off, left), Our Hero displayed nowhere near so much—even to the closest Stalls seats—as most female members of the audience will display with equanimity nowadays in the Bar during the intermission.

But with modern shirt-tails hardly long enough to cover bare essentials, and men's underpants whittled to a minimum, the dramatic verities have to be reconsidered in terms of an adulterous hotel room. For one thing, one must be careful regarding the possibilities of anti-climax:

At a menswear exhibition only a year or so ago, a manufacturer of men's underwear brought a touch of Rabelaisian reality to the display on his stand by padding out the fronts of the various pairs of pants with a generous addition of foam rubber. And as recently as in 1971 a swimwear firm launched a range of swim trunks with plastic inserts at the front which it promised would smooth out the liberalities of a man who in polite society might be considered as over-endowed *but offer visual consolation to the man who wasn't*. Since then, the fashion for wide-bottomed but tightly crotched jeans among the Permissive section has sometimes been further romanticised by the addition of similar falsification on everyday trousers.

Less impressive physiques taking recourse to such a camouflage should bear in mind that should the dissembling constitute the basic characteristic of his attraction for the girl in question, ultimate success for him must only bring ultimate disappointment for her. He will be no more honest than the sad young lady who wears falsies in order to lure men who might otherwise leave her untouched, but who, having touched her, realised it was hardly worth the trouble. Perhaps the prime example of this feminine wile was the one which also underlined the average woman's cupidity, when a *brassière* manufacturer placed on the market a bust-bodice which boosted the apparent bosom of its wearer by incorporating two small coin-purses in the zip-fastened compartments of the frontal cups. How many young men later discovered that the flamboyant figure they had for so long admired added up in truth to no more than a handful of coppers?

The best way of compounding such physical felonies is simply to train yourself to undress in the dark, and there are still certain young ladies brought up in a Victorian tradition which prompts them to divest themselves of their underwear after they have actually donned their all enveloping night-dresses. The see-through nightie largely put paid to that archaic approach, but it is interesting to note here that the development of attractive nightdresses for women only began in the 1880s—when the dissemination of a general knowledge of the principles of birth control first began to be discussed.

Previously the Victorian wife, exhausted by a series of interminable pregnancies following swiftly one upon another, regarded looking attractive at bedtime as a calculated risk. The hazard of even neglecting to screw her hair up in crackers was regarded as a partial threat, and the voluminous flannel nightdress—which even threatened to itch the amorous husband if he came too close—was shapeless and unsuggestive for very basic reasons.

Since the advent of The Pill—which overcomes even the dangers of a passionate urgency neglecting to fumble with fiddling little packets of rubber goods—the Baby Doll and transparent robes are worn by women simply for Honeymoons and the kind of situation we are here discussing. There is, after all, small point in trying to look attractive after the lights are out—and seductive nightwear has obviously been produced all along for the immediate pre-bed period; to be dispensed with as soon as the trap has been laid and the fair game is about to be.

What a man should be prepared for, though, is the trauma of seeing the young lady in the harsh light of the following morning—when an absence of cosmetics has planed her face into a plateau of flat desert land, her eyelashes lie on the bedside table like a pair of inanimate centipedes, and a resolutely active night has tangled her coiffure into the wild disarray of an involuntary 'natural'. Coupled with the man's inevitable guilt complex and his post-sexual remorse, these are the reasons why a woman is ninety-five per cent correct when she coyly suggests: 'But, Darling—you'll hate me in the morning ...'

THE YOUNG LADY
AND SOMEWHERE TO COME,
OR MY PLACE

OFFHAND, I CANNOT RECALL A WESTERN WHICH DIDN'T HAVE A happy ending. From 'Bite on this bullet, Ma'am. Doc'll be here real soon' to 'Stand fast, men; here come the cavalry now ...' the cliché dialogue is deliberately calculated to remove instantly any audience anxieties deliberately induced by the cinematic action.

The poison and the antidote are thus administered practically simultaneously. Even as the baddie smashes his pistol butt down on the oblivious hero's head, you know deep down that Everything Is Going To Be All Right.

For one thing, it is unlikely that the star is going to be killed off within ten minutes of the epic's commencement. For another, years of training in the four and sixpennies has brainwashed us into knowing that, finally, Good and Bad alike always get what they deserve.

Our day to day life outside the cinema should have taught us that life is seldom so rewarding—yet no cinematic cliché could ever produce in a man's soul the soaring revived hope engendered by the simple query: 'Would you like to come in for a cup of coffee?'

There she stands in the darkened porchway; her eyes cast demurely into the fairy grotto of her handbag and her fingers dredging nervously for her latch key. Your Good Time Charlie spending during the evening, and your mental arithmetic in the taxi, assures you that the rest of your financial month must be dedicated to a regime of austerity; your last bus has gone screaming down the road twenty minutes ago; and it is just beginning to rain ... Then she says: 'Would you like to come in for a cup of coffee?' and suddenly you know Everything Is Going To Be All Right.

In such a context, it would be fair to categorise Nescafé as an aphrodisiac—for what bubbling depths of erotic anticipation are plumbed by its mention. How wide the chasm between a blue and white striped beaker of Maxwell House and the surging passion its image irresponsibly releases. In that simply worded offer of camouflaged hospitality, before the hot brown stuff has taken the skin off your drying lips, there is more lascivious suggestion than in a full bottle of the hard stuff.

Too often the invitation is just a little camp as well. The cynical experiences of a handful of dashed hopes inevitably teaches a man that all he is likely to get *is* a cup of coffee. 'Come up and have a cup of coffee' bears absolutely no relationship to its equivalent male cliché: 'Come up and see my etchings ...'

But at least about the latter there is a certain honesty. Any woman over the age of twenty years must know perfectly well its meaning—and can acquiesce only in a complete knowledge of what the invitation entails. It is almost as brazen as the time saving policy of the man who enquires within a minute or two of being introduced: 'Can I go to bed with you?' He gets his face slapped occasionally, but he gets to go to bed with a whole lot of women.

I am not ashamed to reveal that I have asked girls up to my place on the basis of a set of apocryphal etchings—not because I know anything about Art but because I know what I like. Among the younger generation, however, the old faithful seems to have been supplanted by an invitation to 'come up and hear my L.P.s or listen to my new transistor'—an alternative of lures which readily establishes all you are trying to find out as whether she is looking for high fidelity or whether she is simply more interested in frequency.

Personally, I love doing what comes naturally—and after Nature, Art. For one thing, a basic collection of etchings can come a whole lot cheaper than a full set of hi-fi, and even a fraction of a night on the town. It is only necessary to learn how to use them to proper advantage.

The simple and relatively unimaginative method is to keep your etchings in a portfolio which you and your companion can examine together with your heads in intimate juxtaposition as you sit on the yielding upholstery of your patent 'Deep in the centre' settee. But progress here can be obstructed by what might be called the 'premature shock' syndrome. Women react very differently from one another to the sudden production of erotic pictorial stimuli. Some enjoy the honesty of cards on the table early in the game. Others may never have seen Aubrey Beardsley before, and be unprepared. Even the spectacles it is advisable to wear, in order to stimulate a studious aspect may not save you from a stinging back hander before you can whisper 'Circa 1897' with all the suggestiveness such an announcement can contain.

Such retribution can be qualified in the early stages of the game by a simulated search for the etchings when you first arrive back at your place. A hunt through various desks and drawers in histrionic exasperation can ultimately lead to your throwing open a cupboard door behind which you have concealed a bottle or two of Dom Perignon and a couple of glasses. Regard them with absent minded astonishment for a moment and then pull them out with resigned acceptance.

'Well—here's a little something to be going on with whilst I find the damned things,' say. As she draws down a few glasses of happy juice whilst you make searching sounds in the kitchen, and maintain the differential with a bite or two at the cooking sherry, she will never realise that whilst the etchings may not have been framed, she has.

And the expense of framing your etchings need not be discouraging, for the the cost of the frame can be offset by the fact that it is now necessary to purchase only a single etching. And the singular 'Will you come up and see my etching?' suggests not so much parsimony as a uniqueness and rarity value, unmatched by more plebeian collections which rely on simple numbers for their impact.

Having acquired your etching, it is now only necessary to set it in its pre-planned position within The Trap. It should be illuminated splendidly by a long tubular picture light, which must be controlled by a long, dangling ON/OFF string positioned immediately above a club sofa.

The whole should be positioned against the far wall of an otherwise darkened room which should have no other furniture than an ancient, ragged rug. The Trap is now ready to be sprung.

I believe that when confronted by the poorly illuminated illustration (and handicapped by the short-sightedness which seems to be an inevitable facet of any young lady prepared to spend time with me) the young lady of necessity makes tracks across the room to submit the picture to a closer examination.

Her foot will catch in the torn rug, and she will stumble.

The stumble, aggravated by the inconsistencies of the rest of the rug's surface, will develop into a head-down forward trot which will be terminated only by a sharp contact between the wall and the top of her head.

Nothing dangerous, you understand; but a blow of such surprise and suddenness as to render her slightly more stupid than when she agreed to set foot across your threshold in the first place. She will fall gently into position on the club sofa so thoughtfully provided.

All anxious condolence, you are beside her in the instant, taking her in your fond arms and insisting that you kiss it better. The ON/OFF light cord is situated at a level immediately above the sofa and your hand finds it without even stretching your arm. All injuries to the head are aggravated by too strong light directed upon the retina of the eye, explain, and can you be blamed if your consoling kisses fail to find the exact location of her bruise in a room which has been plunged into darkness?

To be truthful, the tiny Bloomsbury *pied a terre* which I dignify with the description 'my West End luxury flat' in the hope that girls might be persuaded to visit it, is so diminutive in its proportions as to forbid such ploys as are here outlined. This is not necessarily a disadvantage—for like Sonny Liston's reference to the boxing ring when asked how he would cope with a constantly retreating target, I can always say: 'Man, they can run; but there ain't no place they can hide.'

My current town flat isn't big enough to swing a cat in and, perforce, I have had to give up the pastime. Consisting as it does of a single bed-sitter room (usual offices adjoining), the first thing to greet a visitor's gaze upon opening the front door is the bed. And faced with such a confrontation, the average female's defence mechanism clicks resolutely into operation behind the bland inscrutability of her baby blue eyes.

'I'll wait in the car,' she says icily, backing out like a shying dray horse, 'bring the etchings out and show me there ...'

The immediate revelation of a bed can also be included in the 'premature shock' category, and must be avoided wherever possible. I await the invention of a thoroughly disguised divan with impatience. Attempting seduction in a single-roomed bed-sitter is difficult enough without adding the female resistance induced by a great, smirking, brass bedstead over there in the corner. A rich friend of mine with a flat in Devonshire Street has an impressive construction which is all bookcases on one side but which revolves on a central pivot to reveal a double bed attached to its back. I have seen such in a dozen cinematic murder mysteries and am hesitant to recommend them. In each case, whenever anybody revolved the mechanism, a dead body came round with the other side —and three's no company.

I experimented recently with one of those ingenious wall-fixtures where the fully made bed is pushed up into the vertical and left to stand on end until the pressure of a button releases it to fall down into the horizontal.

Neutralising its hazards is child's play to a really resolute female. I discovered that any time I made a move towards closer *rapprochement,* the girl would beat me to the control button and the bed clang down on my head—stunning me for long enough for her to make a getaway. There *are* convertible couches, I know, but they do not allow for sheets and pillows to remain in place, at the ready, *but hidden from sight,* whilst you go through the motions of altruistic hospitality in the evening's early stages. And a man's intentions are immediately transparent if his quarry returns suddenly from repairing her make-up in the bathroom to find him smoothing out a pair of Winceyette sheets and politely enquiring, 'Do you like hospital corners?'

A recent Russian invention may supply an unhappy ending to the whole problem by rendering the bed largely obsolete. Soviet researchers are reported to have perfected a Sleep Simulator which plies the system with electronic impulses to disperse the fatigue toxins accumulated in the human frame during the day. They estimate that it should ultimately reduce the amount of necessary slumber to about one hour in twenty-four and will add to its users' lives the equivalent of about twenty years of waking time.

In a permissive society it might be argued, of course, that such freedom for increased leisure will make the bed more necessary than ever—and its copulation connotations will be

even more fully emphasised. Couches, sofas, settees, even the
flat surface of a carpeted floor or a dining table, could take on
the stigma of seduction equipment once the Sleep Simulator
takes over. To *really* lonely men the news that the Simulator
also ensures its users are not subjected to dreams only
threatens to increase the frustrations—but possibly they will
be comforted by another recent scientific discovery: that the
average man dreams far more about other men than he does
about other women, and that the main subjects of such
nocturnal hallucinations are close male relatives.

For my money, the Sleep Simulator cannot be faulted on
that score. With hundreds of millions of women in the world,
I can forego the doubtful pleasures of dreaming about my
Uncle Joe.

Sometimes, however, the problems resulting from going to
bed are not fully emphasised until the time comes to wake up.
Then, it is often a coming to your senses in more ways than
one.

I recall with a kind of dazed affection a piece of fascinating
journalism by my old friend John Hillaby (in more recent
years to become famous as 'The Walker') and published in the
(then) *Manchester Guardian* in the early nineteen fifties. It
dealt with How a Bee Wakes Up.

There being a traditional affinity between the Bees and the
Birds, I might well at this stage parallel Hillaby's learned
scientific treatise with a corresponding consideration of How
a Bird Wakes Up; for any man aspiring to persuade a young
lady to spend the night in ultimate intimacy could be grateful for the warning. For one of the basic reasons behind the
fact that a man is liable to hate her in the morning is because
of her behaviour when that time arrives.

Usually, when the average male wishes to do nothing so
much as go on sleeping, *she* is up and about, clanking through
his china cupboard, swooshing the entire contents of the im-
mersion heater into a bath for herself, and forcing upon him
squares of hard, dry toast when his mouth is all leather and
glue.

Presumably, it is all part of The Tender Trap. Show him
how handy I am about the house, reasons that *rara avis* the
Domesticated Morning Bustler and he will soon see the error

of his lonely and independent ways. In fact, all a man sees stretching in grisly prospect through the years ahead is re-iterated morning semi-sensibility shovelling scrambled egg into his ear whilst the *Morning Bustler* coyly tickles the soles of his feet.

For myself I wish to wait for my eyes to open of their own accord—even though a sense of responsibility may have me walking carefully and blindly about the house beforehand, and no sound to be heard until the soft hiss of the shower prepares my eardrums for the harsh twank of female complaint.

Not that the *Domesticated Morning Bustler* is by any means the worst bird in the dawn chorus. There is also the *Full Breasted Warbler*—whose busty similarity to an operatic contralto has through the years convinced her of the im-pressiveness of her vocal chords.

Charm him, believes the *Full Breasted Warbler*, with the mellow tones of a morning aria from the bathroom, and he's yours for ever.

Akin to this latter species is the *Long-Legged Disc Wallower*, or *Go-Go Bird*—who cannot face the day without a fix from Tony Blackburn; and who spills coffee over your clean sheets as she performs what she imagines to be a seductive Bossa nova to the tinny strains of the transistor without which she goes nowhere. A man watches her with the maximum courtesy he can conjure—a kind of glum nausea—and she jiggles back to the kitchen only in time not to be strangled.

Worst, possibly, is the *Blue Tat*. Haunted by a dread com-bination of post-sexual and alcoholic remorse, she wakes in such despair she cannot scrape together enough self respect even to comb her hair. She says nothing, looks infinitely re-proachful, leaves in such a hurry she goes without her knickers, induces in you a sense of bottomless guilt, and is calculated to lay the kiss of death on the next twenty-four hours as surely as a final tax demand. She is related to the *Night Howl*, who always cries afterwards.

That species surpasses in hatefulness even the cloying giggles of the *Dovelike Darling*, who wakes you by blowing gently on your eyelids, cooing at you, and pressing her foolish face against yours for a breathy good morning kiss with no thought for her last night's indulgent foray into the garlic.

There are others to be discovered in the dedicated pursuits of pure research: like the *Lesser Metallic Coif*, whose bobby pins at the foot of the bed have to be explained to whomsoever takes her place the following night, or the *Greater Metallic Coif*, who has only to turn over to gouge a channel down your cheek with her metal rollers. They are as much to be avoided as the *Nocturnal Water Bibber*, who is for ever stretching her arm across you to the water jug on the bedside table—fighting her nightly battle with drunken dehydration and shoving her charm bracelet up your nose every time she reaches out.

The *Many Ringed Ex* is even more traumatic. Her succession of unsuccessful marriages inevitably sets you up as a possible comparative, and she is inclined to wake early in order to contemplate your possibilities whilst you are yet at an insensible disadvantage. Nothing is quite so embarrassing as opening your eyes to find someone studying you when you have been incapable of putting on your best personal projection. Was your mouth open? Were you dribbling out of one side of it? Were you grinding your teeth? Were you snoring obscenely? No girl is so undesirable as the one to whom you feel at a disadvantage.

Then there is the *Dark Belted Phoney*, who must get up without putting the lights on or drawing the curtains—so that she may cram her self indulgent avoirdupois secretly into the roll-on it needs to give sexual symmetry to her Junoesque housecoat. And the *Morning Screech-Hack*, whose first cigarette wakes you with the panicking smell of house-on-fire and whose horrible coughing prophesies a horrible coffin. Or the *Early Nag-Prod* who pecks you on the cheek and stabs you in the back with her grisly call of 'Less-ave-sum-tee; less-ave-some-tee!' How they all make the nights lovely and the mornings hideous.

One curious and not altogether welcome aspect of a young lady that you may notice as she gets up in the morning is that her neck is thicker than it seemed to be when she went to bed. As recently as in 1972 a report was published establishing the thereto little known fact that the human neck thickens after sexual intercourse and remains in its increased state for a considerable period thereafter.

The theory seems backed in reality by the fact that Spanish husbands in the old days used to measure their wives' throats with lengths of string when they left them in the morning, and submit them to the same calculation when they returned home. It was a check without the fool-proof security of the chastity belt, of course, but possibly it had something to do with the origin of the term 'necking'.

Of course, had the Spanish husbands simply had the good sense to tie the string tightly round the morning neck as they departed for the office or the battlefield, an unfaithful wife would have contributed to her own retribution by merely throttling herself as the throat swelled.

Connected with the neck swelling could be the fact that lovemaking generally takes place in a lying down position, which—in effect—causes a rush of blood to the head. It is worth remembering when a man is seeking that extra smooth personal image projected by a very good shave.

It is a fact that a young lady's face will be rendered sorer by making love in the afternoon or evening than in the morning—unless the man concerned has had the forethought to shave beforehand.

If you have been lying down asleep (or even awake) for several hours the heart has less difficulty pumping blood into the brain, and whereas the standing position offers an immediate drainage system to combat the upsurge of fluid forced upwards, a supine body spreads the gore out equally across a lateral plane. Face and head tissues thus become swollen during sleep from the relative excess of blood inside the head.

That is why your face is all puffy when you first rise. It isn't only the alcohol of the evening previous. If you want a really close shave to last you as long as possible during the day you should wait for about twenty minutes after rising before putting razor to face. If you shave before then you are shaving at a skin level which is higher up the whisker than it will be when your face has contracted. Then, when the outer cover twangs back into place it will leave the lower and unshaved portion of the stubble for all to see. The thoughtful man will shave before going to bed because he is showing the effects of a day's growth plus the shrunken skin of a day in the upright position. He will scratch the lady less. Too, the swollen face of the next morning will seem smoother because it will be coping only with the whisker growth which has taken place since last night—and a face swollen by several hours in a horizontal situation will almost cover the bristles. The lady will be scratched less *then*, too. It is these tiny attentions to the ritual which make the great lover.

THE YOUNG LADY
AND COITUS INTERRUPTED

WE HAVE ALREADY EXAMINED THE IMPORTANCE OF THE MALE wardrobe in terms of a normal seduction. It seems pertinent at this point to give thought to the plight of men unfortunate enough to be caught in one.

The interrupted lover discovered standing foolishly in the suddenly returning husband's wardrobe seems an unlikely cliché; but just think about it: Where else is there to go? For the life of a man (and that, after all, is what is at stake) it is difficult to think of an alternative retreat on the spur of the moment.

As I write this, there lies upon the desk before me the report of an Italian gentleman trapped in a *signora*'s bedroom when the *signore* thoughtlessly took an unexpected afternoon off and blundered home from the office a couple of hours earlier than expected. The seducer wildly followed the pattern of a hundred cartoonist's creations and leapt into the husband's wardrobe. Unable to leave via the downstairs hall because it passed the open-plan living room, and saved by prayer from the husband opening the wardrobe when he disrobed to go to bed, he remained quietly in the closet for the whole of the rest of the afternoon and evening.

Come about eleven o'clock the husband and wife retired to the bed which lay but a few feet from the guilty wardrobe. The poor wife lay awake all night, too terrified to shut her eyes, whilst the sleepy husband went out like a light.

So, to his short lived shame, did the lover—drowsed into somnolence by the Italian climate and the warmth of his close quarters. It was not until the small hours that the husband was awakened by reverberating snores from the wardrobe, magnified by their echoing confinement. The husband strode to the wardrobe, flung open its door, a scuffle ensued, a shot rang out, and the lover fell dead.

At the hearing it turned out that it was the lover who had first drawn the pistol though one wonders from where—and I would like at this point to advise all readers found in such a dilemma against any resort to violence or its threat. For in the momentary panic at what seems like the invasion of his property, the husband is bound not only to try to kill

177

you—but to be almost certainly excused when the case comes to court, on the grounds of *crime passionelle*.

Play it cool. Take advantage of the fact that surprise is on your side. Enquire politely: 'I'd be awfully grateful if you allow me to leave my Tardis in your wardrobe for the night. I haven't quite got the hang of the controls yet, and I've already come seventy-five thousand years since teatime ...'

Or, 'Thank Heaven you've released me at last. God Bless you! I'll have something pretty strong to say to the Times Furnishing Company about this, I can tell you ...'

Move slowly but purposefully towards the door as you speak. If completely natural behaviour can be affected for some thirty seconds, you will have the husband so completely bewildered as to watch you dumbly and immovably until you are through the doorway.

Close it quietly behind you. The shock of a sudden click can trigger off all the reactions to his temporarily hypnotised daze. Take the stairs four at a time and leap through the nearest ground floor window. Never mind the glass; just cut along.

Your immediate behaviour when a husband opens the wardrobe door and finds you standing on the other side of it is the key to the whole situation. Always take the initiative. Always act in a manner which is at once even more surprising than your very presence—but which also confounds him with the necessity to answer a question and the thought he must give to his reply.

'Does the 47 bus stop here?' is a good example. The more bizarre your enquiry, the more inclined he will be to find himself at a loss. If the erring lady has the *nous* to cry 'Surprise! SURPRISE!' in his face as the door opens, you and she can join hands and dance around him singing 'Happy Birthday To You'.

This can have you moving in a semi-circular direction towards the doorway, and going at a fair lick at the same time. How the wife will explain later on when he points out his birthday is not for another seven months yet is hardly your problem, or even worth considering as you overtake all the traffic on your way home. A TV advertising oriented husband might *possibly* accept the insistence that you are one of those bank managers who are always found in cupboards.

It is far wiser, of course, to remain in clear sight if you are trapped by an unexpected husband's return—and face it out. Bland and brash revelation of yourself can often be satisfying to the most suspicious spouse provided you have the presence of mind to don your Patent Collapsible 'Gas Board Inspector' Cap. No dedicated seducer should go anywhere without one. Provided you are also wearing your trousers, it gives you immediate permission to be on the premises. And if you can sport also a pocket full of heavy tools and a mouth full of nails your disguise is practically impenetrable; particularly as the latter explains at once the inarticulate mumbling and stuttering which such a sudden confrontation inevitably induces.

The main essential in allaying the suspicion of a returning husband is to have all your clothes on when he arrives (see above) and this means that the basic quality of a seducer's clothing should be that they are not only easy to slip *out* of but—even more important—easy to slip *into* as well.

That I am personally an authority on this little-studied area of sartorial research is perhaps not widely appreciated— but a plaque of silver and mahogany awarded to me as long ago as 1962 by the British Clothing Manufacturers' Federation bears ready witness.

I was nominated at that time alongside a variety of public figures (including David Jacobs, Terry Thomas and Cliff Richards, etc.) as one of the Year's Best Dressed Men, and the nomination included a brief citation by the CMF announcing: 'Mr. John Taylor is a fluent and easy dresser and always appears, even late in the day, as though he had just finished putting his clothes on ...'

I feel bound to state in all fairness that when late in the day I appear to have just finished putting my clothes on it is probably because I generally just have. I would emphasise, too, that the dictionary definition of 'fluent' embraces the meaning of 'Easily' and 'with rapidity', and, at the CMF Public Citations, when one of the Presentation Committee was kind enough to mention to a young lady present, 'Doesn't Mr. Taylor dress nicely ...' she was so unguarded as to volunteer: 'Oooh! Yes! And ever so quickly too ...' However you may feel that the advice I am about to impart may seem irrelevant to the citation by the Clothing Manufacturers' Federation, there is little doubt that it has clear bearing upon the fact that I have never been cited by anybody else.

The seducer's ensemble needs functionalism first; and the steady trend during the early 1970s towards a fashion for wider trouser bottoms cannot but be regarded as an advantage. This was first suggested to me during a wartime spell in the service of His Majesty's Royal Navy, when I initially experienced the ease of entry of a shore-going booted foot (a basic tenet of Seduction Survival in foreign countries is *Never Take Your Boots Off*) into a bell-bottomed trouser leg. Later on in life I discovered the hazards of the 1950s and 1960s, when fashionable drainpipe trousers required the doffing of even a winkle-picker before the foot could achieve fluent 'through' travel.

Should your sensibilities, or hers, divine an unromantic incongruity in the juxtaposition of stark nakedness and a pair of snub-nosed platform-soled Desert Boots, I can recommend with enthusiasm the elastic gusset or the Moccasin. These deserve their place up there alongside the zip fly— for whereas it is *possible* to both run and button one's trousers up at the same time, there is little likelihood of effecting any real measure of progress if you are having to stoop and weave your bootlaces around those curious metal stanchions which take over (like on skating boots) where the lace holes come to a stop. On the other hand (or foot), a pair of trusty Chelsea Boots has enabled many a calm cuckolder to be placing one leg over the windowsill before the heavy tread of the returning husband has reached the first landing.

Suits should be two-piece at most. Fiddling with five or six buttons up and down the front of a waistcoat, and then laboriously threading a watch chain through the middle, quickly reminds us that Coming Face To Face With Her Husband need not be regarded as a formal occasion. The collar-attached shirt is clearly an improvement on those antediluvian models which required the separate insertions of both a back and a front collar stud; and the hang-down, four-in-hand necktie is inestimably more practical than the finicky and blind fiddling of a real Bow Tie.

The four-in-hand can be slid down into a loose loop and taken off over your head when you are initially disrobing—and can be slipped back over your head in the same way, with the knot still intact, for a quick getaway. The clip-on bow tie would seem to offer rather vulgar advantages; but the true gentleman would be loath to adopt for such a romantic occasion accessories which in more normal times he would prefer not to be seen dead in. Indeed, that he would not wish to be seen dead in a made-up bow has pertinence, in light of the fact that there is never any real guarantee that somebody's husband is not going to catch you sooner or later. Such a denouement must be faced with dignity on both sides. It is no more sporting for an escaping lover to hasten his exit with the assistance of *mechanical* contrivances than it would be for a husband discovering his wife *in flagrante* to shoot her lover on the rise.

For all its relative modernity the belt is little to be favoured. Even braces—though they have the visual absurdity which is a disadvantage in the earlier stages of the courtship—can be more easily slipped into position than can a flaccid belt be thrust through a succession of belt loops. The need to raise and fasten the trousers rapidly, though, and be assured that they will stay firmly around the waist whilst the wearer is in movement, is a basic essential to a rapid retirement from the field. The difficulty of movement of any kind whilst one's trousers remain like halters around one's ankles is emphasised by the ancient adage of Confucius: 'There is no such action as Rape. Woman with skirts up runs twice as fast as man with trousers down.' A more modern expression: 'Caught with his pants down' offers final proof that the self-supporting trouser is the only style which should be seriously considered for circumstances such as we are discussing.

In an attempt to establish the maximum period necessary for dressing fully enough to be accepted on the public highway without the interference of the constabulary, I recently researched into dressing times based upon a commencement, naked, from a supine position in my own bedroom. My own timing—and readers are welcome to improve upon it for the next edition of the *Guinness Book of Records*—was as follows:

SOCKS: 7 seconds. Leave socks flat on dressing chair with heels towards the floor. Eschew suspenders and use only short style of sock with elasticated tops.

SHOES: 8 seconds. This can doubtless be improved with a pocket shoehorn and constant practice. Only Moccasins, slip-ons, or elasticated styles, though. Laces invite danger.

UNDERPANTS: 3 seconds. Use Jockey style which has no buttons and whose legless design allows easy access of socks and shoes.

UNDERVEST: Zero seconds. No singlet should be worn, summer or winter. This not only saves time but offers a far more virile image in the early stages of seduction.

SHIRT, COLLAR, TIE: 27 seconds. This is clearly the great time waster, and can be kept at a minimum through the use of short-sleeved shirt which needs no wrist fastening buttons or links. Even better, though approaching the maximum in informality, is to substitute a pull-on roll-neck sweater for the shirt collar and tie. This latter was timed as only 4 seconds including waist adjustment and turn down of collar.

ROLL-NECK SWEATER (in lieu of shirt, collar and tie): 4 seconds. The extra advantage to the roll-neck sweater is that in the action of pulling it over your head your face is covered —a by-product which can be regarded as useful in terms of confusing witnesses.

TROUSERS: 5 seconds. These must be self-supporting, pre-ferably even without the minor addition of the extension band at the waist. A zip fly is essential.

JACKET: 3 seconds. The only recommendations here are for nylon sleeve linings (more slippery than alpaca and there-fore more conducive of easy arm entry) and a single-breasted styling. This latter has fewer buttons, of course and, anyway, it is a double-breasted model that got you into this situation in the first place.

A formalised version affecting shirt collar and tie and jacket would thus account for some 53 seconds, or less than a min-ute. More informally, the use of a roll-neck sweater and, in summertime, the lack of need for any kind of jacket, could cut this to only 27 seconds—or less than half a minute.

A knowledge of how to dress at full speed, however, is only necessary to the man caught in the toils of the adulteress.

If the young lady concerned is simply a spinster of this parish, the awakening need be neither so rude nor so rapid. The concern in this latter case should be to achieve departure with dignity, without commitment, and with an additional possibility for the brightening of lonely evenings to come.

The routine when one wakes up in a bedroom other than one's own varies according to the situation in which you find yourself at first sensibility: If you are lying on a sofa, a settee, or in one big armchair with another drawn close to support your legs, and you are wearing all your clothes except for your jacket and shoes, there are two possible explanations:

Either (a) you are at the flat of a male friend, or (b) you and your male friend are at the flat of a mutual girl friend and you lost the toss.

But if as you waken you realise you are in a room you have never seen before in your life, and you open your eyes upon a gently breathing female face which as far as you can recall has never previously been numbered among your circle of intimate acquaintances, it is time to collect your thoughts.

Get out of bed as gently as possible, to avoid waking the other occupant. The most urgent move is to check the contents of your pockets. This is in no spirit of suspicion. It would be churlish to grudge her the screwed-up pound note and the one hundred and forty-seven pence in copper which are the inevitable legacy of a drunken evening. What you are looking for is a marriage licence, a pocketful of confetti, or some evidence of the ultimate indiscretion.

Should it not come to light, you may breathe more easily, though not so loudly as to wake your room companion. Your next step is to reconnoitre the living room.

If there is a man on the sofa with only his jacket and shoes off, lift him so gently as not to disturb his insensibility, carry him into the bedroom and lay him softly beside the young lady. Tippytoe back to the sitting room, put on all your clothes save your shoes and your jacket, and go to sleep on the sofa until they come out of the bedroom and wake you.

Your attitude should be half rueful for yourself, half happy for them. The girl may be puzzled, but will be too vague in her memory to question the bewilderment sustained by finding your companion beside her on waking. Certainly she is not likely to voice publicly a dormant suspicion that she has slept with *both of you* on the same night.

Your male friend, on the other hand, will be so proud of the evidence of his preferment as to leave the situation unquestioned. You can underline his bravado with a succession (when she is not looking) of those heavy winks which constitute such an important part of the unspoken language of knowing admiration of one male for another. He will feel such 'a Hell of a fellow' that he will thrust from his conscience the shame of waking up still wearing his socks, shirt and trousers.

The young lady, meanwhile, is at your disposal. If the cold light of the morning finds her not so attractive as did the night before, you can detach yourself via your clear understanding that it was *your friend* she preferred.

Should you need her to fill in an empty evening at some future date, you have but to contact her to find her pathetically grateful for your ready forgiveness at (a) her mistaken preference for your friend, or (b) her sluttish behaviour during a night of dual service.

If, however—when you make your initial reconnoitering of the sitting room (see above)—you find no other man asleep on the sofa, crumple its cover and flatten its cushions to suggest that your heavy body has lain there undisturbed throughout the night. Pull the sofa up to the fire. Leave two or three small coins lying in the corners of the seat as though they had rolled from your pockets during slumber. Now make for the bathroom. You should have a vague idea where it is. After all that drinking you are certain to have used it last night, and you will feel better able to cope after a shave.

There is bound to be a razor in there somewhere, though because it is designed for using on legs and armpits it will not offer the efficiency of your normal Gillette. Shaving soap and brush are no problem either. Trapped at a lady friend's house for the night, it is worth knowing that a pot of cold cream or a tin of Nivea will serve perfectly as the lubricant of a shave. It is more difficult to clean the razor afterwards, but the resultant smoothness is in some ways more comfortable than the results of ordinary shaving soap. And you will smell very attractive should the sight of the young lady when you take her in her cup of tea tempt you to further indulgence.

If you are determined to avoid lasting involvement by the suggestion that you have slept alone, however, dress fully before making the tea and knock purposefully on the door before entering. Better—wait until summoned to enter, and thus establish that you regard a young lady's bedroom as territory hardly to be encroached upon without formal invitation.

On entering, look around curiously—as though the room is a new sight and you are naturally interested to see what kind of background she can boast. With luck, such a ploy may be unnecessary—as many young ladies at that time in the morning, especially after a heavy evening's drinking, are loath to show their unmadeup face and uncombed head above the sheets. And there is small chance of success for a maintenance order if she cannot swear, without fear of perjuring herself, of ever having seen you in her bedroom.

To make assurance doubly sure, announce 'Morning Tea!' in a heavily disguised voice, swiftly wipe your dabs from the saucer, and melt from the scene.

All that is necessary now is to get out of the house (a) without besmirching your companion's reputation among her close neighbours, and (b) without offering to nearby window watching witnesses the memorable image of a strange man. Here is more work for your Patent Collapsible 'Gas Board Inspector' Cap. If in about nine months' time a squad of innocent Gas men are lined up to undergo the social stigma of an Identification Parade, it is simply one small way at getting back at them for power cuts.

THE YOUNG LADY
AND PREGNANCY

WOMEN SENSE MALE RELUCTANCE TO ACCEPT THE
responsibilities of parenthood and play upon the culpability,
as a dog smells your fear and bites you. The position is in no
way alleviated by the massive guilt complexes which inevitably bedevil a man once he achieves a relationship of ultimate
intimacy, but which somehow never disturb the female
psyche.

'Miss Lettlove has phoned seven times since you went
out to lunch,' says your Secretary as you ease down into your
chair with all the careful dignity of the slightly drunk. The
cold hand of incipient funk plucks momentarily at your
heart strings. Seven times?

But you dive back into the internal dregs of your alcohol
for courage. 'What is this fatal fascination I have for women,'
you ask with cool bravado. 'God! Will they never give me
peace?'

'I thought she sounded pretty worried about something,'
says your amanuensis, with the impersonal deliberation of
someone bringing the bad news from Ghent to Aix. That
swooshy feeling that turns a stomach to jelly swamps through
a body suddenly wet with sweat and a mouth suddenly dry
with fear.

'I think I'll call her back,' you say.

'I think you'd better,' says your Secretary.

'Darling, I *must* see you as soon as possible,' says Miss Lettlove from the other end of the line. Do you detect a note of
hysteria? 'I can't speak over the 'phone,' she adds without
comfort. 'See me in the bar at the Savoy at six o'clock ...
Please be there, darling. You absolutely *must*.'

You replace the receiver with waves of panic splashing
about inside you. What on earth can she want?

It *couldn't* be. *Could* it? The damned things are supposed
to be electronically tested. But, then, so was Starfighter. No,
it *can't* be. It wouldn't be fair. Posed with the mystery of a
woman wishing to see him urgently a man's imagination
will inevitably lead his conscience into the black areas of
guilty despair. Even if no physical grounds for such a situation can possibly obtain, a man builds in such a store of

guilt from previous liaisons that his mind fixes on the potential guilt rather than the reality. A neurotic afternoon begins to play out its tormented hours.

'Why the Devil can't she say?' you snarl petulantly at yourself. But Guilt catches you by the conscience and smooths your cowardice into sweet reasonability. You are caught between surges of irritation, heights of optimism, and periods of resigned pessimism. Here and there decency inserts passing moments of self-pitying affection for the girl.

You will stand by her, whatever, you tell yourself; hoping vainly that God has heard and will be satisfied with instant repentance rather than protracted retribution.

Anyway, it's *her* fault. Heaven knows it's simple enough for women to look after themselves nowadays, you think.

You heartless, irresponsible swine, you think. Poor little love, you think. We'll make out, somehow, together, you think.

Anyway, how does she know its you? you think. After all, a girl who carries on like that has clearly had some practice previously, you think. I bet the bitch is using me as fall guy, you think.

I love her, you think. Make it all right, God, and I'll marry her anyway. Just make it all right. *Please.*

The afternoon passes in a dizzy state of semi concentration, one eye on Heaven, the other on the clock. Everything you read, every paper or magazine you cull for interest or instruction features somehow a coincidental comment on the blackest of possibilities. Every joke a colleague drops makes some oblique reference to your latent situation. A scream lies ready in your stomach to leap through your throat should you relax the tight clench of teeth which otherwise might begin to chatter.

You leave for the Savoy with the sun shining and the birds singing. You are deeply conscious of the beauty of this world you have thrown away, this life you have smashed, this career you have wrecked with your irresponsible sensuality. You pat small boys on the head and give them small coins. You smile at men who jostle you, stand politely aside for thrusting homegoers, and generally try to make up in a quarter of a mile walk for a lifetime of black sins whose retribution you are now convinced you approach. You pause at the door of the Savoy and, to his intense surprise, tip the Porter generously. For you, the action has the symbolism of making a will. You square your shoulders like a man and, very circumspectly, push through the swing doors.

It transpires, in the event, that it is not really important at all. She simply wants to give you up and marry another man. Flooded with relief, you offer her congratulations with such deep conviction and sincerity that she is a bit fed up. Fondly kissing her on the cheek—for her lips are now another's—you make off in search of an alternative young lady.

Though making a girl a mother induces tremendous guilt complexes in a man, a certain rough justice arranges that a girl has no guilt about making a man a father. The cynical fact is that it is necessary for her in some way to officially establish male responsibility, and one of a woman's hardest tasks in life is proving to a man that his intentions are honourable.

In the United States a system has been perfected recently whereby maternity homes can overcome those sad Mother/Baby mix-ups. Fingerprints are taken of the Mother and the child simultaneously before they are wheeled out of the delivery room. One plate contains both sets—so it becomes a simple matter to establish which baby belongs to which mother. But so far no fingerprint system has been evolved whereby the identity of the male parent can be so readily established.

Luckily, too, a husband is unable to dust over his wife for your dabs following upon her return from that illicit assignation, and even in breach-of-promise cases there is no record of the betrayed maiden displaying the cad's finger marks all over her.

It is in the intimate revelation of personal physical characteristics normally hidden by clothing that a man can too easily be identified. A coin spot strawberry mark on your left buttock not only establishes personal identification, it establishes that she is in a position to know it is there. Most magistrates would draw logical conclusions. A man wishing to avoid the consequences of wild promises made whilst under the influence of soft lights, a bottle of wine and a hot dinner, should be careful of the wide dissemination of his more intimate identification marks. All the facial plastic surgery in the world will not stand up to an assertion in Court: 'If he's got three moles in a row between his navel and his groin he's the one who owes the alimony ...'

If the job of tracking a man down is left to the police, of course, you are halfway safe. Every Identikit picture looks much the same as any other and the average police description of a wanted man offers absolutely no assistance in the recognition of an individual.

'... The man is believed to be of between twenty-five and thirty-five years of age and of average height. He has mid-brown hair greying at the temples, and when last seen was wearing a grey/blue suit and a beige raincoat. He is clean shaven, brown-eyed and of medium build ...'

Who isn't? Whilst establishing the innocence of all flashily dressed negroes, or dandified gaffers with jet black or albino white hair, who are tragically emaciated or diabolically overweight, the description could have about a third of the male population nicked on sus.

There is a curiously coincidental linkage, as a matter of fact, between pregnancy and established birthmarks. For most women are firmly convinced that such marks are the result of some trauma experienced by the mother whilst she was still with child. I have long used the excuse that my mother was frightened by a naked man to explain my reflex action of automatically trying to get a young lady's clothes off, and the myth that maternal impressions affect the shape, size, colour or condition of the infant is strongly entrenched in the philosophy of the majority of the female sex.

Crocodile men, Turtle men, Rabbit men, have all—according at least to an army of fairground barkers—developed individual physiognomies because their mothers were scared during pregnancy. Barnum's world famous Elephant Man firmly believed that his appearance was the result of a traumatic brush between his mum and a pachyderm—as clear an instance of Mumbo-Jumbo as ever the world witnessed—and greater minds than his have followed a similar trajectory.

Hipprocrates, the father of Medicine, is related to have saved the reputation of a contemporary princess versatile enough to have been delivered of a coal black baby by citing it as a case of Maternal Impression. She had been gazing at a painting of a negro during her pregnancy, he explained, and paternal honour was satisfied. By contrast Persina, a one time Queen of the Ethiopians, fobbed off the presentation of a snow white child as being due to her admiring study of a portrait of Andromeda.

In similar terms we might expect romanticisation of the normal human image as an automatic result of the increased viewing figures of the annual Miss World Contest— but the flip side to such easy improvement comes from the fact that opposite effects can also be expected. The exhibition of Freaks and Freak Shows has in the past been forbidden in some countries due to the hazards of pre-natal impression. Thus the Siamese Twins were forbidden to exhibit themselves in France for a time and, taking the opposite view, Spartan women were compelled to gaze steadfastly at statues of Castor and Pollux three times daily after meals in order to ensure producing children worthy of the race.

The medics have themselves been guilty of an inclination to believe such theories in the past—and medical literature abounds with primitive assumptions of such a nature.

In 1726, for example, a certain Miss Mary Toft as a result of being startled by a rabbit in a field 'when five weeks gone with child' unaccountably gave birth to a Bunny. And so successful in arousing public interest was this remarkable visitation that she subsequently claimed to have produced a litter of considerable proportions. Her claims did not stand up to official cross examination finally, though locally the legend died hard.

Dr. James Blondel, a man of medicine practising in the eighteenth century, quotes in his published work the popular recommendation that 'all frightful and ugly objects be re moved from the sight of pregnant women'. That was a year after the miraculous conception of Miss Toft, but it might have been today in the opinion of many an old wife or young. Dr. Blondel also referred to the widely held belief that 'the mere longing for Mussels is sufficient to transubstantiate the true and original head of the child into the shape of a shell fish'. Were this true, many of us might have joined the crustaceans—for a perverted desire for shellfish has in modern times been claimed as practically diagnostic of pregnancy.

Birthmarks are the most readily accusable in terms of pre-natal impression because they lend themselves to the imagination. Along with large hairy moles and port-wine stains, they are the commonest birth disfigurements and are due to dilation of the small blood vessels in the skin or to excess of normal pigment. They may range in size from a new penny to a soup plate and may be said with the application of a little fancy to resemble any animal, bird or fish you care to name. A common form of *naevus*—the medical term for such a birthmark—is one with radiating extensions like spiders' webs. The mother of a child with such a birthmark rarely has to think for long to remember being upset by a spider during a pregnancy. Mugging up on her nursery rhymes in anticipation of the happy event, indeed, could psychologically impress her with the fate of the sad Miss Muffett.

Nowadays, the medical profession is inclined to be sceptical of the influence of a mother's processes on the shape and colour of her unborn baby. If the child, when delivered, is not quite so handsome as the egos of the respective parents are inclined to expect, it is probably because the poor little devil simply takes after its Father.

There is no doubt that prior to the advent of The Pill, the fear of pregnancy kept most young ladies, and quite a few young men, on the straight and narrow path—the removal of which hazard has simply redirected most young feet down that path called Primrose.

The general acceptance of The Pill to a degree emphasises the slight difference between the basic decencies of the two sexes. There is no doubt that promiscuity is rife nowadays because the woman feels she has control of a situation she was always supposed to be averse to, but which in actuality was simply one she couldn't trust. Often too bashful to present himself to a chemist's shop for the unwieldy contraceptives of the past, the young man was inclined to buy his little paper packets from the barber's shop. The variety of cutting instruments in the vicinity, sharp pointed scissors, razor blades, etc., inescapably induced neurosis via auto-suggestion that perforations could be all too easy, and one way and another many immature males inclined towards the happier frame of mind resulting from celibacy. In such a case, he might decide, not only did he not have to wrestle with the girl—he didn't have to wrestle with his conscience. Thirty years ago young men were far more honourable than young ladies have taught them to be today, and the gallant misgiving which threatened an idyllic love affair with the chastening reminder that Familiarity Breeds Contempt, emphasised the hazards of The Act with the supplementary reminder that Familiarity Breeds.

Remembering his Scouting days, a young man simply had recourse to a cold bath as a means of deadening his wicked thoughts—but later research has shown that in this mis-conception (if that's the word I want) we were simply adding to the vast army of factually unfounded old wives' tales. In recent years it has been pretty conclusively established that if you wish to fornicate without retribution the proper answer is a very hot bath.

Dr. Howard Gabriel, director of the Health Planning Council in Wichita, Kansas, discovered upon research that there was a tendency for infertility in men subjected to, or partial to, hot working conditions and hot baths. Research in America had already suggested that exposing the testicles to more heat than they enjoy inhibits sperm production, a situation which may be reversed by exposing them to the cold. Apparently the normal temperature of the testes is, or should be, lower than that of the rest of the body, and hot baths at a temperature above about 98.6 Fahrenheit is suffici-ently hot to inhibit sperm production. A man who had been used to regular, 25 minute long, hot baths daily, and who worked in extreme heat for two hours a day, successfully fathered a child after merely replacing the hot baths with cold baths at 65 degrees Fahrenheit. Alternatively recom-mended as treatment in such cases is the sudden application of an ice bag to the scrotum, but a consensus of opinion largely conceded that most men would prefer the bath. And the whole theory raises doubts concerning the wisdom of the Esquimau's traditional generosity with his wife.

From the Wichita research also emerged the suggestion that tight-fitting trousers which were dark coloured and so would absorb radiant heat (an important consideration in tropical climes) might emphasise the sterility effect. And here we have a precedent, outlined in Britain, with a pertinent parallel.

During the stint of Duncan Sandys as Minister of Defence in the Tory Government which fell in 1963, Sandys had replied to a question in the House of Commons regarding atomic fallout by referring to a contemporary report issued by Swedish scientists engaged upon mutation research. He quoted the Swedes as suggesting that the unnatural heat caused by the wearing of trousers is likely to have a cumulative serious effect upon the male organs, and that the kilt might be sensibly and advantageously adopted by the Western world. The Swedes backed their premise with a belief that trousers could cause 1,000 times more genetic harm than would the amount of atomic radiation then present in the atmosphere; and that people habitually wearing trousers would have a spontaneous mutation rate 85 per cent higher than that of nudists.

The Swedes had aimed their criticisms especially at the very tight jeans which were contemporaneously popular, and it seemed ironic that the social group most marked for the adoption of such crotch-grabbing garments were the Beatnik and Ban-the-Bomb agitators who for so long sacrificed their comfort and freedom by sitting down on cold wet roadways as a protest against the atomic tests.

Had they but known it, their defiant passivity was exposing them to more than simply a sharp attack of haemorrhoids. The confining structure of the trousers which were a badge of all their tribe was, even as they sat there, threatening them with the same grisly mutative effects which their whole protest programme was aimed at negating.

The connection between garments and pregnancy is more acute than the simple production of Maternity Dresses would lead us to consider. Night dresses—*pretty* night dresses, that is, are a virtually modern manifestation which only began to be generally appreciated following upon the 1880s and the first general dissemination of a knowledge of birth control among women. Prior to that, Victorian housewives worn out by an interminable succession of pregnancies following one upon another, had regarded looking attractive at bedtime as a calculated hazard. Nowadays, the advent of the electric blanket has relegated pyjamas to archaism in the menswear trade—except where they are romanticised and used as lounge-about wear at home.

In America especially, where the urban citizen is reluctant to leave his home in the evenings because (a) it will be burgled, or (b) he be mugged on the street outside his front door, there is a tendency to stay home. And coupled with the general acceptance of central heating (which requires on average an additional degree of heat annually to sustain relative comfort, once you have become used to it) the U.S. family sits in a state of nightly seige in a temperature of around eighty degrees Fahrenheit. There, day clothes are substituted by garments based on the nightwear of a quarter of a century ago, and their very flimsiness is inescapably erotic. How high the birth rate would soar were it not for the distractions of Radio, Television and the Gramophone is clearly emphasised by the result nine months later of the New York electrical breakdown some years ago, and by the baby boom resulting from the Government's decision to cut TV short during the 3 Day Working Week crisis in Britain at the beginning of 1974.

Why babies are born is a confusing study. Even taking all the scientific evidence into account does nothing to explain the report by Bertrand Russell that the Trobriand Island woman, whilst enjoying free love quite naturally, seldom conceived before marriage—and that if she did, the visitation was regarded as a severe social stigma doubtless sent as a Providential punishment. In such a savage society there might have been certain heavenly omens to observe, of course, and it is true that even the highly civilised London *Sunday Times* published a report in early 1974 stating that an unusual method of contraception—Birth Control by Astrology—was adding daily to its devotees.

Like the traditional Safe Period method, it depends on

the avoidance of fertile periods in the woman, but in this system these are calculated by observations of the movements of the heavenly bodies. The *Sunday Times* reported: 'The principle is simple. Women who wish to use the Cosmic Rhythm method must first find out what was the angle between the sun and the moon at the hour of their birth. Each lunar month, the moon moves into the same angle; and this is the peak fertility moment which must be avoided. For example, a woman born at 8 p.m. on 28 March, 1944, had a peak fertility hour of 4 p.m. 27 February.'

I realise that for many of you, especially those born at 8 p.m. on 28 March, 1944, this news may have come too late; but you may console yourself with the insistence of practitioners that the method researched by a Czech and a Hungarian doctor gives a 15 per cent chance of pregnancy, and as the *Sunday Times* went on to say, the figures have not been recognised by any family planning agencies in the West.

When one considers the influence upon women of the phases of the moon, the idea seems to have a logical basis hanging about there somewhere but, personally, I would have thought the only sure way of avoiding pregnancy astrologically is to be born resolutely Virgo. Only slightly paraphrased, Shakespeare might well have put into a woman's mouth—rather than into that of jealous Cassius—the observation that: 'The fault is not in our stars but in ourselves, that we are under things ...' In a woman's mouth, indeed, the whole problem seems to be being resolved one way or another. The Pill is there for all to swallow, and one of the wisest aphorisms of the Old Wives is the recommendation that the finest and most reliable oral contraceptive is 'No!' One emerges, finally, with the reluctant conclusion that generally speaking it is largely a matter of a fellow's luck and it's better not to push it. This particularly in face of the fact that a pregnant woman is not the loveliest of sights. Admittedly she takes on a curious kind of fulfilled completeness—which can be mistaken for beauty if you happen to be the man concerned and are succumbing to the rather smug assumption that such a situation has never happened before simply because it has never happened to *you* before. But the misshapen bulk of the young lady concerned is not only aesthetically unacceptable to the true student of form—it is irritating in its relative immobility. Its bulk induces that kind of *laissez faire* resulting from simply waiting for something to happen. Nothing else matters until 'The Time' comes. It is like standing in a queue, and queues are degrading because they suggest that the service is more important than the customer. Queues suggest that it is right that the latter should stand about endlessly until the former is ready to serve him.

Taking your turn is supposed to demonstrate the just equality of a democratic society, but all it does in actuality is sharpen up the Fascist beast within the man-in-charge.

Witness the arrival of any bus at any bus-stop; how Jack-in-Office, in the full bureaucratic glory of his Young Conductor's Set, selects, with what imperiousness, the portion of the waiting customers he is prepared to embark. Or watch a cinema commissionaire, done up in the seedily absurd finery of a Ruritanian Admiral, chivvying his management's clients with the sour hauteur of an 'Officer of the Day' sniffing out haircuts.

Emergent bullies are manifested at the root of every queue. Only people in a kind of doped expectancy—like rummies waiting for their Meth, housewives waiting for their turn in the fish queue, and pregnant young ladies waiting for their babies will accept with equanimity the arrogance of the working-class clod temporarily in power. The testy shopkeeper who doles out packets of fish fingers as if he were dispensing gifts to the needy and brushes aside a customer to whom he should be politely grateful with the ignorantly dismissive 'Next ...' should be held firmly with his face four inches from the till whilst a queue of his clientele lines up for the privilege of ringing up NO SALE and whacking him in the moosh with his own money drawer.

It is no surprising coincidence, to me, that one of my most traumatic experiences resulted from the converging circumstances of standing in a queue and accompanying a pregnant young lady. I was attempting to escort the latter on a number 159 bus from St. Leonard's Church bus stop in the Streatham High Road to the Thornton Heath Clock Tower, and had manoeuvered her eight-months-gone bulk into a position some seven or eight places back from the head of the queue. Her own face a mask of contented expectancy, my own atwitch with the possibility that junior might arrive at any moment, we waited for the bus.

As is often the case upon a bus's arrival, no one ahead of us in the queue wished to take the 159, so levering my companion out of our position, I began to steer her laboriously up the outside of the line towards a position where she might be heaved with relative dignity up on to the platform.

But clearly irritated at the apparent lack of interest in his bus's route, and not bothering to check as to whether travellers at the rear of the queue wished to avail themselves of his service, the conductor rang the bell and started his vehicle on its journey before we were hardly half way to his used-ticket box.

My irritation with my lady's immobility was possibly sharpened by the guilt complex deriving from my being responsible for her condition, but it merged with my natural antagonism for all bus conductors in a sudden flooding fury as the bus belched exhaust and made off down the road. But a flush of wild triumph engulfed me as I saw it suddenly brought to a halt at the traffic light placed only some twenty yards beyond the bus-stop. Scenting the miraculous intervention of Providence, I shouted, 'Come on ...' at the girl and sprinted full pelt for the arrested omnibus.

Even as I started my run the lights changed and the driver noisily let out his clutch. But at full gallop I am the match of any London transport heap in Second, and I flung myself on to the platform before its speed had reached the 15 m.p.h. mark.

Alas—I had disregarded the natural immobility of my young lady companion, who had hardly by now succeeded in turning her globular frame even in the right direction. I could only attempt to make the bus stop and wait for her. Reaching up to the bell push I furiously punched it in a staccato reiteration which I know to be the emergency signal between conductor and driver. Convinced of the urgency of my peremptory ringing, the driver threw himself against the brakes and the bus came to a skidding, screeching stop no more than one hundred and fifty yards beyond the lights, but well out of the sight of my pregnant companion.

Temper, frustration, the fury induced by disinterested thoughtlessness, concern for the lady, and an overweening hatred of London Transport, all came together in a red wave. It was not a good time for the bus conductor, who had mounted to the upper deck to collect fares once he had dismissed the St. Leonard's queue from his mind, to leap down the stairs and confront me with a querulous: "'Oo rung that bell? 'Ere—did you ring that bell? You got no right ringin' that bell ...'

My passion clearly surprised him. My retort, even more. 'Ring that bell,' I repeated in neo-hysterical fury whilst amazed passengers inside the bus studiously avoided catching my eye. 'I'll ring your bleeding neck. Don't you have any consideration for pregnant women?' I shouted, through foam flecked lips.

Obviously terrified, he drew back—his eyes darting down confusedly to my waistline clearly convinced that I was raving on about myself. He looked wildly about the bus for assistance and began to back up the aisle in the direction of the driver and possibly a handy spanner. 'What pregnant women you talkin' about?' he queried desperately.

I looked about me. There was none in sight, of course. The lady had hardly trundled herself more than five yards along the pavement in the few split seconds it had all taken to happen. I was a mad, solitary wildman, alone on a stranded bus, surrounded by a conductor and some twenty seated passengers who hadn't an idea in the world what in God's name I was on about.

I took recourse to the only possible action of a man in my situation. Grabbing the conductor by the lapels of his jacket, I raised him up off the ground until his grey face and rolling eyes were no more than an inch from my own. Then 'Watch it!' I hissed. 'Just you bloody well watch it!'

Flinging him from me, I disembarked from the bus and walked off into the night—conscious but unconcerned about the mass of bewilderment I left behind on the lower deck of the number 159. Stamping back to the bus-stop, I encountered the lady making her painful, self-satisfied, pregnant perambulation in slow pursuit of me. She had just about reached the lights. I turned her round and pointed her back at the bus-stop. We had, of course, lost our place in the queue.

I retail this story for two reasons. One, to demonstrate how the fear of pregnancy is not all dissolved even once you know the worst, and, two, to offer a long overdue explanation to anyone aboard the bus that night and into whose hands a copy of this book may happen to fall.

YOUNG LADIES
AND DOGS

LOST IN THE MIST OF MEMORY IS THE MOMENT I FIRST discovered how babies came. I conclude, therefore, that the intelligence was imparted without submitting me to any particular trauma. Probably the general picture of the human mating ritual had come to me piecemeal, and the final link in the system occasioned no special surprise in consequence.

Who instructed me in the esoterics of reproduction is also past recall, but certainly it was neither my schoolteachers nor my Mummy and Daddy. Had my current knowledge of the procreation of species depended upon any or all of those worthies, I should still be scanning the horizon for the approach of a stork, or searching feverishly under gooseberry bushes for the miraculous manifestation of the last of the Taylors.

I am sprung from parents born of a Victorian generation which concluded that the less you knew about sex, the less likely you were to push your luck, and the less likely you were to get into trouble. Children of my generation were left to find things out for themselves.

The fact that this in no way seems to have obstructed the production of subsequent generations suggests that an enormous amount of nonsense is talked about the need for sex education in the schools. Whether or not biology classes embrace the human scene, the human scene continues. And the fact that we are currently plunged into a permissive society, and that the incidence of venereal disease rockets as official sex education increases, suggests that the induced feelings of illicitness which the parental conspiracy of silence brought to my age group, seemed to bring also a respect for sex and its consequences which today's adult blabbermouths patently fail to instill in their own offspring.

Parental attitudes of Yesterday seem epitomised by my own father's reaction towards my healthy curiosity in how our Alsatian bitch Aquila produced pups.

She had whelped during the night whilst I was fast asleep, but my delight at the surprise litter on the following morning in no way diminished a natural interest in where actually they had come from.

Reluctant to become involved in an embarrassing Andy/ Judge Hardy man-to-man, my Father side-stepped the issue with a vague 'I don't know, Son,' and a demand for a second cup of tea. Impatient at his lack of curiosity, I decided to find out for both of us by recourse to Harry Hookway—a boy some three months my senior and of all the worldly confidence such seniority imparts. Harry knew about such things and was at pains to put me right.

Puppies are born, he explained, by the startling process of a large lump of fat disengaging itself from the mother, sprouting little legs and a tail, and gradually assuming the shape of a miniature dog.

Intrigued with this new knowledge I loyally shared it with my Father, who listened with some interest, gravely thanked me, and returned to his newspaper.

He neither denied the Hookway theory nor attempted to elucidate with an explanation which (if you consider it seriously) is hardly less ludicrous than Harry's. He realised instinctively that at the age of seven one miracle is as good as another. Instinctively, too, he knew that in all good time I would get the message.

I am delighted that I finally did, of course. Things would have been hardly the same, otherwise. But like my Father, I realise there was never the slightest danger of my not finding out.

It would be an interesting experiment to raise a boy and a girl together in a sex-knowledge vacuum where no instruction nor suggestion on the subject could reach either. I am prepared to wager a considerable sum that with the arrival of puberty they would quickly discover the natural method of perpetuating their images. For I believe we no more have to teach children the basics of sex than we need to teach them that if they do not eat they will die of hunger.

What we teach children is not *how* to eat—or even when —but simply the ritual of etiquette which will make their eating habits less than disgusting. It is an approach which we might with advantage transfer to the subject of sex education.

Via the matter-of-fact indulgence of sex education films and lectures, we skip the delights of close personal relationship, skirt the deep satisfaction of sharing intimacy, ignore the declensions of love and affection, and concentrate simply on biological principles.

This tends not to encourage lovers into a beautiful and shared experience, but to project a kind of factory-belt production line where each plays his or her separate role in what should be a dual cognition. From such selfish individualism emerge the frightful tragedies of clumsiness on the one hand and ultimate frigidity on the other.

What we should teach in schools is not Sex, but Romance; not the academic basis of the act but the loving and beautiful connotations of the approach to the act and its fulfilment.

Might it not be far more sensible to instruct boys in articulate flattery, girls in coquetry, boys in gentleness, girls in relaxation, boys in patience, girls in understanding? For seduction should not be simply the coldly sighted target of a lecher aiming at a virgin's deflowerment, but a sharpened spiritual appreciation of the romantic love attainable via a shared physical experience.

If such appreciation comes at all, it comes slowly and by stages. It does not come in a grotesquely matter-of-fact lecture where only the slightly distasteful practicalities are emphasised. It does not result from a thrashing for not paying attention, or from being marked nine out of ten.

Personally, I am glad I learned the long way round and that—for the sake of Alsatians everywhere—I was wrong the first time.

All the hazards—normal, financial, physical and psychological—considered, it is probably better to give a girl a dog than a baby. For she finds in such all the qualities which men are reluctant to guarantee—Obedience, Adoration, Resignation, Loyalty, and something she can drag around on a leash.

It is possibly because of a growing disillusionment with a succeeding variety of men that women generally end up with a dog as the last sustained affection of a lonely twilight of their years. With men, it is the other way round: to most small boys a dog is their real first love.

The majority of the male sex, therefore, carry with them through life an abiding nostalgia for what was their first experience of obedience to them. When you are only little, to have something littler is perhaps your first positive achievement. To demand attention to your command without being on the receiving end of a hearty clout necessarily implants a strong affection for the subject of the emergence of your expanding juvenile ego. A boy's first dog is his initial introduction to 'responsible relationship', as his first bicycle is his introduction to the rat race of status.

My own projection into the canine scene came when, finally overcome by the inevitable nervous breakdown, my third Nanny was taken off in a plain van and my father divined the need for a change.

Doubtless influenced by the family set-up in *Peter Pan*— an institution to which, and to our chagrin, he insisted upon exposing my brother and myself annually—he decided to replace Nanny III with a large dog. Not only would this remove us from the effeminising influence of womanly indulgence, he reasoned, but with the animal sustained to some extent by occasional bites at itinerant hawkers, the food bill should be less.

As happened with many of Father's bolder ideas, the plan was far from foolproof. The great, soppy Alsatian which finally arrived to take over the care of my brother and myself came from a Continental family, was already four years old, and understood only French.

What to a more normal family might have seemed a drawback, was lightly disregarded by my father, who himself spoke fluent French and had a vague feeling that exposure to the hound might in some way either encourage or improve his children's linguistic studies. He would engage the dog in esoteric conversation for hours at a time whilst I sat on a sitting room chair watching in a dull incomprehension largely shared by the animal. Sometimes, as a special treat for our 'Nana', he would even switch the wireless to Radio Normandy and indicate the movement with triumph when the bored hound nervously and quite coincidentally turned her head in the direction of the loud speaker.

To some degree, though, the advent of the Alsatian did improve my knowledge of the languages. Its name turned out to be Aquila, which I learned early in life to be the Latin equivalent of *Eagle*—though we pronounced it as *Ar-keeler* initially and eventually shortened it to a fond diminutive of

'Keeler'. This was in itself no social handicap as small boys without the advantages of my early brush with the classics translated the *Keeler* into 'Killer'—and I may well have escaped some bullying as a result.

But being the youngest of the family, I was the last ever to reach any full communion with the dog. At seven years of age my knowledge of French was confined to only a few of those curiously useless phrases contained in the Conversational French text books of the period. Attempting to bring Aquila to heel, I would often inform her in prep. school French that '*L'homme a bu la lait derrière la porte de l'église,*' but the beast seldom evinced much interest in the information.

Seeking a reasonable linguistic alternative, I would sometimes address Aquila in English superimposed with my precociously juvenile impression of Mr. Maurice Chevalier (then all the rage) thrusting out my lower lip, dropping my H's in a ecstasy of Gallic charm, and even as a last resort putting on my father's straw boater.

It seemed to have small effect other than rendering her rather anxious, and Aquila would shift uneasily from front foot to front foot, staring deep into my mouth in a desperate effort to get the message. And meanwhile, from her great brown eyes there shone the unmistakable enquiry: '*Quel kind of a nut avons nous ici?*'

But though she never comprehended me, God bless her old heart she always understood me. She became my constant, resigned, attentive and tender comrade for every day of the following five years; and there arose between us an affinity which Heaven witnesses I never experienced with man, woman or beast before or since. And when one cold rainy day in December she lay sadly on her side, blinked the glazed eyes of a dying dog, wagged her tail faintly twice, and slipped away to the happy hunting ground, I thought my little heart would break.

And for a man it is in the departed nostalgias of childhood that a dog's charm lies. A dog was his first lieutenant—even his First Lieutenant—and therefore his initial memory of growing up. To a woman a dog is often a child substitute—and there remains around the man who gives her one the aura of having given her a baby without giving her the attendant miseries of pregnancy and childbirth. Too, a man is unlikely to contest custody when the romance has ended and the thrill has gone. Though the affair is over it will never therefore sink into that animosity which follows upon the humiliation of divorce. Just a wag of the little tail, the roguish larceny of a fluffy slipper, that fascinating little lapping sound as it gets itself a drink from under the kitchen table—and you're freshly back in her mind.

There is a nostalgic little sigh, a bravely brushed tear, a sudden seizure of the irritated pup before he has had more than a mouthful—and if you could just 'phone her at that moment you'd be in all over again, Meredith. Happiness *can* be a warm puppy.

In establishing contact with women, dogs can be invaluable too. Walk in the park, or enter a bar, carrying a twelve-week-old Poodle puppy in that uncut stage where he looks like a bundle of fluff from under the bed, and you will receive as much attention as a current hero of teeny boppers. To the predatory male, the old dictum might easily be conveniently paraphrased into 'Love my dog; love me.'

The way to a girl's heart when she owns a dog already is a simple elaboration of your interest in all the canine species, and the simple forethought of filling your ticket-pocket each morning with a handy selection of Spiller's Shapes against the random associations of the day ahead. Get the dog on your side and you are halfway home. Only in the decision as to which dog to give a girl friend do we find a problem.

Asking her to choose is as hazardous as asking a girl to pick out her own engagement ring. Necessarily you are exposing yourself to paying a bill for a highly expensive thoroughbred beyond the budget of a man of wider interests. Better by far to attack her sentimentalities by persuading her of the humanity of selecting an unwanted animal from the dog's home.

It may be beyond house training at that age—but that is hardly your problem. Too, a hybrid puppy could well grow into an ugly hound of ugly temperament—but you can always blame her methods of care. The only clear advantage to buying a specific and clearly distinct breed is that you can in a way thus control how it is going to turn out. In consequence, you can select a dog which may be easily overcome should an estrangement in relations later produce a situation where she attempts to use it against you. There is little menace in a pointing female finger and the peremptory command to 'Kill; Caesar!' when all that confronts you is a chihuahua or a hairless mexican.

If we seek a warning, though, we can find one in the story of a middle-aged swinger of my acquaintance who though irrevocably chained in the locks of matrimony cheered a couple of nights a week via an illicit association with a young lady some twenty years his junior.

Hubert (the facts are true, only the names have been changed to protect the guilty) marked his appreciation of this liason with the presentation of a pyrenean mountain dog puppy to the young lady in question, and what at first sight presented the projection of a modest feather duster finally grew into a hairy monster with the appetite of a Woolmark dragon.

Its perpetual need for exercise became a handicap, particularly as the young lady lived on the third floor of a block of what are unfailingly described by the popular press as 'West End luxury flats', and Hubert found to his chagrin that often in the later stages of the evening his exploratory persuasions in the direction of the bedroom would inevitably be countered by the sly riposte: 'Heavens—is it bed-time already? Time for Rover to have his Bye-Bye Walkies ...'

Typical of the category in which women embrace dogs is the fact that they inevitably address them in Baby Talk, but Hubert was unconcerned with such Freudian trivialities. His problem was that once the girl had galloped Rover several times around the greensward of Regent's Park, she was far too exhausted for the more intimate exercise he had in mind for the later stages of the evening.

Finally he hit upon the idea of plying her upon her return with a glass or two of reviving Brandy, and one evening he repaired to her flat with a couple of bottles of the happy juice and a determination to outwit circumstances.

When the usual time for Rover's Bye-Bye Walkies arrived the girl and the dog departed for the adjacent Regent's

Park and Hubert unwrapped his bottle of brandy in readiness for her return.

Unhappily, a heavy rain storm forced the young lady to take shelter in the middle of the exercises, and her absence from the flat expanded from the usual half hour to one of some hour and a half.

Realising what had happened, and conscious of the bad weather outside, Hubert meanwhile decided to break open the bottle and cheer his lonely vigil with a bite or two at the cognac. Inevitably as her absence became protracted and his own loneliness emphasised, he found more and more consolation in the brandy and ultimately fell into a deep slumber with his face resting nose first in a slowly drying pool of the Bisquit.

Meanwhile, the rain had ceased and the young lady returned to the front of the block to discover she had left her keys on the dressing table.

Confined within the deepest regions of relaxation, Hubert responded in no way to an incessant ringing of the door-bell, and faced with the alternative of a night out with Rover, the young lady resolved to enlist the assistance of the local constabulary.

Down at the nick, she explained the problem of the missing keys; but loath to induce embarrassment through any suspicion that the male occupant of the flat might be other than legitimate company, she glibly referred to Hubert as her 'husband'—persuading the desk sergeant that if he would be kind enough to continue ringing her flat by telephone, she would in the meantime return and add the jangle of the door-bell to the noise of the telephone and the shouted reiteration of his name. Thusly, she reasoned, Hubert might be prompted into sensibility.

The plan was successful. Even Hubert's condition found it impossible to ignore the cumulative cacophony, and he roused to a fuddled state of mind where he concluded the telephone to be the more urgent summons and instinctively reached over to answer the instrument whilst vaguely wondering who could be ringing the door-bell at this time of night. Clearly it couldn't be the girl—because she had her own keys.

His reply to the 'phone engendered a polite greeting from

the Desk Sergeant and the innocent information that, 'I think you ought to know Sir, that your wife is trying to get into that flat . . .'

Innocent to the Desk Sergeant, that is. With all the guilt complexes of an instant hang-over crowding his befuddled mind, Hubert could only conclude the worst. He was discovered! Pausing for but a split second to register a terrified 'Thanks for the tip . . .' he moved stealthily to the window to register a shadowy female figure in the darkness beneath and a stentorian bellow of 'HUUUUBERT!' echoing down the street.

In clear panic he retreated to the rear of the flat, leapt from the open bedroom window without bothering even to replace his Chelsea boots, and succumbed to a grisly death impaled on the pointed palings surrounding the area beneath. If there is a moral to this tale it is perhaps the only moral with which Hubert was ever associated in his untiring and ubiquitous pursuit of the opposite sex.

YOUNG LADIES
AND THE GREAT OUTDOORS

NOTHING OCCASIONS DELIGHT SO MUCH AS THE SMUG APPRECIA-
tion of catching Homer nodding, and I will take to my death
the rosy glow I once experienced at hearing an instant Television pundit, recruited for his popularity rather than his
expertise, refer on a horticultural programme to a flower
by the name of the 'Cotton-easter'.

Full-flooded with the patronising esoterics of an expert
who happens to know it should be pronounced 'co-tone-e-
aster', I suddenly realised that I am one of the few gardening
gurus who never gardens—possibly the only one who sees in
the great outdoors far more specific advantages than the need
to spoil a manicure with an underlay of the good earth, or
soil a pair of thirty-five guinea snakeskin two-tones with
seepage from the mulch.

Yet there is hardly a single idiosyncrasy of the *saxifragaceae*
(hydrangea), *guttiferae* (hypericum) or *leguminosae* (labur-
num) to which I am not privy; no aspect of the English country
garden on which I may be quizzed without the answering
enlightenment of versatile expertise and academic precept.

This is because I am a punctual as well as a punctilious
diner, and the BBC Radio programme *Gardeners Question
Time* is transmitted promptly at two o'clock, rain or shine,
every Sunday as I sit down to lunch. Useless as its rustic
esoterics might seem to a seasoned metropolitan, it seems
infinitely preferable to the tired comedy alternatives on Radio
Two, Radio Three's abstract cacophonies of some obscure
Bulgarian nose-flautist, or an Open University lecture on
The Orientating Influences of Alkali Metals on the Reaction
of Carboxylating Carbonate Compounds.

A captive audience of *Gardeners Question Time* for some
several summers now, I have become to a degree satiated by
the round of reiterated, only slightly differently worded calls
for assistance from the amateur gardeners in distress, and am
inclined to shrug off with irritation the plaintive bleats for
help on subjects dealt with only a few months previously.
And as its originality palls, I begin to envisage potential im-
provements in a programme which offers unplumbed
versatility to a Producer of more elastic invention.

More challenging, I find, are the extraordinary pleas for assistance featured in those specialised magazines which invariably identify their patronage via the gatefold illustration of undebilitated (and undepilitated) young ladies in latter stages of undress. Their search for definitive instruction in sexual practices which are often idiosyncratic, seem to me a model of initiative in the search for human enlightenment. I would be interested to listen to a merging of the serious specialised instruction of *Gardeners Question Time* and the serious specialised curiosity of contributors to the letter pages of, say, *Penthouse* magazine. I believe such a programme might project the discussion of subjects far beyond the consideration of a volume, such as this is, circumscribed by its very moderation.

There are, nevertheless, fringe subjects concerning both Young Ladies and the Great Outdoors which we might examine on these pages and which, indeed, might be utilised eventually as acceptable programme material for a *Question Time* daring to extend its repertoire beyond the prosaic.

For example, the men's 'girlie' magazines, searching desperately for the largely unread pages of type which punctuate the pictures of naked ladies, are inclined to project a regular essay aimed at advising upon the essential furniture and furnishings seen as most likely to grace the bachelor flat of a young male seducer. And it seems to be automatically assumed that every red-blooded young man extant lives out his life on the twelfth floor of a West End domestic complex. Beyond twelve miles from Hyde Park Corner, runs the legend, no woman need go in hazard of her virginity. Conception in rural areas is immaculate. Only she who comes to town ends up a bad lot.

Lady Chatterley knew better, of course. So did Mellors. The theory that a romp in the long summer grass inevitably ends in disciplined morality might well be the traditional reason for the needle in a haystack but it hardly helps in the national effort to re-populate the rural areas. Seriously considered, why should the hot thrash of seduction take place only in the cooling shadows of a town pad? Tweed trousers come down as easily as worsteds. A young lady, indeed, is on her most cynical *qui vive* in urban surroundings, and the exercise becoming the more calculated becomes the less romantic. Let us bring more natural joy to the sex act by airing it proudly and openly in the sunshine and open air. Not to sell tickets, you understand, but to bring to it a beauty as appropriate as the beauty of the flowers, as natural as the seeding of a tree, as burgeoning as the full-bodied blossom that cometh after.

The question I would like to ask *Gardeners Question Time* is 'How would the panel plan a bachelor's back garden (50^x by 20^x) to give sexual potential to a suburban or rural swinger lumbered with a two-up, two-down, desrble rsdnce, semi-det, dcnt-szed gdn.'

To pre-empt the panel members' embarrassed replies, I should like to suggest that a young man's garden ought to be planned as far as possible bearing in mind a drive in the country and the intimate picnic which is its ultimate climax. When one thinks, indeed, of the essential circumscription of the interior seduction (dealt with in another chapter), one only begins to realise that the real wealth of imagination is only called into play by the initiatives required for the out-door assault.

Basics may seem obvious, but are worth mentioning if only because their apparency might lead them to be ignored. And the need for high walls; quick-growing, sky-aspiring *cupressus* hedges; and the enveloping canopy of evergreen foliated trees are essential to the prevention of being overlooked by out-raged suburban neighbours whose own sexual deviations are represented by the guilty consideration of the possibility of more than once a week on Saturdays.

These visual obstacles will also serve to hide from view that other heinous suburban crime; a neglect of cutting the grass—which, coupled with a generous preponderance of shrubbery and bushes supplies that essential cover without which any young lady divested of her upper and outer garments retreats into non-cooperative embarrassment. It is the twentieth century equivalent of the female Victorian insistence upon making love only when the lights are out, even in bed.

Talking of beds, flower beds are largely superfluous in this type of garden, apart from the possibility of their perfume inducing an exaggerated romantic mood. But it seems pertinent that it was recently established by Professor Francis Ebling, a distinguished zoologist, in a paper to students at Sheffield University, that most of the commercial perfumes at least are more likely to excite the woman wearing them than the man at whom they are traditionally considered to be aimed.

More of that elsewhere, but the Ebling paper bases its theorising on the fact that most commercial perfumes are based on the extractions of male animals—scents which leave the normal man, at least, virtually unaffected. Female excitation is more likely, therefore, to result from flowers smeared with the exotic brews of the couture houses than those allowed simply to stand there and exude their own natural odours.

Other beds, too, are debatable. It is a curious fact that beds traditionally regarded as suitable for the garden or the out-doors are highly unsuitable for the purposes of sexual inter-course. The garden Hammock is too contortionate to be anything but a waste of space to any but those exhibitionists determined upon the achievement of some kind of bizarre intimacy in a standing position. The very title of the 'Camp' bed implies an unspoken homosexuality with which our average hero would hardly wish to be associated in such circumstances; and experience soon teaches that those tubular metal constructions mostly discovered in the vicinity of private swimming pools are far too weakly constructed to bear the weight of more than one person at the same time. Research has failed, indeed, to discover any improvement upon the old-fashioned groundsheet. It is impossible to fall off it, and a certain charm may be added to its seemingly basic practicality by imbuing it with a Hefneresque sophistication and cutting it circular. Certainly it will serve to save the young lady from the foggy, foggy dew—if not from that which you will doubtless regard as your right and proper.

The garden swimming-pool is ideal in that it encourages in these days of the Bikini a divesting of the clothes to an absolute minimum—with all the diminished need for effort that such a state establishes—but has the essential drawback of needing pretty open ground and a lack of lush foliage if you are not to be constantly breaking off from your blandishments to go and clean out the filter. And the absence of trees, bushes or long grass immediately subjects you to the hazards of neighbourly inspection.

To be truthful, the successful seduction garden should be planned in slightly bizarre terms. A collection of those large stone prehistoric beasts such as are playfully dotted about the Crystal Palace Gardens would be ideal in that their sudden encounter around a bushy corner can scare the pants off her, and have her running fearfully into your protective arms. And there she is in your arms in the bushes and no pants on.

A pair of large rocking horses parked in a shady corner might seem juvenile at first consideration, but could offer the companionship of a country gallop without undue exhaustion. And these could be placed in close juxtaposition to an intimately small summer-house decorated on the outside with a swinging Inn sign, and on the inside with a few engraved mirrors, a 'fridge full of drinks, and a cold table. It's nice here. All you need to ensure that your garden is as close to Eden as this life is likely to encounter is that there should be only one rake around and he you.

If the garden seduction represents the aspiration of the suburban young monkey, though, the foray into the country will be a mollifying experience to the urban gorilla unless the approach is properly poised, properly practised and strongly advised. To the man whose idea of roughing it is going three days without a manicure the beckoning of the authentic *country* picnic is a challenge that stirs the heart whenever (as Chaucer so neatly put it) *May is comen and that I hear the foules singe and the floures ginnen for to springe.*

Chaucer may have been a poor speller, but he was a great one for assessing the weaknesses of the human condition. His *Canterbury Tales*, with all their Rabelaisian license, were prompted by a group of people leaving the disciplines of town life behind them—and it is a handy fact that morality decreases in direct proportion to the removal of a person from her natural habitat.

So be undeterred by the report that the local populace

recently ate a missionary in Amersham. Divorced from the smoky air of town you can find a new kind of loving in the polluted air of the countryside. A hundred miles (less, even) from London lie fish and chip shops, take-home Tandoori, hoardings, neon signs and detergent packet architecture in profusion. Every metropolitan comfort is offered—plus the estimable advantage that in a paired picnic a young lady is a relative pushover.

A romantic in town, a young lady becomes sentimental to the edge of lunacy once transported more than eight miles from Hyde Park Corner. A verminous wild rabbit; the sun going down in exactly the same way it does over the Tottenham Court Road; a sheep deeply matted with grease and his own excreta; a grey squirrel which can be fairly regarded as nothing more than a tree-rat; all these manifestations of the fact that urban civilisation has not yet arrived can push the female reaction into an unending succession of silly-ahhhhhhhhs appreciations which automatically soften up her cynicism for your sudden attack.

Perhaps the main advantage of a date in the countryside is the enormous opportunity it affords a man of seeming heroic. Assume a deep knowledge of all natural things which allows you to identify everything with horns—from a goat to a hat rack—as a ferocious bull, and everything that moves in the undergrowth as a deadly snake, and one needs only a normally ignorant town girl to be able to scare the pants off her at will (see above).

Steady assaults on the ecology sometimes necessitate your taking along your own wild animals, of course. A variety of harmless grass snakes may be purchased relatively cheaply from local pet stores, and one of these can always be secreted in the boot of the car to be released at a propitious moment. It is unlikely that she will know it from a Puff Adder and your image will be greatly improved if you simply tread towards it warily and prod it off into the bushes with a cleft stick.

Slightly more ambitious is the plan whereby you secretly stick her in the bottom with a tea-fork as she turns her back on the luckless reptile and flings herself into your arms for protection. Or you can press a holly-leaf into her thigh as

you place your arms comfortingly about her. Greet her involuntary scream with a grave assurance that there is only
one known cure for snakebite—and you can insist on filling
her up with whisky as a precaution.

It's even worth a try at getting down and offering to suck
the poison out of the wound at great hazard to your own
well-being. There would seem to be fewer personal intimacies
more emphatic than getting your lips on to her thigh, and
the clear danger from the venom could be used as an excuse
for having a couple of Scotches yourself.

A car is essential for such an outing, so a car coat is an
automatic accessory to give your hired Cortina the ring of
ownership. In fine weather it may be superfluous, but in
cold or rainy days it is extraordinary how deep are the intimacy connotations of shared male garments borrowed by
women. The prime example of such is the helpless attractiveness projected by the sight of a beautiful girl in a pair of
far-too-large men's pyjamas, and whilst we are on the subject,
reasonable foresight will have urged you to carry a pair of
pyjamas constantly in your car against an emergency overnight
stop (book well in advance in the tourist season) at that superb
little country inn handily close to where you simulate gear-
box failure on the way home. With but one pair of pyjamas,
one of you will have to sleep with no clothes on, but that's
hardly your fault.

The basic essential of the picnic site is the Fire. It is necessary for drying out after that illicit nude swim in the icy
lake ('Here, darling; you're blue with cold. Let me give you
a good towelling ...' is quite as effective as 'Shall I rub you
with sun-tan oil? ...') and is of course the instrument for your
barbecue later on. But it can be a problem.

My own rather outdated copy of *Scouting for Boys* (1936
edition) promises that for tinder to get it started you may
utilise dead bracken, newspaper, pine cones, heather, or
even dried orange peel. This is worth knowing, though the
problem about the last is that you presumably need to have
a fire going already in order to dry it out. Be careful, certainly, of the casual dollop of petrol cavalierly flung into
smouldering beginnings. Look what happened to Yul
Brynner. The only advantage to using petrol from the car

is if you can persuade the young lady that your allergy will not permit your siphoning the stuff. Acquiescing, she will find the petrol leaves a revolting taste in her mouth which of necessity can be removed only by another pull at the whisky bottle. What with the snake-bite precaution, she will by now be well on the way to being at least slightly tipsy; which is a prime facet of your operation.

One essential is to spring the picnic on her as a surprise if possible. She will not then be properly dressed for it—which is better for yourself. With high heels or platform soles she will be incapable of walking too far or running too fast. You will not be shown up for you're out of condition condition and she will find it more difficult to get away. In certain circumstances, too, impractical clothing in countryside terms to a degree puts her at the mercy of your assistance. At obstacles such as fences, hedges or streams, you will gain the personal and intimate contact of lifting her over bodily—ensuring she experiences, as they say in the novelettes, 'his hot breath upon her'—or she will have to hoist her skirts thigh-high and climb over independently. Either way, neither way is bad.

Your own dress should be calculated in ultra-masculine terms if your physique is worth showing off, or in more academic and specialised terms if it isn't. The Norfolk jacket, knickerbockers and deer-stalker hat of the countryman will emphasise your claims to a knowledge of natural history and distract her defence mechanisms to a degree. For example, 'I know where there's a lark's nest,' is a transparent enough way of luring her into a handy field where, because 'all that neck-stretching can bring on a double chin,' the best way to look out for larks is from ground level. 'I suggest we lie down here in the long grass where they can't see us and won't become suspicious ...'

The very word 'lark', however, is likely to rouse her own instinctive suspicions. Perhaps 'I know where there's a pheasant's nest' may be better. That's more reason for dodging off into the underbrush.

Occasionally, you can strike lucky quite unintentionally. A relatively inarticulate young man, stumped for conversation in a simple pastoral *tête-à-tête* a couple of years ago, murmured rather fatuously: 'Ah—back to Nature's the thing!'

and the girl answered very seriously: 'I'm absolutely delighted that you share my belief in the efficacies and health-promoting properties of Naturism,' and immediately took all her clothes off. They now have a small son who, doubtless in deference to the pre-natal influence of the mother's Naturistic beliefs, was born stark naked.

Food plays an enormously important part in your country campaign. For a full stomach brings a friendly sense of cosy satisfaction and, coupled with drink, a stirring realisation that all the sensual delights have been experienced and enjoyed, save one. A sense of repleteness induces that winking feeling—and that drinking feeling. And whether you be prosaic (bottled beer), a novitiate (vin rosé), transparently sophisticated (straw flasks of chianti), utterly cynical and impossibly impatient (gin), or simply a big show off (champagne), there is nothing so conducive to getting her to see things your way as getting her full of the happy juice.

Barbecue all the natural juices out of a couple of rashers of salt bacon, feed it to her between two slices of a crusty, toasted roll, and she'll be croaking for a drink of water before you can wrestle the plastic covering from the processed cheese.

But ('Dammit!') you never brought any water with you, did you? Only wines and spirits. And the risk of typhoid would never allow you to agree to her slaking her thirst at the brook. 'Here, darling, help yourself to a long, cool drink from this carafe. NO—really—we've plenty ...'

How, then, to prepare burnt food. First the fire: Good kindling woods are Birch, Cedar, Cypress, Scots Pine, and Spruce. Avoid Chestnut, Elm, Oak, Poplar and Sycamore.

The kindling and quick burning woods are good for boiling; the slow burning woods (best are Ash, Oak, Plane, Sycamore and Yew) are better adopted when the fire is burning properly and you wish to start cooking in terms of baking or barbecuing.

For quick firing, I can recommend the following procedure: Place a kindling stick about ten inches long upright in the ground, heap tinder (paper, dead bracken, dried peel, etc., see above) around it as far as possible up the side of the stick and then lean pyramids of shorter kindling sticks against the centre. Leave the opening for lighting the tinder where a helpful breeze will fan it for you, and rub two boy scouts together until the necessary spark is produced.

For the type of fire I can offer two alternatives: *The Channel* or *The Reflector*. You make *The Channel* simply by placing two rows of bricks or flat stones at an angle which produces a narrow, open-ended vee—with the wider end towards the wind but not plumb into it. This is perfectly adequate for frying or boiling or, provided the bricks or stones are high enough to ensure the food isn't burned, for a kebab of small morsels you can spit on a skewer. Pots and kettles are simply rested on the stones.

The Reflector is slightly more ambitious in that the grate is made from bricks set in a square and the fireback from two stout pieces of green Ash or Oak (it's unlikely to burn) sunk into the ground with other pieces fastened across them at right angles. More ambitiously, you could use a flat sheet of metal here—you could even increase the reflection with a shape something akin to three sides of a box kite. Then you arrange a spit across the grate (stiff wire mesh, or a gridiron) where the meat will catch the maximum heat.

Remember that much of the fat is lost in the process—so baste regularly—and confine yourself to simple dishes like hot-dogs, steaks, chops, and kebabs which consist simply of alternated pieces of meat, bacon, onion, mushroom, thin slices of potato, apple, liver, kidney, etc., brushed with fat and basted regularly. Ensure the wind is in the right direction so that the meat may be smoked but not your Game, and interest her in the cooking just when the food is about bad enough to arouse her maternal instincts.

At that stage she will offer to take it over, and it is wise to surrender to her apocryphal superiority as a female caterer. Help her into the barbecuing apron—it is a sneaky way of getting your arms around her and is another of those psychological touches which affect a woman without her ever realising. Her sub-conscious will appreciate that you have helped her to dress and will be at least halfway towards a mental acceptance of the possibility of your helping her to undress. What is more, it is better that she should cook the food because it will give her no possible grounds for complaint. A curious aspect of the average human being is that

even the most burnt-up morsel tastes oddly satisfying provided
you have yourself taken a hand in preparing the sacrifice.

Keep your cool, and take it easy whilst she busies herself
about her little open-air chores. Encourage her to have the
meal ready as the blood red penny of the setting sun balances
on the slot of the horizon. Then watch the shadows drift up
to the periphery of the firelight and softly sip the wine you
have cooled in the gurgle of the running brook.

Permit the small birds to sing and wonder not whereof
they sing, but attend to the swiftly passing friendship of the
pine-scented steak whose memory you will cherish long after
he has departed.

The Loaf of Bread is handy, the Jug of Wine is at your
elbow, she is there Beneath the Bough, and Omar knowest
full well what he may do with his book of verses. Lean
closer in the firelight, and melt the silence into quiet companionship with a whispered, 'Pass the Thou ...'

THE YOUNG LADY
AND THE MIDDLE-AGED
SWINGER

ALONG WITH THE REALISATION THAT GROWING OLDER TAKES
a great deal longer than just growing up, comes the realisation
that 'dirty old man' is simply a *relative* term. It is a term
your relatives use for you—those dried up spinsteresque aunts
and uncles who have lived lives of suburban rectitude and
ever felt that somewhere along the way fulfilment had
evaded them. There is in every family a cheerily decaying
roué or an irresponsible middle-aged delinquent who goes
his way unaffected by the disapproval of righteous conform-
ists; knowing not only that 'the best is yet to be' but that it
hasn't been half bad so far either.

At about forty-five years of age, indeed, a man is at the
optimum of his female appreciation quotient. Almost nothing
is too young to admire, and very few are too old to desire.
In recent years, indeed, the potential in the field has been
considerably expanded by the tendency for young girls to
achieve Puberty at a much earlier age than was hitherto
regarded as decent. Whereas the pre-war girl technically
became a woman at about fourteen years, the modern miss
begins sprouting breasts at around the age of ten.

Memories of the opposite sex during what were miserably
referred to as The Happiest Days of My Life, recall schoolgirls
of smalle Latin, lesse Greek, and a minimum of sex appeal.
The black-sack gym-slip with the saggy and shapeless sash;
the thick and wrinkled worsted stockings; the flannel blazer
unpadded either at shoulder or bust line; the hat like an
inverted chamber-pot; the navy blue, elasticated Bloomers
which, when exchanged for a Bathing Costume on Swimming
Days, left a curious scarlet ring around every little girl's
thigh—so unaphrodisiac was the image that it is small wonder
little boys regarded their female equivalents simply as a race
of reluctant tree-climbers who—even when so persuaded—
hardly warranted attention even to get a surreptitious peep
at their knickers.

But grow up: A man has but to attend Prize Day at a
local Academy for Young Ladies nowadays to realise how
suddenly and urgently the blood is pumping through his

temples, and how he can hardly keep his hands off the prefects.

Indeed, to a middle-aged man, the adult social scene is hardly safer. His forty to fifty-year-old acquaintances invariably boast daughters of anything from fourteen to seventeen years, and he slowly realises that these children with whom he used to play Bear are becoming the objects of his guilty desire. Reflecting on how much more fun it would be to play bare with them nowadays, the Humbert Humbert in a man emerges like a salivering Mr. Hyde.

At a friend's one day for casual Sunday morning drinks, your neighbour lightly mentions that young Cynthia is back from College for half term and is beginning to think about her A levels. When she enters the room you know at once that you are in love. With the instinctive sadism of a woman she knows it too, and does nothing to alleviate your inward distress at this mental betrayal of her father—your finest and best friend.

'John!' she squeals in high delight—dropping the once mandatory prefix of Uncle and increasing your unease at the familiarity. She flings her slender young arms around your neck, filling your susceptible nostrils with that fresh, young, feminine body-odour which is so much more compelling than the headiest scent; pressing her bosom *manqué* against the chest at which she used to fire her rubber-sucker arrows. You extricate yourself with careful hands, looking around nervously in case a policeman has entered the room and is reading your mind.

How can you find such a child so desirable? you ask yourself fretfully. Only a few years ago she was too sticky to be touchable, and so ill-tempered and spoiled that you would have gladly smacked her bottom then. Come to think of it ...

No use to remind yourself that when you were already an experienced rake about town this wanton was lying on her back in her pram with her legs in the air—nothing on below the waist, and happily covering her face with spit bubbles. You peck her casually on the cheek with feigned disinterest, wondering what would happen in the household if you suddenly bent her back over your right arm, shifted the lip contact to dead centre, and gave her a thirty second exercise in adult education.

I can never understand the average father's complete unconsciousness of the sexual attractions of his teenage daughters. Are fathers virtual eunuchs once they have fulfilled their parenthood? Is there some law of Nature—obviously aimed at the minimisation of Incest—which renders a male parent blind to the gorgeous thing that is growing up in his house? Is a father incapable of appreciating the jade he has personally fostered? Is he utterly insensitive to the diabolical surmise throbbing through the psyches of his men friends? The novelettes keep us well supplied with constant warnings regarding the tendency for best friends to run away with their best friends' wives—but for my money my best friend is welcome to hang on to his old lady. I want to run away with my best friend's daughter.

The attitude may seem indictable, but it also seems inevitable. Coupled with the general Youth Cult which urges older women to reduce their apparent ages as much as possible, and such little girl manifestations as the Mini Skirt and Hot Pants on older women and ankle length gowns on younger ones, there is a great ocean of women around between the ages of fifteen and thirty-five who look pretty much the same as one another. At the older end of the age-scale a man may feel he is acquiring a bonus, but woe betide the man who tastes the delight of a nymphette of less than sixteen summers and ends in the hands of the constabulary. Simple justice suggests that in the face of the difficulty of knowing a girl's age without recourse to her birth certificate, it is high time we adjusted the age of Jail Bait to somewhere closer to fourteen years.

One imagines the Age of Consent as being originally established at sixteen years because such an age was regarded as an average balance between capability and responsibility. Now that capability seems to be starting several years sooner, and earlier responsibility seems to have been acknowledged officially by the decrease in the age a girl is given the vote (and remember that sixty years ago she wasn't given it *at all*), middle-aged men should be protected from the increased nubility of juveniles and also from another unforseen effect of modern social developments—namely, their own increasing attractiveness to the kind of girl who can get them in serious trouble Thirty years ago, age groups were isolated and as in-breeding as the social classes, but modern democracy has precipitated the greater mingling of Colour, Class and Age. The spread of 'sophistication' via the Media, prepossession with cosmetic and beauty aids, and inexpensive and increasingly titillating dress fashions, all make common entry to most social functions easily accessible to any modern girl of normal sensitivity. And a growing and encouraged taste for expensive life, coupled with increased confidence and a talent for instant *ennui*, impresses upon younger women more and more the advantages of an affair with a mature, prosperous, and worldly middle-aged man—as opposed to the naive relationship with a callow youth whose economic situation inevitably demands they go Dutch.

Let not the middle-aged roué bother himself with bourgeois moralities. Snide suggestion that he simply seduces a young lady's interests (or a young lady herself) via his suavity, his money, his fame, his connections, his sophisticated knowledge of how to give her an expensive good time, or all of these, hold true enough as factual statement—but lack all validity as a moral attack.

Is there, after all, less reason to be proud of such romantic ammunition than there is to be proud of an attraction based entirely on the accidental and entirely hereditary appeal of good looks? (*There* is an hereditary principle the Socialists might well examine now they have practically dissolved the unjust passing on of family wealth. Should beautiful babies be disfigured at birth to prevent the advantage their looks might give them in years to come?)

But if a man is prosperous, famous and worldly wise nowadays, the chances are that he achieved such a state on his own via talent, application and hard work. Attract a girl by such achievements and you may console yourself you did it your way. You aren't just a pretty face.

The confusion in the male mind on this point was emphasised to me not long ago when I read a letter in one of those sad 'Let Me Help You' columns purporting to come from a young man who feared his girl friend was only going out with him 'for a good time'.

Why does he go out with her, I wonder? For a bad time? In defence of the Gold Digger (whatever became of that phrase?) I cannot see that a man should *care* why girls go out with him as long as they do. A middle-aged man who has come to terms with himself and the world need not be concerned that his cavalcade of lovely escorts are there beside him because he can feed and wine them expensively, introduce them to the delights of sophisticated places and sophisticated people, and make the evening a sybaritic delight. That is part—if not, indeed, the sum—of his attractiveness.

Is aura less praiseworthy than high cheekbones in a man? The attractions of a man's looks and physique are purely sensual, but the attractions of his background and professional connections are intellectual. Any decent chap would prefer to keep companionship on this higher plane. It is the intrusion of emotion flavoured by romantic aesthetics which inevitably spoils a love affair. Marriages last longer than love affairs because the party of the first part has come to *need* the party of the second part. Whether the need is based on female dependence or on the male acknowledgement that a housekeeper would cost more than a wife does, the basic glue is economic.

What seems as clear as the current tendency for young women to manifest an increased interest in older men is a curious tendency among young men to manifest a decreased interest in girls of their own age in favour of (a) older women, and (b) other young men. Are we commencing in the human race a subtle readjustment of our mating principles? As social barriers break down between the sexes and the classes; as steady female emancipation neutralises the one time superiority (*sic*) of young men over young ladies, are we heading for a time when men and women will find natural companionship more readily and more enjoyably among vastly different age groups of the opposite sexes?

In twenty years time, will sex between a sixty-year-old man and a fifteen-year-old girl be no more socially reprehensible than sex between a white woman and a black man is today? In the general *mores* of little more than half a century since, both were pretty well unacceptable. Copulation between the races and the colours today holds no more social hazard than did a Mixed Marriage fifty years ago or a Morganatic Marriage fifty years before that. Who knows how soon the ultimate favour will be bestowed upon a man simply for helping her with her homework?

It is possible that intimacy with middle age will inevitably lead to a diminishment of respect for middle age; and a far more levelled society will emerge in all classification categories. It is possible, indeed, that a welcome disappearance will be manifested in the vanishing of the Middle-Aged Old Buffer.

When I was a schoolboy, it was the habit of Headmasters in those days to invite down to the school once a year a curiously pompous middle-aged old gentleman to present the Prizes. I suspect now that his pomposity derived from an inverted inferiority complex due to not having a bit on the side; and invariably the gentleman in question would hand out the trophies, congratulate us on the achievements of the school's sporting year, and deliver a final homily on the essential godliness of self denial and the inevitable perils of self abuse—a peroration from which, as I recall, few of us ever profited.

Like a Mayor, or a Prime Minister, or a Chairman of the Board, or a Union Seckerterry, the Man Who Presents the Prizes has remained a traditional figure of fun—and my chagrin was intense not long ago when I found myself in his shoes via an invitation to present the prizes at The London College of Fashion.

In my speech of encouragement, any references to the hazards of masturbation seemed misplaced in terms of teenagers of the current generation, and I wisely excluded them. But it was more than that which seemed to suggest to me that the chasms between the generations of thirty or forty years ago have narrowed amazingly.

Far from seeing the girl students as things beyond the pale of my interest or experience, I found myself anxious to be accepted by them. When some of them manifested that acceptance by the use of my christian name, I was disproportionately delighted. It is easy to see—if you were brought up in times when the Middle Aged ran the world and the

Young were kept resolutely in their place—how neatly the positions have been reversed.

For a knowledge of diet, an increased concern with appearances, improved medical and dental science, and general acceptance that the difference between Middle Age and Youth is not so marked as we once suspected, inevitably produces the welcome and balancing acceptance that once suspected differences between Youth and Middle Age are not so marked either. With young and older men looking as much like one another as are young and older women, a man needs some reference points to which to refer in order that he falls not too readily into the trap of becoming mutton dressed as lamb.

Note that:

(a) a man is middle aged when he can affirm sincerely that it is fifteen years since he saw an unattractive woman;

(b) a man is middle aged when he neglects running fifteen yards to catch a bus, which is beginning to move off, because there will be another one along in fifteen minutes;

(c) a man is middle aged when he realises that oysters are delicious, after all;

(d) a man is middle aged when he freely acknowledges that dinner and a bottle of wine with a woman is infinitely preferable to a night on the beer with the boys;

(e) a man is middle aged when the focal point of the evening is the food and the wine rather than the entertainment. To the young, it is the film that matters; and the fish and chips to follow is simply a supplement;

(f) a man is middle aged when good looks in younger men are suspiciously effeminate;

(g) a man is middle aged when a fashion for short hair comes in just as he has at last decided to grow his long;

(h) a man is middle aged when trousers begin to narrow again just as he has taken delivery of his first flares;

(i) a man is middle aged when even the Police*women* begin to look young;

(j) a man is middle aged when he can call every girl or woman he addresses 'Darling', and neither she nor her fellow be affronted.

A hasty perusal of the list will show that being middle aged is not all disadvantage, and such disadvantages which arrive via what may seem like diminished virility, diminished good looks, or increased premature baldness, can often be recruited towards improving one's personal image.

A receding hairline need not make you sick (*transit gloria mundi?*) nor handicap your rivalry to a curlier and younger man, if you propagandise its arrival with scientific authority. For according to research by the State Medical Centre in New York, experiments were carried out which seem to link baldness with sexual virility.

A study by the Centre of a cross-section of men deficient in male hormones revealed that nineteen out of twenty failed to develop 'maturity' hair recessions at the temples—those early patches of the receding hair-line which begin to appear on a male only after he has come to puberty and which reshape his forehead into something like a rectangle rather than a semi-circle. Given gland treatment and injected with male hormones, the men all began to develop the balding recessions—and it has been established thereby that there is some connection between the old wives' tale about virility being established by hair on the chest and not on the head.

Unthinking vanity can sometimes disregard what can be an advantage. There is no doubt that some people look *right* bald—in the same way that some people look *right* fat. Women are made up of a contradictory jumble of desires and wistful acquisitiveness, and whereas a man is polygamistic in that he likes to enjoy a number of different women, each with a single emphasised attraction-characteristic to suit his passing moods, women are monogamistic and incline to seek one man with all that they require cumulatively presented.

The Father-figure and the Little-boy image satisfy their insecurity and their maternal instincts respectively—and a man who can manage to project both images is practically irresistible. A slightly aging façade with an emergent bubble of chubbily irresponsible fun-loving can embrace premature baldness and advancing obesity without too much stretch of her imagination.

Avoid the wigs and hair-pieces, therefore. A sudden realisation that she can see the join is as traumatic to an admiring woman as watching her lover take down his trousers and reveal a cork leg. When hair recession arrives at a point where the bare sectors predominate over the hirsute, it is better to pre-empt Nature by shaving the whole head clean; thus projecting your virility symbolism to the maximum.

Eschew at all costs that desperately thin camouflage sometimes resorted to—of carefully laying thickly greased and separated strands of hair in evenly parallel array across an otherwise naked pate. It looks like a dish of spaghetti served by a fantastically tidy waiter. As a riposte to the chaff of younger men, point out benignly that a head bald on the outside is infinitely preferable to a head bald on the in.

Even the traditionally accepted attractions of wavy and curly hair can be countered by a sincere and serious discussion of medical principles. It is true that in strict medical terms only straight hair, with the perfectly rounded follicle which is needed to extrude it, is regarded as 'normal'. Curls and waves in the hair are produced by a misformed irregularity in the hair follicle and are properly regarded in technical terms as local deformities. Loving a man for his deformity can sound rather sick if you explain it to her in the right way.

Neither is failing eyesight the handicap you might expect it to be, if you bear in mind the cinematic cliché of a few years ago. After some brotherly horse-play had accidentally shaken out the girl's hair bun, a look of burgeoning bewilderment would begin to creep across our hero's face as with sudden sincerity he reached out and gently removed her spectacles. 'But, Miss Tomlinson,' he would murmur in reverent realisation, '—you're beeyoutifull ...'

That she inevitably fell in love with him back might well be attributed to the fact that without her glasses she couldn't see him all that clearly, and with middle-aged eyesight you can at least butter up your ego by taking off your own spectacles and realising how much better she looks in soft focus. If enjoyment of the sexual act is heightened by a belief that it is taking place between two Beautiful People, we have a possible reason why men seldom make passes at girls wearing glasses. Who can afford to be examined under a magnifying glass?

A further balance seems extant in the fact that human

eyesight generally is deteriorating—or, at least, higher and wider degrees of rectification are being more generally employed—and more and more men are wearing spectacles nowadays. It is certainly to the middle-aged man's advantage that he has normal access to a range of frames which can be used actually to improve the apparent proportions of his face. The younger generation, if they are to be accepted in the image terms of their contemporaries, are required to adopt those grotesquely archaic little lenses with the thin wire rims and ear supports—something akin to spectacles handed out by 'The Panel' in days before the National Health Service bowed to the right of non-paying patients to be 'in'.

Consequently, the myopic young man looks like nothing so much as a mediaeval Swiss watchmaker, whereas the heavy rims of Father Figure spectacles, especially when supplemented by deeply tinted lenses, immediately emulate sunglasses and all the film star connotations they involve.

Above, I suggested that spectacles, far from necessarily disfiguring the face upon which they have to be imposed, can actually be used to improve its visual proportions—and any girl cursed with small eyes will know how much more acceptable is her personal projection when she offers the suggestion of great, wide, round eyes via the simple process of wearing huge tinted glasses which deny any examination of the proportions of the actual eyes behind them. In similar vein, a male profile can be romanticised by the right choice of glasses. Short snub noses out of proportion to the rest of the features can be visually bettered by means of spectacle frames which fit a very high bridge. This tends to suggest a longer, unbroken line to the bridge of the nose itself, and therefore offers a visual image of a longer proboscis.

In the same way, a very long or very large nose can be visually rectified by arranging for the bridge of the spectacles to rest further down the bridge of the nose itself. Part of the nose is then hidden from view behind the bridge of the spectacles and the size and length of the wearer's nose is thus visually modified.

But the kind of spectacles most likely to keep a middle-aged man on his toes are those which blot out all through-visibility from the outside via reflective mirrors. Girls should be encouraged to wear these in company of older men, for they reflect his own image back at him constantly and influence his self respect in much the same way as does a man's reaction when he suddenly comes across a mirror placed in a situation where he was not expecting to encounter it.

For a split moment he wonders cheerfully enough who that flabby, curiously familiar, stooping old party waddling towards him can possibly be. He has met him before, but where was it? There is something peculiarly, even intimately, memorable about the body and the features. They stir a chord of distant familiarity. Could it be a relation? A rather seedy old uncle, perhaps ...

With a flood of horror he realises it is himself—and in a flash the shoulders go back; the guts are pulled in; the head is thrust up and out to neutralise the pendulous chins; the cheeks are sucked flat against the orbed protruberance of the jowls; the back is straightened; and he is conforming once again to his mirror image—the lie he lives in all his moments of reflection save those in which he is caught unawares.

This curious vanity in the presence of women younger than ourselves is possibly the origin of the expression, 'A silly old fool making a spectacle of himself,' but why should he not. The middle-aged swinger today comes of a twilight generation which has to a degree lost out at both ends of life. When he was an adolescent it meant nothing more than thirty bob a week, at best, and an inevitable crucifixion to Acne. Now he has come at last to solvency, achievement, success and prosperity to find that in the meantime the world has changed gear and slipped almost imperceptibly into motivations which worship the accident of being under Thirty.

He remembers that when he was young he hung back from women in respect for their vulnerability, and in a dual fear of V.D., pregnancy, and going to Hell when he died. Brought up by generations of parents who were Victorians, he was instilled with the belief that nothing is so honourable as the Waiting Game. Now he finds that the generations who are his sons acknowledge only the sexual tenet that he who hesitates is last. The Pill, gratis french-letters, the dissolution of sexual stigma via the cynical anarchy of liberalism, all see middle teenagers indulging themselves in climaxes which, when he was their age, came to him only in dreams.

He knows it is not an era for hanging about. He sympathises, as he is abjured to by politicians, that young married (or unmarried) couples are unable to buy their own houses—forgetting that he waited until he was about thirty-five before he seriously contemplated buying his own—but he wonders from whence will come the enjoyment of Life if everything is experienced before you come to man's estate. Will today's youngsters enjoy their own mature years when it seems they supped all human delight in early life. Can a fun-time really last forever?

Or is a steady evolution of sexual behaviour carrying us towards a time where all the lust will be used up by the time a man *becomes* a man? Could it be that Nature works towards an arrival where the sexual satiation of the teens and twenty year age levels will dissipate all lust and leave us free in later years to broaden the spirit, the reason and the intellect; untrammelled by resurgent urgent promptings for another session of time wasting, emotion wasting, strength wasting copulation?

However we may experience little rises and falls in the graph of relative morality over, say, a hundred years, it is more interesting to look back to half a millennium since and wonder at the difficulties of sexual intercourse in the four-teenth or fifteenth centuries. In your average stone castle, the women were generally discouraged from eating with the men of the house and often required to serve themselves in an adjacent hall where they would not be exposed to coarse male behaviour or become a nuisance through their presence demanding the little courtesies which so take a man's mind off his food and drink.

Nowadays, when a meal and a bottle of wine are the essential and prime facets of ritualised courting, it is difficult to see how the sexes ever used to come together. Your sweet nothings, your whispered endearments, would be drowned in the thunderous belches which were regarded as the natural concomitant of communal living. And eating with the fingers relegated the most passionate groping to little more than wiping your fingers on milady's gown.

Useless to attempt to lure her away for a prolonged petting

session in the secrecy of the transport you had parked just outside the castle gates. However short the Volkswagen may fall in terms of room for intimate relations, try it on the rear end of a tournament shire-horse. And even glib tongued persuasion in the direction of a Ye Dirtye Weekende inevitably ended in the frustration of a chastity belt.

Anyway, motels had not yet been invented, there was no back row at the cinema, and feudal communal living ruled out even the simple possibility of borrowing the front room for the evening. If there *was* a front room it measured 150 feet long by 75 feet wide by 50 feet high, and was crammed with sweating licentious soldiery and elk hounds.

It may be that all the apparent enthusiasm for hunting in those days was simply a manifestation of the necessity to get off somewhere deep in the undergrowth. Even at the risk of being trampled to death by the follow-up, it was nevertheless the only chance a feverish couple had of achieving any sort of privacy.

For if you read up on the amenities of the average ideal home some five hundred years ago you will find it was only the king of the castle who enjoyed a room to himself, and who could in consequence carry on with the propagation of the species without at best considerable embarrassment and at worst the coarse observations of a cheery host of interested spectators. The feudal lord's privacy may have led initially to the perpetuation of only the strongest strain, but surely it did more than anything to encourage the acceptance among less elevated but more frustrated wives the welcome experience of *droit de seigneur*.

So if you are past the forty-year-old mark, and sometimes fretfully reflect that changing moralities have caught you with your pants up, try to count your blessings. Accept the era into which you have been born and ponder how much more preferable, nowadays, are the middle ages to the Middle Ages.

HOW TO GIVE UP A
YOUNG LADY

THERE IS A CURIOUS BELIEF AMONG A LARGE SECTION OF THE population that there is nothing quite so tragic as losing the love of a young lady. Fostered by milk-sop poets and wet romantics, and perennially sustained by the female ego everywhere, it projects the highly unlikely proposition that once a man escapes from the smothering constriction of two cool, slender arms, he wants nothing so much as an end to living.

In films, books, poems, plays and operas, we are constantly submitted to the spectacle of a chalk-white misery who has just received his come-uppance via the recent delivery of a 'Dear John' letter, but to keep the situation in a proper perspective it is necessary to realise that all the media listed above constitute branches of *fiction*. In real life there is nothing quite so elevating as that roaring sense of freedom which envelopes a man when he holds in his hand conclusive proof that the way is open once again to play the field.

For once a young lady has run her time and served her purpose, a man's motto should be Stop and Go. Where is the sense—as the sexily diminutive Andy Hardy once asked in juvenile soliloquy—in faithfully making one girl miserable when by a generous and wholesale distribution of favours you can make hundreds happy? What a man needs is not advice on how to cope with the reception of a 'Dear John' letter, but a sustained course in how to ensure such.

For it is a curious paradox of human nature that the world has been desperately pursuing the discovery of a love philtre for centuries, but has never apparently given any serious thought to the production of a handy little draught that will kill affection stone dead on the instant.

It should be realised that giving up one woman is by no means the end of your serious sex life. Like advancing Chinese, there is always another woman marching towards you and ready to fill the gap. But the need to rid yourself of a female when her company begins to bore, her giggles begin to pall, her looks begin to fray, her mannerisms begin to irritate, and her possessiveness gets in the way, must give you pause to consider practical steps to take.

First of all, it is pointless to tell her to go away. She will not only ignore the demand, she will love you all the more for it. For nothing is quite so attractive to a woman as a man who does not want her. Here it is impossible by way of illustration to better the observation of George Bernard Shaw who protested: 'The fickleness of the women I love is only equalled by the infernal constancy of the women who love me ...' The technique required for giving up a young lady is to make her give you up.

It is here that the first obstacle of ego intrudes—for if you are really at a loss it is very simple to break a girl of her constant and adoring attentions: It is only necessary to cultivate one or two slightly disgusting personal habits and parade them before her and her friends whenever the opportunity presents. Few women could sustain romantic affection for a sustained belcher, an habitual spitter, or a dedicated nose-picker. There is a clear way out there for any man.

You will find, nevertheless, that this simple technique will be automatically rejected by ninety-nine men out of a hundred. No man wishes a woman to be *glad* about the severance. Her carrying on a normal happy life after you have left her hardly bears consideration. It is far pleasanter to picture her mulling wistfully over your photographs and letters, pink ribbon lying fondly on the floor beside her, in the long lonely evenings to come. You do not really want her to stop loving you so much as carry on loving you at a convenient distance where her nuisance quota is diminished to a minimum but where she is ready to be reclaimed in perhaps a year or two when you are temporarily going through a thin time womanwise. There may be years of wear in her yet, after all. If only you could put her in the deep freeze ...

Economically, too, it is better to be rid of the old love before the new love has become a regular expense. It can be wearing on the nerves as well. Finding a regular evening or evenings, lunch time or lunch times, for the new young lady whilst the pattern of the old mistress is still being sustained often takes more time out of the week than even the most understanding wife is likely to accept without suspicion.

The break must be made as quickly as possible and as definitely as possible; and for this purpose I have perfected the technique of the 'Dear Marcia' letter.

This consists of your composing a series of passionate epistles anonymously despatched and delivered from some point of near locality with which you will not in any way be personally identified. They should be typed and worded in such a plethora of hyperbole that your own occasional grunts of communication as you motion her to pour you another drink will be furthest from her mind as she gloats over a penned adoration she has long suspected as her rightful due.

At first she will act reticently—feeling in her secret enjoyment of the affection and admiration of another that she has unwittingly betrayed you; but concentrate with the Dear Marcia letters and become even more slipshod in your normal everyday treatment of her. Chagrined at your apparent indifference and femininely unable to keep her secret any longer to herself, she will petulantly reveal in a burst of illtemper that despite your lack of appreciation there are *others* who are at her whimsical disposal for the asking.

Do not overplay your hand yet with a sweep-out. Remember, she does not yet know the author of her love-letters, and leaving her alone before they have made any contact simply leaves you open for her tearful suppliant reconciliation next day. Play it hot.

Insist upon seeing the letters. Examine them with jealous ferocity, simulate a belief that her refusal to name the writer is simply her transparent shielding of his treachery, and threaten suicide unless she makes him known to you.

Alarmed at your attitude, she will seek vainly down a list of male acquaintances in an effort to name a man who might be responsible. Choose the name of one you most dislike, and concentrate upon him. But allow your anger to cool and adopt the unlikely self-sacrificing role one sees in heroes in cinematic romances but never in real life. Protest that your only true wish is that she should be happy—and assure her that the moment she feels her life can be better fulfilled in the arms of another man your retiral from the scene will open the gates to all her lovely tomorrows. Only your need to be sure he is *worth* her, will keep you—for the moment—an interested observer of her new acquaintanceship, you say.

Having established a likely victim, with her virtual agreement, you can emphasise the possibility of his involvement via the dropping of a few clues in subsequent correspondence. Post one of the letters from his nearest locality post-office. Introduce a figure of speech, a simile, or a flattering reference to her that might possibly be traced to him, and trace them to him whilst she is listening. Seem to be whisked up in a determination to identify the man positively. When finally you have achieved the identification to her satisfaction, promise to investigate his reputation with women (in her own interest) and finally reveal to her that he is an absolute rotter with the ladies.

No woman can resist such. She will realise at once that his philanderings are, after all, simply the cynical reflection of a restless search for perfection which he has discovered at last only in herself. Your cold criticisms, reiterated *ad nauseum*, will begin to get on her nerves—and gradually her loyalties and infernal constancy will be transferred from Nagging You to Romantic Figure Him. You are almost off the hook.

Your next and practically final step is to arrange a meeting between the three of you where the man in question may be confronted with his anonymous epistles. As there is at least slight acquaintance between you, this should present few problems. Explain your presence in terms of being the young lady's 'best friend', with only her best interests at heart. He will be flattered by the clear attentions she will pay him from the outset of the meeting—for it is certain that nothing is quite so attractive to a man, or to a woman, as the fact that a woman, or a man, finds him, or her, attractive.

He will deny having sent the letters, of course. He is shy, you acknowledge. He will bluster whilst she demurely and understandingly smiles at his transparent dissimulation. It is now time to play your role of 'best friend' to the hilt.

Draw him aside into the gentlemen's toilet and whilst you are standing in sympathetic juxtaposition of adjoining stalls, and he has his mind at least partly on his privates, be blunt and honest with him:

'Look, chum,' advise him, 'you *say* you didn't send the things—though I have my doubts on that score—but why submerge your good luck in a rush of honour to the head? The girl is clearly dotty about you. Spread a little happiness as you go by. If you can lay somebody as you go along, then your living will not be in vain, and all that sort of stuff.

'Take what the Good Lord offers, and be happy ...'

At this point employ that secret sign known to men whereby the flat of the left hand is laid upon the right bicep and the clenched right fist and forearm is brought sharply into an erect position. As you both return to join her at the table, he will be thoughtful.

Plead a sick headache and insist that they must have much to discuss anyway which hardly warrants your presence. As you rise to go, look into her eyes for a long moment, smile sadly (but bravely), squeeze her shoulder, turn quickly on your heel and walk out of her life.

Leave a letter for her explaining that you are called away for a few days on a business trip—or to the dying bedside of an old war comrade whose life you once saved—and leave town for the rest of the week and the weekend that follows. Soon after your return you will be shuffling through the bills one morning when you will come across an envelope addressed to you in her firm (Thank God!) but sentimentally tear-stained handwriting. It will begin: 'Dear John ...'

Without reservation, I unhesitatingly recommend the soft sell-out as allowing you to disengage with dignity and without too much hard feeling. The inevitable result of telling a girl you love her so, is that in about two months at most you will be realising that you love her only so-so—and *forcing* a girl to give you up has as much chance of success as trying to push toothpaste back into the tube. I can relate personal experience of many years since—when my youth and lack of understanding encouraged me to attempt a hard sell-out. Apparently foolproof in its theoretical construction, it fell down in that it needed ultimate moments of Good Fortune— which is never to be relied upon in dealings with young ladies. Simple reflection, after all, will at once reveal that it is only bad luck that got you in this situation in the first place.

I had been attempting to terminate a luke-warm affair for some weeks, and, hoping that we might gracefully drift apart, had neglected to report for a couple of luncheon appointments and even directly refused a dinner at her place on the outspoken (and one would have thought unforgivable) grounds that I was spending an evening with some male acquaintances. Her eyes hardened momentarily at this last brash challenge— but she clearly consoled herself with the egotistical female belief that I was simply playing hard to get. Desperate, I resolved to take a more positive line.

Approaching her flat the following evening, I ruffled my hair into a simulation of *laissez faire*, held my breath for several minutes in order to redden my face, induced a slight stagger, and sucked hard on a rum and butter toffee.

She was at home, waiting, her lower lip slightly tremulous from the humiliation of my hour and a half's late arrival. I threw my hat at her hall-stand in abandon, deliberately missing, and struggled to doff my overcoat with enough physical abandon to reveal to her that I had neglected to zip up my trouser fly. Leaning uncertainly forward to kiss her in seemingly drunken affection, I brushed her cheek spitefully with the stubble of my Five O'clock Shadow, and exhaled into her face strongly enough to allow the aroma of the rum and butter toffee to make its point.

'Ugh!' she said impatiently, pushing my hand away, 'don't start *that* the minute you get here. You're an hour and a half late, did you know?' She was icily polite now, to emphasise the depth of the accusation to follow:

'Furthermore you've been drinking.' She turned her eyes to Heaven in interrogative supplication. 'Why, oh why!' she asked God, 'do men drink?'

Her Creator remaining impassively reticent on this point, I summoned a handy remembrance from De Voto's *The Hour* and replied for Him in superior but deliberately slurred tones:

'My dear, the Water of Life was given us that we might see for a while we are more nearly men and women; more nearly kind and gentle and generous; pleasanter and stronger than —without its vision—there is ever evidence we are.

'It is the Healer, the Weaver of Forgiveness and Reconciliation, the justifier of us to ourselves and to one another ...'

She looked away momentarily, with a *sotto voce* 'Pompous ass', which I shrewdly suspected I was meant to register. Then she turned imperiously and fixed me with a stare of cold disappointment.

'I thank the Lord,' she snapped, 'that we women are not constrained by the weaknesses of our personalities and our inability to cope with life to be constantly full of alcohol ...'

I held my hand up in silent reproof. Then, pretending to roll a cigarette with fumbling fingers that sent flakes of tobacco floating into her cup of Ovaltine, I lit the crooked result with an uncertain match.

'A woman's hypocrisy,' I remonstrated coldly, 'a woman's *hic*-pocrisy, is equalled only by her curious ignorance of the elements of matter and emphasised by her lack of knowledge of the workings of her own constitution.

'Know, then,' I went on, 'scientific research has proved that chemical reaction to carbohydrates within the human system ensure a constant conversion of certain food stuffs—such as ordinary bread and butter—into blood-stream Alcohol.

'You, my dear, are in effect a human rum-pot distilling for the involuntary use of your body a ready supply of the liquor your existence demands but which you so crassly affect to despise.'

I smiled blandly in anticipation of my elegant play on words, unwittingly flicking my cigarette ash into my open fly: 'We,' I said, 'are such stuff as drams are made on ...'

In my verbal triumphs she began to sense the steady establishment of my debating superiorities and the foundations of her own defeat, and as women do in moments of uncertainty she retreated into the wheedling truce of resigned acceptance: 'Oh, come on, Sweetheart,' she offered, allowing a rueful smile to play treacherously upon her lips but come not within two inches of her eyes. I tore down her white flag of surrender and stamped it into the mud.

'According to *Chambers's Etymological Dictionary*,' I coolly retorted, giving not one inch of ground, 'the term "sweetheart" means a *Lover* or *Mistress*; neither of which salutary situations it has so far been my fortune to fulfil in our combined experience.' I leered broadly. 'May I conclude that here in the confines of your domestic *pied-à-terre*, your bedroom being but five paces from where I stand, your brazen offer of sexual intimacy is to be seriously considered?'

It was a brilliant innovation on my part; slightly distracting, but worth a try. She paled momentarily in the panic of every woman at last faced with the sixty-four dollar question, and began instinctive prevarication:

'Naughty, naughty, Darling,' she fenced with the wag of a coy finger.

'*Darling* is a pertinent observation upon our present relationship,' I continued remorselessly. 'A mediaeval corruption of the term "little dear", which finds ready parallels in "yearling" or "lordling", it reminds me that you *are* a little dear ...'

As she built her hopes suddenly, I as suddenly dashed them.

'... and emphasises, indeed, the fact that you are frightfully expensive.'

I turned my ruthless, impassive face upon her.

'In view of the flood of criticism to which I am invariably expected to subject myself via the simple social contacts your attitude leads me to believe will never achieve more intimate relations, I must reveal I consider you a luxury I am able to afford no longer.'

The thought of an easy if occasional meal ticket galloping off into the far distance will wreck a woman's pride quicker than you can say, 'Bring me the menu.' She was at once all mollifying, placatory desperation.

Holding my hand to her cheek, ignoring the smouldering end of my crooked roll-your-own as it stubbed out against her ear-ring, she dived into the last-ditch pacification of idiotic baby talk.

'Lovey dovey mustn't talk to his poppet like that, or Mummy smack,' she mumbled through my itching fingers.

'You are indeed a Poppet,' I acknowledged with a cruel mirthless smile twisting my handsome features. 'For a Poppet, according to the omniscient Mr. Chambers, is alternatively *a piece of timber* or *one of the heads of a lathe.* The combination clearly categorises you as a wooden head ...'

Even in the face of a retreating meal ticket, a woman has her pride. Stung at last into the simple invective which is a lady's last resort, she fixed her blazing eyes upon me and snarled a final rejoinder:

'You conceited, opinionated, priggish, pompous, inebriated, glib, lying, sadistic sot,' she catalogued with a suddenly outstretched arm and an index finger stiffly indicating the door.

'Bugger off out of this flat before I phone the Sex Squad and
have them book you for assault ...'

Knowing her threat to be idle, I composed a straight face
with all the desperate dignity of a drunk and strode firmly
and proudly in the direction of my dismissal—laughing
inside harder than at any time since my Aunty Ada caught
her tit in the mangle.

The door slammed behind me, and I stood there for a
moment congratulating myself upon the success of my
machiavellian duplicity, zipping my fly, tidying my necktie,
straightening my overcoat, and generally preparing myself
for the short journey to the young lady I had planned to visit
hot upon the resolution of the denouement I had just experienced. It was only as I went to walk away that I discovered
the tails of my coat had become inextricably caught in the
door jamb as it slammed behind me.

It took at least ten minutes dedicated bell-ringing before
she deigned to answer. Then her mascara streaked cheeks and
her red rimmed eyes could never hide the blaze of triumph
in the haughty stare that told me she knew I'd come crawling
back within the hour.

Useless for me to attempt to explain my sartorial predicament. Useless to protest that it was no fear of separation which
forced me to keep my elbow on her buzzer in peremptory
summons. She dismissed my testy explanations as juvenile
pride, and throwing me over her shoulder carried me circumspectly back to her sitting room to sit me down and plan
another damned, cosy, frustrating, boring evening together.

In some ways, suicide seems more logical as a means of
escaping from a young lady rather than as a means of balancing
up any misery which may accrue from your separation, but
I can offer no recommendation for it on either grounds. We
are all going to die, after all, and there seems little merit in
impatience. Via Tobacco and Alcohol we are assured that
inevitable doom awaits—and though Smoking and Drinking
are widely indicted as Slow Death, I am certain, on the whole,
that they are immensely preferable to a quick one. As one
who never had enough courage for the coward's way out (*sic*)
I think that when my time comes it will be no more than
partly hastened by that poison which neglects even a govern-

ment warning on the label. Paradoxically, it is the one poison which induces in a man that artificial optimism which makes an end to living no longer attractive. If a broken affair urges you towards the poison bottle, choose Gin or Whisky and we'll have you up and about in no time.

A study of suicide statistics, not surprisingly fails to list either Smoking or Drinking. A slightly out-of-date tabulation which I studied recently put self-inflicted death by Firearms as the chosen method of 42 per cent of suicides, and easily most popular. Hanging came in second with 21 per cent, and High Speed Gas a poor third with only 11 per cent. Nowadays the specific chemical poisons account for only about 10 per cent. They were far more popular in the olden times, but are difficult to come by unless you can claim some definitive professional requirement.

Drowning attracts only about 4.5 per cent, and 'Cutting and Piercing' (grisly phrase) but 3.7 per cent. Jumping from High Places can account for perhaps 3.4 per cent and odds under the sods look after the more individualised methods of the rest of the percentages. Crushing, apparently, was quite a popular form of suicide in olden times, but now seems entirely out of fashion. The finding occasions small surprise. How do you crush yourself, anyway? Try, and you will have yourself shouting 'Stop it, do you hear!' within seconds.

Strangely enough, women, drinking, and smoking can all be to a degree sickening—even to the point of dark despair—but the fourth estate in wickedness, gambling, is regarded as an almost certain antidote. None less than Bernard Baruch once wisely pointed out that 'you never see a suicide who owns a yearling or a lottery ticket'. Owning either, to a degree bespeaks the kind of idiot optimism which believes that things have at least a chance of getting better. And it is this eternal optimism which rests at the base of the ordinary man's belief that though every woman with whom he has had a relationship has invariably treated him badly, he nevertheless should continue his search for the perfect coupling. He has about as much chance of success as the lottery ticket holder or the bright-eyed owner of the gee-gee.

This blind belief in his own infallibility induces rather than is caused by conceit—but it is certain that whilst a woman is instinctively prepared to believe a man has lost his fondness for her (it is the root of a woman's natural suspicion) a man will generally conclude that an affected lack of fondness towards him by the young lady he adores is a ploy to sharpen his desires, or a simple temporary punishment for some recent shortcomings in romantic protocol.

For pretended animosity is as paradoxical as pretended affection. A man is vastly confused by one as he is by the other. Georg Groddek, the German analyst, for example, has observed in his book *The Unknown Self* that 'almost always the words "I love you" are spoken only when hate or indifference is pressing forward. They are uttered in order to keep the vanished feeling of love a little while longer, and cover the first promptings of dislike ...'

Examined in depth, the theory is perhaps too sweeping. But certainly the assertion 'You never say you love me any more', inevitably produces a grudging, churlish and self abasing 'I *do* love you', which brings satisfaction to neither party—and often prompts the first realisation that you don't.

At the same time, at the moment of sexual climax it is difficult to think of anything else to say other than 'I love you'; and one would presume that at such a time the affections are clearly enough directed. 'What do you fancy in the Three-Thirty at Lingfield?' or 'I say, what a pretty button-backed bedhead', would surely rouse more suspicion than romantic clichés. In my youth I was warned by a roué of uncertain years that a woman had clearly lost interest in you when she simply lay there eating an apple. Then, he opined, was the time to begin to look elsewhere.

But as was pointed out above, when the cooling of affection originates in the female there is an inevitable reluctance on the part of the man to believe in his fate. And even when my first *inamorata* began to manifest more interest in her Cox's Orange Pippin than in any 'Core!' produced by me, I too fell into the trap of conceit. When I received her 'Dear John' letter, I concluded her pretence that love had died was simply her spiteful reaction to being taken too much for granted. But with true *noblesse oblige* I paid her sex its due homage with an apologia couched in terms of sincere regard, an appended poem to her attractions lifted neatly from the lesser known works of a minor poet, a gummed envelope moistened with the tongues of angels, and all emblazoned with the protesting legend SWALK.

Her immediate recognition of my handwriting unfortunately meant that the persuasive content went disregarded and, determined to sulk on at least a little longer, she returned my letter marked 'Delivery Refused'.

It seemed to me that the time had come for firmness, and with the sting of more positive action decided that the quickest way to bring a woman to her senses is to hit her where it hurts most. But fears of an assault charge persuaded me that it might be more prudent to hit her where it hurts second most —i.e. her acquisitiveness—and dispatched a solemn demand (with the name and address typed) insisting that if our relationship was indeed at an end I would expect her to formally establish the parting by the immediate return of all gifts and presents she had accrued during the enjoyment of my generous affiliation.

The gambit was largely unrewarding. In reply I received an answering epistle from her solicitors instructing me that painstaking research on their part had managed to establish that what my letter referred to as 'presents from the party of the first part' amounted in total to a quarter of a pound of Black Magic I had purchased as part of a dutch trip to a local cinema in the July previous—and which by dint of more rapid mastication, I had managed to acquire mainly for myself.

It was now clear that a personal rapprochment was essential. Experience of her weakness for what she had always affectionately described as my 'Little boy lost' look, urged me into what (with hindsight) might seem an overtly absurd emphasis, but what (in retrospect) might still be deemed a noble try. Not only did a pair of short trousers, a shoulder satchel and a schoolboy's round cap seem to me to underline the juvenile appeal, but even if the worst came to the worst she must surely fall about laughing—and there is little which more establishes rapport than a round of hearty giggles. Supplementing the juvenile projection with a practised expression of hurt bewilderment, I presented myself at the front door of her flat and rang the bell.

Even as the hall light was switched on, I fell victim to the temporary panic which inevitably precedes a confrontation, and before the door had opened I had fled. She arrived to see only a satchel, short trousers and small school cap disappearing hot foot up the drive.

At the end of the drive, I came to a halt and mentally castigated myself for cowardice. The sudden fear was ridiculous, I told myself, as I turned and retraced my footsteps —determined this time to face it out and establish how resolute her rejection might manage to be in face of the melting appeal of my actual presence. I scorned my former panic. What can a slender, five feet two inches, twenty-two-year-old girl do, I asked myself, to hurt a man my size?

My answer came almost instantaneously. Her recognition of the satchel, the short trousers and the school cap was immediate upon her opening the door for the second time. She flew at me across the porch and dealt me a stinging box around the ears which deafened me so much as to allow only a faint appreciation of the accusing words which followed:

'How dare you play Knock-Down-Ginger at my door, you little horror,' she screeched. 'A boy as big as you should be ashamed. Go away at once or I'll call a policeman ...' And the door was slammed in my face before I could say as much as, 'Penny for the Guy.'

Twenty-four hours' reflection found me back on her doorstep but reluctantly acknowledging that the naive approach had not been a success. Second thoughts suggested that where we had gone wrong had been in not attributing enough sophistication to one another. She had not seen my inevitable philandering as a projection of worldliness, I had failed to recognise in her urge to snub me the resurgent spirit of a modern woman who seeks self assertion. A civilised approach suddenly offered itself as far more advantageous.

In top hat, white tie, tails, a *boutonnière* illuminating my discreetly wide lapels, and a gold mounted, 18-inch-long onyx cigarette holder clamped between my shining teeth; I lit a Gauloise, blew a romantic puff of Paris through the letterbox, adopted a pose of lackadaisical nonchalance, and rang the bell.

As she opened the door, I cast my features in a mould of half smiling mockery and leaned towards her with a waggish bow. She took but an instant to register recognition, and then slammed the door so hard it jammed the top hat hard down over my ears and sheared a good seven inches off the end of my onyx cigarette holder, taking the Gauloise with it.

Some kind of reconciliation had now become imperative. Not only was my pride beginning to fester, my self confidence to waver—but I wasn't sure whether or not you can weld onyx and anyway you know how much a Gauloise costs. I must get into her flat at all costs—if only to retrieve all four. Desperation called for Plan Gable.

It had always worked for Clark. Rejected, he would suck the corners of his mouth into smiling dimples, push his wide-brimmed Fedora to the back of his head, seize the recalcitrant young lady in his arms and kiss her long and firmly on the lips. At first her furious fists would beat a wild but ineffective tattoo on the padded shoulders of his Full-Drape, but as his muscular frame proved impervious to her frantic struggling, the blows would steadily decrease in intensity until her slim and shapely arms hung in sweet surrender by her sides. Then, only gradually, her hands would begin to creep a return journey up over his back, around his neck, until the intensity of her embrace became at last as fierce as his own. When she opened the door at the next ring, I decided, I would be over the threshold as speedily as a bailiff, grasping her firmly round the waist, kissing her in a way that would stir old memories and waken new delights, frogmarching her firmly down the hall and into the bedroom, gently but firmly back and down upon the bed.

Unbeknown to me, however, she had been entertaining that evening the young man who had replaced me in her affections—a knottily muscular second-row forward of some twenty-eight summers and some two hundred and thirty pounds. Reluctant to face the embarrassment of a verbal parting, she had sent him to answer the door and reason with me in favour of leaving them in peace.

I was not to know this, at least not immediately. As he opened the door the need for rash initiative had me already committed to a course of action from which it was now impossible to withdraw. My hot, wet lips were upon his on the instant, my arms about him, my breathless voice whispering through the saliva of my searching intimate tongue: 'Don't fight this, Darling. We were meant for one another ...' For but a brief moment we tasted the joys of the love that dare not speak its name.

His surprise was short-lived. Mine was to be more long lasting. First I felt his right hand grab deep into my hair and jerk my head back effortlessly in what seemed a resolute attempt to pull it off at the neck. Then his left hand dealt me a blow in the stomach so severe as to leave the imprint of my waistcoat buttons etched deeply for a fortnight. Then he held me out at arm's length by the skirts of my tailcoat, spat noisily through the open door in an effort to purge himself of the disgusting consequences of our recent intimacy, eyed me with deep nausea, and flung me across the doorstep in the direction of his expectoration.

'You dirty old pouf!' he shouted at my retreating figure. 'You want to go and get some treatment ...'

I did not stop to argue. I remember reflecting that if that was the sort of lout she pretended to prefer to me in an effort to make me jealous, she would be justly served by condemnation to a longer lease of his affection; and as a matter of fact that's the way it turned out.

She married the muscular young man about three weeks later and they had four children in the next three years. They all emigrated to Canada in 1957 and, though I can easily sympathise with the way she has spoiled her life, and the way in which a proud and misguided heart will always try to hurt the one it loves the most, I sometimes feel that she is taking her role of playing hard-to-get a little too far.

CONSUMERS' GUIDE TO YOUNG LADIES

It seems a pity that the Consumers' Association has not hitherto applied their critical faculties to an organised comparison of the wide variety of types available in the open market.

Dedicated to the proposition that the merits of goods available are far from created equal, the CA has effectively guided our hot hands for many a year as we reached out acquisitively in the self-service store. Frozen peas, binoculars, hired dress suits, washing machines, paper handkerchiefs—hardly any everyday commodity has avoided their stern inquisition and come out better or worse. On only one aspect of good living—the young lady—has the Consumers' Association remained resolutely silent, and it has seemed to me that in a work of this magnitude I might well rectify a service hitherto unfulfilled and dedicate its findings to the further honour of the CA.

WHICH WITCH?
(Types of Brands investigated)
I chose six different brands, as covering the wider range of types. Generally speaking, I considered these as being representative of the majority of specific styles available.

Certain facets of each product are, of course, unavoidably duplicated; and there are doubtless other brands on the market which may share or overlap many of the merits or disadvantages listed here.

All the tests described here were carried out under a variety of conditions and a variation in depth of heating, lighting, and relative propinquity. All brands, I discovered, reacted strongly to the atmosphere in which tests were applied; and though it was difficult to establish similarity either in price or weight, a certain degree of comparison could be fairly assessed in terms of suitability for purpose and pocket.

Brands tested were: DEBUTANTE, HIPPY, FEMME FATALE, SECRETARY, SPORTSGIRL and HOMELY.

Test 1: *Packaging*

In this category two brands were immediately outstanding in aesthetic terms—FEMME FATALE and DEBUTANTE. A third—HIPPY—was also persuasive in visual impact, but might be regarded as appealing to a clear minority interest.

Considering the brands in terms of status symbolism, FEMME FATALE emerged obviously as the superior product, though DEBUTANTE—particularly where the product was identifiable with one of the older established houses—was a close second in the field.

The four other brands had little to offer in terms of pure status but often had packaging attractions clearly aimed at specific area, class or requirement declensions of the market.

HOMELY, for example, had a loyal following based mainly on its handiness and on the fact that its relative unpopularity in the mass market often urges its promotional drive in the direction of an appeal based on the 'inexpensive' bargain image.

SECRETARY, especially in the more expensive ranges, often commanded considerable interest, but an image sometimes over simplified in search of an Efficiency projection inclined to bespeak an unswerving functionalism which was not necessarily the case.

SPORTSGIRL—a title which, like HIPPY, I felt was not necessarily in tune with actualities—was inclined to roughen and discolour into unattractive red shades after violent movement, and under warmer atmospheric conditions often inclined to lose its freshness.

FEMME FATALE, on the other hand, whilst easily the most impressive and colourful in its original presentation form, inevitably seemed to require considerable and regular repaint jobs.

Shape retention factors once unwrapped were superior in DEBUTANTE, HIPPY and SPORTSGIRL; though the last, whilst solid in construction and basically perhaps the strongest of all, was not perhaps aesthetically well made. FEMME FATALE, unwrapped, was often a surprising disappointment—particularly among vintage models—and there were sometimes surprising advantages to SECRETARY which the too practical packaging was disinclined to suggest (see above).

It is worth pointing out that the shapes of FEMME FATALE and DEBUTANTE were too often derivative; the former almost inevitably reminiscent of certain Italian and Continental models, and the latter esoterically uniform and inclined to an appeal to nostalgia.

Most HIPPYS, examined in the unwrapped state, offered the disadvantage of a dangerous over delicacy; and HOMELY inclined to wrinkle easily.

Test 2: *Performance*
HIPPY started more easily than any of the others and FEMME FATALE did not always offer the ready efficiency its streamlined appearance might lead the consumer to expect.

DEBUTANTE reacted strongly to atmospheric conditions and seemed inclined to start only when environmental situations were suitable. HOMELY was often reluctant and when cold sometimes refused to start at all.

SPORTSGIRL, though quick to respond, gave an impression of wasting much of its energy in supplementary activity. Too, its basic construction in terms of more utilitarian duty appeared to unsuit it for the more delicate requirements of this particular test.

In the matter of Performance, all types tested reacted well to inductions of alcohol; though whilst this generally facilitated starting it by no means guaranteed improved efficiency. Here it is important that the user himself experiment to discover the correct dilution suitable for each individual type.

Too much alcohol in the case of SPORTSGIRL, for example, produced a power which was often difficult to control, and I would recommend this type under such conditions only to users of considerable strength and extreme experience.

Too much alcohol applied to SECRETARY, particularly during post prandial periods, induced lazy and lethargic working in terms of the duties for which this type is basically designed, but the exactly balanced proportion soon had FEMME FATALE purring smoothly. HOMELY, on the other hand, inclined to cough and splutter after initial alcohol induction, and DEBUTANTE stalled.

Test 3: *Disposability*
Unfortunately, none of the brands considered here is easily disposable, least of all HOMELY. FEMME FATALE, which usually has a ready second-hand value, and HIPPY (which is often acquired or regarded as community property) are best in this category.

SECRETARY is disposable only in its entirety. Once its duties have been expanded to embrace the extra-curricular it is to a large degree spoiled for the work for which it was initially designed, but by its very adhesive properties it becomes controllable only to the firmest and most practised user.

Clutch control is difficult once DEBUTANTE's motivation is engaged, and leaving SPORTSGIRL involves clear personal hazard unless a substitute owner can be swiftly put in charge.

Test 4: *Availability*
SECRETARY and HOMELY make up between them perhaps 80 per cent of all known brands in terms of availability. As a result, their images suffer slightly through easy accessibility.

Consumers devoted to these brands generally explained their devotion as being the result of the handy package. Many wished they might switch allegiance, or occasionally experiment in terms of other brands, but the ease of supply and demand in each case rendered the user so susceptible to the brand's power as amounting to neo addiction. If, indeed, the user of either of these brands inclined to try another type, it was almost inevitably the other one.

In each case, consumers seem inclined to go on using the brand whilst it is easily available. In most cases a change is only made by a substitution of another style in the range of the same brand.

For irregular use and as an occasional stimulant,

FEMME FATALE seemed overwhelmingly the most sought after. Only this brand has been tried by almost every male consumer in the country at one time or another, but in terms of sheer weight of numbers HOMELY will probably capture the interest of most men eventually.

DEBUTANTE's appeal is esoteric and cultivated and not widely available as a result. HIPPY also appeals to only a minority interest, though it is easily the most popular among types of consumer inclined to try anything once. SPORTSGIRL constitutes a kind of market contradiction, to a degree—its manufacturers seemingly perversely more interested in the condition of the bodywork itself rather than the functions and uses to which that bodywork may be put.

Test 5: *Motivation*
Easily the cheapest to run was HIPPY. HOMELY, though by no means extravagant in its requirements of fuel or liquid induction, involves extra responsibilities in terms of housing and upkeep expenses. Too HOMELY, as its name suggests, is a domestic model and seldom suitable for taking about. This is why so many regular users of HOMELY are inclined to use SECRETARY as a console model.

DEBUTANTE often has the advantage of its own motivation, as do certain types of SPORTSGIRL and the more expensive brands of SECRETARY, but for transporting FEMME FATALE it is generally expected that a limousine or taxi is the necessary adjunct.

With FEMME FATALE, gear changing is often a frequent and elaborate process and considerably time wasting. Coupled with the regular necessity of re-painting, this constitutes one of the great disadvantages of this style.

HIPPY is rather circumscribed in its environmental suitability. It cannot be taken *anywhere* because of its jarring image in juxtaposition to most conventional backgrounds. Its great advantage in terms of natural economy, coupled with occasional contributions of profitability even, are at least partly neutralised by the fact that one may seldom afford much pleasure from its appearance alone. In terms of transporting it, one advantage of HIPPY was that it was the easiest to pick up.

Test 6: *Fuel Consumption*
HOMELY was the least extravagant in these terms and
ran for hours exclusively on regular intakes of simple
carbohydrate. In the absence of this more solid fuel, it
could work quite well on a regular injection of strong
tea. After too much alcohol induction, it was inclined
to leak.

FEMME FATALE suffers from the disadvantage of re-
quiring very regular injections of the most expensive
liquid spirit, and though HIPPY clearly required filling
up just as often, I found that its catholic acceptance of
almost any liquid fuel established it in the true economy
class. DEBUTANTE not only proved itself a voracious consumer of both liquid and solid fuel, but points of sale
dispensing the only type of intake it seemed prepared
to accept were both expensive and generally situated only
in urban areas.

SPORTSGIRL seemed reluctant to absorb anything other
than protein and natural juices, whilst SECRETARY needed
only to be topped up at half hourly intervals with regular
dispensations of caffeine to offer quite remarkable efficiency. But it should be noted that under such conditions
it smoked almost continuously.

HOMELY was the only brand to falter seriously under
the alcohol test. Provided the mixture was suitable for
type, all other brands came readily to the boil.

Conclusions
The best all-round purchase seemed to be FEMME FATALE,
provided the vintage of its production ensured good
bodywork when unwrapped. Generally it offered reasonable efficiency, a background of experience, undisputed
status symbolism, smooth moving parts, highly attractive
packaging, and the simple if expensive need for little
more than raw spirit.

It is impossible to beat HIPPY for cheapness of running,
but small status results from its acquisition and it is
difficult to keep clean. HOMELY was also one of the least

expensive of all brands in running terms and quite the most useful in any application to general duties. A good *practical* model this, but suffering generally from a neglect to its packaging. To a man able to afford two models, advice would be to run a FEMME FATALE and a HOMELY alternately.

DEBUTANTE offered clear attractions, but suffered the disadvantage of being difficult to get hold of and generally difficult to handle. Uneconomic to run except to the wealthiest consumers, its general appearance was not always what might be expected from old established houses of long established reputation. Too much stress, it seemed to me, was attached to what one might call the 'By Appointment' syndrome. It should be appreciated that even previous Royal patronage, though clearly dispensing status, increases the value only in the second-hand market.

SECRETARY offers ready availability and a handy pool of temporary replacements in the event of occasional breakdown; but habitual users interviewed on their experience with this type invariably seemed to wish they had started on another brand. Too, there seemed a tendency in the sales force of this brand to power-house the consumer should he ever show an inclination for another brand. Main advantage here seemed to be convenience and a ready suitability to the purposes of the business trip.

SPORTSGIRL had a widely dispersed but loyal enough following; its main attraction being that under no conditions did it smoke. It seems commendable to the experimenter in various brands if only as a reminder that he makes all kinds to take a whirl.

SYMPOSIUM

A few second opinions; with a woman having the last word

Love is that delightful interval between meeting a beautiful girl and discovering that she looks like a haddock—*John Barrymore*

Marriage is a ghastly public confession of a strictly private intention—*Ian Hay*

The most difficult task in the world is convincing a woman that even a bargain costs money—*Ed Howe*

Women inspire us with the great and noble aspirations they prevent us from accomplishing—*Alexandre Dumas*

Love is based on a view of women that is impossible for anyone with experience of them—*H. L. Mencken*

Oh, what a tangled web we weave when first we practice to conceive—*Don Herold*

A woman at forty should be changed for two twenties—*Douglas Jerrold*

A woman's intuition is the result of millions of years of not thinking—*Rupert Hughes*

No one ever got so much conversation out of his surgical operation as Adam did—*Artemus Ward*

Bevare of vidders. Vidders is vicked wixen—*Toby Weller*

The fickleness of the women I love is only equalled by the infernal constancy of the women who love me—*George Bernard Shaw*

No lady is ever a gentleman—*James Branch Cabell*

Brigands demand your money or your life. Women require both—*Samuel Butler*

Women are but children of a larger growth—*Lord Chesterfield*

She who hesitates is won—*Oscar Wilde*

A woman believes that two and two'll make five—if she cries and bothers enough about it—*George Eliot*

If only we could fall into their arms without falling into their hands—*Ambrose Bierce*

Marriage is inconsistent with the liberty of the subject—*George Farquhar*

A woman not only expects the worst; she makes the worst of it when it happens—*Michael Arlen*

Chaste is she whom none has asked—*Ovid*

A girl's best friend is her mutter—*Dorothy Parker*